# Spices and Tourism

## TOURISM AND CULTURAL CHANGE

**Series Editors:** Professor Mike Robinson, *Ironbridge International Institute for Cultural Heritage, University of Birmingham, UK* and Dr Alison Phipps, *University of Glasgow, Scotland, UK*

TCC is a series of books that explores the complex and ever-changing relationship between tourism and culture(s). The series focuses on the ways that places, peoples, pasts and ways of life are increasingly shaped/transformed/created/packaged for touristic purposes. The series examines the ways tourism utilises/makes and re-makes cultural capital in its various guises (visual and performing arts, crafts, festivals, built heritage, cuisine etc.) and the multifarious political, economic, social and ethical issues that are raised as a consequence.

Understanding tourism's relationships with culture(s) and vice versa, is of ever-increasing significance in a globalising world. This series will critically examine the dynamic inter-relationships between tourism and culture(s). Theoretical explorations, research-informed analyses, and detailed historical reviews from a variety of disciplinary perspectives are invited to consider such relationships.

Full details of all the books in this series and of all our other publications can be found on http://www.channelviewpublications.com, or by writing to Channel View Publications, St Nicholas House, 31–34 High Street, Bristol BS1 2AW, UK.

TOURISM AND CULTURAL CHANGE: 38

# Spices and Tourism

Destinations, Attractions and Cuisines

Edited by
**Lee Jolliffe**

**CHANNEL VIEW PUBLICATIONS**
Bristol • Buffalo • Toronto

## To Darrell Tschirhart
## (1948–2013)

**Library of Congress Cataloging in Publication Data**
Spices and Tourism: Destinations, Attractions and Cuisines/Edited by Lee Jolliffe.
Tourism and Cultural Change: 38
Includes bibliographical references and index.
1. Spices—Social aspects—Case studies. 2. Spice trade—History—Case studies. 3. Culture
and tourism—Case studies. 4. Heritage tourism—Case studies. I. Jolliffe, Lee, author,
editor of compilation.
GT2870.S75 2014
394.1'2–dc23 2014003187

**British Library Cataloguing in Publication Data**
A catalogue entry for this book is available from the British Library.

ISBN-13: 978-1-84541-443-6 (hbk)
ISBN-13: 978-1-84541-442-9 (pbk)

**Channel View Publications**
*UK*: St Nicholas House, 31-34 High Street, Bristol BS1 2AW, UK.
*USA*: UTP, 2250 Military Road, Tonawanda, NY 14150, USA.
*Canada*: UTP, 5201 Dufferin Street, North York, Ontario M3H 5T8, Canada.

Website: www.channelviewpublications.com
Twitter: Channel_View
Facebook: https://www.facebook.com/channelviewpublications
Blog: www.channelviewpublications.wordpress.com

The policy of Multilingual Matters/Channel View Publications is to use papers that are
natural, renewable and recyclable products, made from wood grown in sustainable forests. In the manufacturing process of our books, and to further support our policy, prefer-
ence is given to printers that have FSC and PEFC Chain of Custody certification. The FSC
and/or PEFC logos will appear on those books where full certification has been granted
to the printer concerned.

Typeset by Techset Composition India (P) Ltd., Bangalore and Chennai, India.

# Contents

# Contributors

**M.S.M. Aslam**, Sabaragamua University, Sri Lanka

**Ana Firmino**, New University of Lisbon, Portugal

**Aaron Francois**, Government of Grenada, Grenada

**Guðrún Þóra Gunnarsdóttir**, Holar University College, Iceland

**Laufey Haraldsdóttir**, Holar University College, Iceland

**Lee Jolliffe**, University of New Brunswick, Canada

**Márta Jusztin**, Budapest Business School, Hungary

**Azilah Kasim**, Universiti Utara Malaysia, Malaysia

**Carol Kline**, East Carolina University, USA

**Obeid Mahenya**, College of African Wildlife, Tanzania

**Melanie Smith**, BKF University of Applied Sciences, Hungary

**Kimberly Thomas-Francois**, University of Guelph, Canada

**Stacy Tomas**, Tennessee Tech University, USA

**Leanne White**, Victoria University, Australia

# Acknowledgements

As I write this, the holiday season is upon us in Atlantic Canada, with thoughts for me of mulled wine, eggnog with grated nutmeg, gingerbread men and a gingerbread house built with my grandson, sage and parsley stuffing in the turkey – all culinary delights that would not be possible without spices. I am sure that my contributing authors share these thoughts as well, from their various cultural perspectives either at this time of year or at other celebratory occasions and I am most grateful to them for joining me in this enterprise of putting together a book on the relationship between spices and tourism. Several authors have worked with me before and it has been a delight to have new authors join in this endeavor – all are listed on the contributor list. These authors were willing to contribute to a volume with a niche perspective of culinary-related tourism, as had the contributors to my previous volumes with Channel View Publications: *Tea and Tourism: Tourists, Traditions and Transformations* (2010), *Coffee Culture, Destinations and Attractions* (2010), *Sugar Heritage and Tourism in Transition* (2013).

As ever, it has been wonderful to work with Sarah Williams and Elinor Robertson at Channel View Publications.

Thanks to my family and especially my late husband Darrell Tschirhart to whom this volume is dedicated for their ongoing support of my work.

Last, but not least, thanks to my employer, The University of New Brunswick, for providing a working environment that is supportive of research efforts such as this edited volume.

# Introduction

# 1 Spices, Cultural Change and Tourism

## Lee Jolliffe

*Along with reasons of practicality and necessity, our practices concerning food and drink are driven by context and environment, belief and convention, aspiration and want to display*

Boniface, 2003: 1

The above excerpt can be applied to the case of spices, used for practical reasons, driven by context and environment and influenced by belief and convention. Spices not only enhance the preparation and taste of food, but also contribute to health and wellness through medicinal uses. Spices are part of belief systems; for example, in Indonesia they are an integral part of traditional ceremonies and festivals (Hall Brierley, 1994). Beliefs about spices have changed over time. Historically, spices were about the aspirations for the exotic and the unobtainable, as with the search for nutmeg (Milton, 1999), which once obtained, displayed a sign of affluence.

As with food and drink itself, as discussed by Boniface (2003), spices and their use in cultural practices play a role in the production and consumption of global tourism. Spices are part of the foodways and cuisine, and Timothy and Ron (2013) argue that spices are important to the tourism system. Using spices in tourism is also derived from cultural traditions geared towards the production and use of the ordinary in everyday life, unless we consider the case of gastronomy, where spices play a role in creating a product for the few.

A creative use of spices and related attractions in tourism reflects on-going changes and evolution in cultural practice, while often exhibiting the original spices in situ, potentially reflecting cultural authenticity. However, tourism itself may also threaten the authenticity of spice-related touristic products, leading to a constructed authenticity (Wang, 1999), as altered uses become perceived as authentic by the tourist.

Exploring the story of spices that acts as a context for today's spice-related tourism and its links to culture, there are the many issues, for example of spice traditions passed on through both trade and the migration of people and groups, changing foci of production, relationship to ethnic and national identity, and the recognition of both tangible and intangible global yet local spice-related heritages.

Global trade spread the use and influence of spices across the globe. As Dalby (2000) observes, spices were among the earliest products to cross the globe in trade networks. A once precious trading commodity has become widely available, and is primarily used to enhance the quality of the everyday diet. Through migration the use of spices in ethnic cultural practices has been passed onto new destinations and territories. Travel has allowed for people to be introduced to new ideas and concepts about spices, beyond their own cultural backgrounds. Parry (1955) indicated that: 'few food commodities have the importance and usefulness possessed by spices and certainly none is as interesting'. The expanded availability of ethnic food and cook books, the growth of travel with associated food experiences and the dissemination of information via various medias also encouraged interest in the use of spices (Farrell, 1998). Globalisation has thus contributed to breaking down the barriers and borders between the cultural use of spices, disseminating knowledge about use through exported and imported spices and related products.

The changing logistics of the production of spices in a global market has in some cases nurtured small farms, but in others has led to the production of spices in plantation-like settings. Spice farmers seeking a higher remuneration for their crops are turning to tourism, instead of marketing the spices themselves; the experience of visiting a spice farm has become a commodity for tourism in our glocal (global and local) world. This situation reflects transitions from modes of production to modes of consumption and the associated tensions reflected in the current trends towards international tourism (Smith & Robinson, 2002: 3). Tourism has directly influenced the nature of spice production, as is evidenced by the growing number of spice farm attractions in Africa, Asia, Central America and the Caribbean. In spice-producing societies such tourism has the potential to affect socioeconomic development, providing opportunities for improved livelihoods at the local level as well as increased cross-cultural communications between hosts and guests.

Spices and their use are closely related to cultural identities at local, regional and national levels. Spices are key to making a dish a national symbol, as for example with paprika and goulash for Hungary. Cuisines that cross cultures, such as the Mediterranean diet, rely on spices. Spices have thus been employed in place-making for tourism, especially at locales that either produce spices or exhibit 'spicy cuisines'. Exploiting culture for tourism purposes such as branding of destinations is identified as a social process linked closely with identity construction, usefully including a commercial product that can be consumed (Hall & Page, 2003).

The tangible use of spices in culinary tourism, cuisine and health/wellness is representative of both global and local (glocal) foodways and traditions that are now incorporated as part of the contemporary tourism phenomenon. The intangible aspects of spices, the knowledge conveyed and passed down from generation to generation, demonstrate the changing role of spices in cuisine. This phenomenon is documented in cook books. A review of historic meat recipes that employ spices (Sherman & Billing, 1999) showed that spice use has been of benefit by cleaning food of pathogens before consumption, thereby directly contributing to health, wellness and longevity of populations.

It is the intent of this volume to serve as a modest introduction to the evolving relationship between spices and tourism and forms of spice tourism, defined as 'being related to the history, production, consumption, and tourist experience of spices at destinations and attractions and through cuisine'. Such tourism represents and reflects the nature of culture and the identity of people and places, although it is not immune to commercial influences that change local spice traditions and customs into products that are easily consumed by tourists. This view takes into account the influence of social change in tourism as viewed through this niche type of food-related tourism. The themes of destinations, attractions and cuisines considered in the book provide a lens through which we can examine the subject of spices, culture and tourism, offering a critical perspective on cultural change evidenced by the current use of spices in tourism.

The book has a few limitations. It does not provide a history of spices, as many other volumes are available for that purpose (see Dalby, 2000; Keay, 2005; Parry, 1955). As a first review of the connections of spices and tourism the volume identifies links and examples, but does not claim to be comprehensive.

# Contemporary Spice Production and Trade

In a contemporary cultural context what are spices, how are they produced, traded and used? Some authors acknowledge that spices can be difficult to define. Spices, is not a botanical term, but a culinary one (Sherman & Billing, 1999). Spices are often defined as the seasonings derived from the bark, buds, fruit, roots, and seeds of tropical or sub-tropical plants (often shrubs or trees) and are usually dried before use (Oxford English Dictionary, 2008).

The FAO (n.d.) describes herbs as leafy spices with some, such as dill and coriander, providing both spice seeds and leafy herbs, noting that many spices and herbs are widely regarded as also having medicinal qualities.

Spices can consequently be defined as the actual spices (such as nutmeg, cinnamon or mace) or by use, in some cases herbs, derived from the leaves of plants can be used as spices, in particular to spice food (Parry, 1955). This book takes a broad-based international definition of spices as being used for flavour, colour, aroma and preservation of food, with herbs being a sub-set of spices (UNIDO & FAO, 2005).

Spices commonly in use today include cinnamon and cloves; ginger and pepper; saffron and chilli (Dalby, 2000). Spices are produced at different global locations with about 40 to 50 spices having global and economic importance. India leads in production, followed by China, Bangladesh, Pakistan, Turkey and Nepal (UNIDO & FAO, 2005). Spices and herbs are produced in tropical and non-tropical areas:

> In terms of world trade value, the most important spice crops from the tropical regions are pepper, capsicums, nutmeg/mace, cardamom, allspice/pimento, vanilla, cloves, ginger, cinnamon and cassia, and turmeric. Coriander, cumin, mustard and sesame seeds and the herbs sage, oregano, thyme, bay and the mints are the most important spice crops from non-tropical environments.

Today the use of spices is especially found in cuisine and also in beauty, health and wellness. In terms of trade and industry both international and national bodies consider spices and herbs together. On a national basis for example the Australian Herb and Spice Industry Association is the industry body for herbs and spices in Australia.

Diversification for small-scale spice producers is encouraged by development organizations and by organizations, such as the organic farmers association in Zanzibar, who are mentoring their members to diversify farm production by adding tourism visits to their farms (see Chapter 6). However, diversification is not without challenges, as spice farms concentrating on production may need to only cultivate two or three types of spices, whereas those adding tourism visits need to grow a broad variety of spices for demonstration purposes. There is also potential for fair-trade spice production to enhance the livelihoods of spice producers. A sustainable spices initiative is developing guidelines for production, beginning with a focus on the seven spices of: pepper, ginger, turmeric, chillies, vanilla, clove and cassis. The overall aim of the project is to 'secure the future supply of natural spices and increase the positive impact of its production by building a sustainable spices sector' (The Sustainable Trade Initiative, 2013). As of 2013 through local workshops with stakeholders in Indonesia, Vietnam, India and Madagascar local interpretation guidelines for these spices have been developed, and eventually will be extended to the 34 spices recognized by the European Spice Association (ESA). Since small-scale farms in developing countries grow many spices, broadening activities and revenue streams through both fair trade and tourism has the potential to contribute to the increased sustainability of spice farms as well as to enhance the experience of visitors.

## Destinations Studies

*And for the international traveller, spices and herbs will be a very real and compelling reason to visit India – particularly Kerala.* (Thampi, 1997: 579)

In particular this volume contains studies of *destinations* that identify themselves as a place with spices. Destinations around the world consequently associated with spices include those located on historic spice trading routes and at the contemporary sites of both production and use. The very mention of Grenada, Zanzibar, Sri Lanka, China and India conjures images of the spice trade and spicy food.

In particular some islands have used their spice production characteristics to brand themselves as a 'spice island'. This includes both the original home of nutmeg, the North Maluku Islands, Indonesia examined in terms of territory branding (Astuti & Ramos, 2012) and a contemporary site of production, Grenada (Nelson, 2012). Another spice island, Zanzibar uses its spice character in branding endeavours for tourism, stating 'We welcome you to Zanzibar, the majestic spice island of the Indian Ocean' (Zanzibar Commission for Tourism, n.d.). Producers in spice-producing destinations are also being encouraged to diversify their spice production and one way to do that is through tourism, either by offering small-scale spice experiences (tours) at the source of production or by processing and packaging of spices into souvenirs. Research on souvenirs has revealed that some tourists look for local goods that they can use once they are home as a memento of place. Spices as souvenirs are particularly characteristic of spice producing locations and are thus representative of the locally produced type of good (Gordon, 1986).

Destinations rely on a sense of place, in particular in the context of cultural tourism (Timothy, 2011) and at a number of places around the world that sense of place is closely related to spices. Many are located on trading routes, others are centres of spice production, often islands, and yet others are defined as trading zones in the form of spice quarters and bazaars. Some destinations have also become known by the spice-related cuisines of either indigenous or migrant cultural groups of people.

The complex history of the spice trade, in both historic and contemporary times has led to the formation of different types of spice destinations that can be delineated on both a geographical and a functional basis. From a geographical perspective spice destinations can be classified as countries, regions, islands, cities, routes and districts. Particular countries and regions of the world have naturally participated in spice production and trade, owing in particular to tropical locations and climates that have nurtured the production and trading of spices. A number of tropic islands in particular (Reunion, Zanzibar archipelago, Grenada for example) have geographically provided the conditions for spice cultivation to prosper. Routes of trade from these spice-generating locations to world markets for spices have also been geographically established. At a local level, in some countries such as Tunisia have been known for their role in the spice trade and individual spice marketplaces known as souks, selling spices in bulk (Citivello, 2008: 252) can also be identified. From a functional perspective a number of destinations are using both their spice history and contemporary production to their advantage in terms of tourism. Grenada as a producer of nutmeg has also used the nutmeg moniker to brand the destination, for marketing employing slogans such as 'Spice Holidays', 'The Spice of the Caribbean' and 'Spice Up Your Life in Grenada' (Daye *et al.*, 2008).

Spice producing and consuming countries thus have a natural propensity for linking spices and tourism, especially as spice production is in rural areas, spice-related tourism can thus be part of rural tourism and agro-tourism initiatives. Other spice producing destinations also have the potential to develop spice-related tourism, creating experiential tourism products related to spices and featuring native grown spices and herbs used as spices in their cuisine.

## Attraction Studies

*It is the end of summer. All alongside roadsides near Hatch, New Mexico there are signs of chili fever. In the fields of this fertile valley near the Rio Grande, bright red chili peppers are ready to be harvested. For a few days each year, the little New Mexican town becomes the chili pepper capital of the world. The Hatch Chili Festival is a celebration of the town's favourite crop.* (King, 1995: 5)

At other destinations specific *attractions* have been developed related to local spice production, such as the spice farms of Grenada, Sri Lanka and Zanzibar. Spices and herbs used as spices are also integral to local cuisines, for example the distinctive and spicy Sichuan cuisine characterized by the use of the Sichuan pepper and other spices is contributing to the image of Chengdu, China as a UNESCO gastronomic capital (Liu, 2011). At spice producing destinations spices have long been available as tourist souvenirs, but now spice activities and attractions are being developed so that visitors can experience spices at their source. Products being developed include spice-themed attractions (such as dedicated spice gardens, museums and routes) as well as resorts, culinary and spa experiences related to local specialty spices, and their use in the cuisines of relevant cultures. For example, a spice-themed route on the island of Réunion (Réunion Island Tourist Board, n.d.) links attractions and producers, offering visitors the opportunity to both experience spices at their origins and to purchase spices and related goods as souvenirs.

Within destinations there are a number of types of spice related attractions with the primary characteristics of either: collection/interpretation, production, celebration or geography. However, some spice related attractions will combine different functions, for example many spice gardens or farms may incorporate small museums or interpretation centres. Spice gardens may also feature processing and production facilities that are open to the public.

Some celebratory events may focus on spices, a particular characteristic of spice generating regions, for example Sri Lanka's World Spice and Food Festival established in 2005 features cooking demonstrations and competitions, live entertainment and museum, with major hotels in Colombo each featuring the spicy cuisines of a country (World Spice Food Festival, n.d.). In 2013 the Ooty Summer Festival in India added a three-day spice exhibition that included a five-foot model of the Taj Mahah made out of 15 varieties of spices, related cultural performances. This event was initiated by the Hill Country Development Association (Times of India, 2013b). From a geographical perspective spice-related features and/or attractions can also be linked or combined in the form of spice routes and/or regions and spice tours. Spice routes can be either historic or can be invented for the purpose of tourism.

There are only a few dedicated spice museums in the world, including Spicy's Museum in Hamburg, Germany (a commercial entity) and the Longstanten Spice Museum of the UK. At other destinations spice museums are under consideration, for example in Kochi, India there is consideration of using historic warehouses as a spice Museum with support from UNESCO and the French city of Lorient (The Times of India, 2013a). Botanical gardens and parks also often both grow and interpret spices as at Kew Gardens in London, England and the Fruit and Spice Park in Miami, Florida.

# Cuisine Studies

*Each nationality has its own special favourite combinations of spices, tradition-*
*ally handed down from one generation to another, and as these are passed from*
*one community to another, the variations become infinite.* (Farrell, 1998: 4)

Spices have historically been used in cuisine (Sherman & Billing, 1999).
Once available only to the rich, as they became more in reach of everyone,
they became for a time less popular (Civitello, 2008). With the globalization
of food and foodways spices are now readily available around the world.
An example is the Tastes of India spice mixes sold in Canadian grocery stores
that are developed by chefs from hotels in India.

Foodways incorporate the intangible traditions regarding food ingredients, practices and customs, and are represented by historic cuisines, and
by culinary routes, sites and landscape. According to Timothy and Ron
(2013) food imbued with a variety of social, cultural and historical meanings are a more important part of the tourism system than simply food
and food services. The authors indicate 'Cuisine is, without doubt, one of
the most salient and defining markers of cultural heritage and tourism'
(Timothy & Ron, 2013: 99). Tourists are seeking both the sacred and
authentic in their food experiences in what (Long, 2006) refers to a food
pilgrimages.

Culinary tourism has become a major theme in terms of developing and
promoting destinations, contributing to the tourism supply (Smith & Xiao,
2008), and some of this tourism can be either related to spices or include
spice experiences. A higher end of culinary tourism, gastronomic tourism
(Scarpato, 2002) also has a relationship to spices. Cuisine acts as a marker
of regional national identity that can be both a lure for food related tourism
and can differentiate destinations (Ab Karim & Chi, 2010). Some destinations are further embracing their spice association, such as evidenced by the
rebranding of Penang, Malaysia as 'Hot and Spicy Penang' a product position reflecting both their tangible (spice production and sale) and intangible
(history as a spice trading route, reputation for a spicy cuisine) spice heritage (Jalleh, 2012). There is a growing recognition of foodways being valued
for their intangible heritage through knowledge embodied by both the
production and preparation systems, as in the instance of Chinese cuisine,
much of which depends on the use of spices (Cheung, 2012). Spices are both
a tangible and intangible part of culinary traditions and foodways
(Civitello, 2008). Tangible spices are used but intangible culinary traditions
guide their use.

# Book Contents

This first chapter provides a background and a research context for examining the connection between spices, cultural change and tourism. The first part of the book then consists of spice destination studies from the West Indies (Grenada and Carriacou), Hungary and India. In Chapter 2 'Spices and Agro-Tourism on Grenada, the Island of Spice' Kimberly Thomas-Francois and Aaron Francois examine the role of spices in agro-tourism to Grenada, a significant producer of nutmeg, also known as the Spice Island. A number of spice farm attractions are profiled as key participants in tourism related to agriculture here. The authors note that the nutmeg contributes significantly to the cultural identity of the country. In Chapter 3 Stacy Tomas and Carol Kline in 'Spice Destination Case Study: Resident Perceptions of Tourism in Carriacou' outline the findings of their study at this small island that is part of the nation of Grenada. Although this Carriacou does not have the same spice production characteristics as the main island of Grenada that support agro-tourism the authors find that spices are related to tourism in here through culture, cuisine and souvenirs. Chapter 4 'Paprika: The Spice of Life in Hungary' by Melanie Smith and Márta Jusztin highlights the story of Paprika and its significance to both national identity and tourism in Hungary. This chapter demonstrates one of the paradoxes of the story of spices, for paprika is derived from a vegetable, yet after processing it is used as a spice. Paprika is a pervasive part of both cultural life and tourism in Hungary, contributing to the national cuisine in terms of the well-known dish of goulash, playing a leading role in the Hungarian souvenir market and starring in tours that reveal its importance through visits to paprika-related attractions. Author Ana Firmino in Chapter 5, 'Agriculture and Ecotourism in India's Goa Province: A Taste of Spices' utilizes the concept of the sustainable forest garden to examine the spice garden attractions in the Goa Region of India. These attractions feature spices and integrate complimentary cultural activities.

The second part of the book has a focus on *attractions* related to spices, profiling a common type of spice-related tourism attraction, the spice farm or garden, from the perspectives of three international destinations. In Chapter 6 'Rediscovering Spice Farms as Tourism Attractions in Zanzibar, a Spice Archipelago' authors Obeid Mahenya and M.S.M. Aslam profile spice attractions on Zanzibar, where spice farms for tourism are being developed to counter a decline in spice production. Here, the spice industry has identified an opportunity to balance spice farm revenues by aiming for diversification from production to tourism. Turning to the next, Chapter 7 'The Role of Spice and Herb Gardens in Sri Lanka Tourism' also profiles spice farm tours. Here author M.S.M. Aslam positions spice-related tourism within the trend towards sustainable rural tourism in Sri Lanka, providing comparative case studies of the spice farm tours, offering insights from both the perspectives of the operators and the tourists. In Chapter 8 'The Tropical Spice Garden in Penang, Malaysia' author Azilah Kasim profiles the role of a dedicated spice garden attraction in tourism to Penang, Malaysia. This well-planned and established attraction along with the spicy cuisine of Penang offers a key attraction for experiencing Penang culture.

The third part of the book has an emphasis on spices in relation to cuisine with chapters from different corners of the world: Australia, Iceland, the Mediterranean, Mexico, China, South Korea and Colombia. In Chapter 9 'Australian Native Spices: Building the 'Bush Tucker' Brand' author Leanne White traces the recognition of indigenous and native spices and herbs. This is reflected in the emergence of a distinctive Australian 'Bush Tucker' cuisine, linking to aboriginal culture, cuisine and national identity, evidenced by case studies both at home and abroad. In this Chapter 10, 'Pure, Fresh and Simple 'Spicing Up' the New Nordic Cuisine' authors Laufey Haraldsdóttir and Guðrún Þóra Gunnarsdóttir trace the Icelandic use of herbs as spices in the New Nordic Cuisine sanctioned by the Nordic ministers. Here chefs are extensively using spices for a cuisine that is distinctively Nordic, reflecting a cultural policy initiative designed to create a Nordic cultural identity through cuisine. For Chapter 11 'Recognition of Spices and Cuisine as Intangible Heritage' author Lee Jolliffe identifies and reviews the UNESCO recognitions of cuisine, linking this movement to a spice related tourism context. As the cultural practices related to spices are often intangible, these recognitions are significant in nurturing the preservation and use of culinary traditions related, especially through tourism.

The concluding Chapter 12, 'Lessons from Spice-related Tourism Destinations, Attractions and Cuisines' draws out the findings from the chapters related to spices, cultural change and tourism, while also identifying directions for further research. This includes an analysis of the current state of tourism related to spices, which is gradually developing around the world reflective of cultural change in relation to tourism.

## References

Ab Karim, S. and Chi, C.G.Q. (2010) Culinary tourism as a destination attraction: An empirical examination of destinations' food image. *Journal of Hospitality Marketing & Management* 19 (6), 531–555.

Astuti, Z.B. and Ramos, R. (2012) *Ternate-Tidore Spice Islands: A Territory Branding Process. Recent Researches in Environment, Energy Systems and Sustainability Conference* (pp. 243–248). Athens, Greece: WSEAS Press.

Boniface, P. (2003) *Tasting Tourism: Travelling for Food and Drink*. Aldershot: Ashgate Pub Limited.

Cheung, S.C.H. (2012) From foodways to intangible heritage: A case study of Chinese culinary resource, retail and recipe in Hong Kong. *International Journal of Heritage Studies* 19 (4), 1–12.

Civitello, L. (2008) *Cuisine and Culture: A History of Food and People* (2nd edn). Hoboken, New Jersey: John Wiley and Sons, Inc.

Dalby, A. (2000) *Dangerous Tastes the Story of Spices*. London: British Museum Press.

Daye, M., Chambers, D. and Roberts, S. (2008) *New Perspectives in Caribbean Tourism*. London: Routledge.

FAO, Food and Argriculture Organization of the United Nations (2004, 2009). Herbs and spices. http://www.fao.org/inpho/inpho-post-harvest-compendium/herbs-and-spices/en/ (accessed 1 July 2013).

Farrell, K.T. (1998) *Spices, Condiments and Seasonings*. Gaithersburg, Maryland: Aspen Publishers Inc.

Gordon, B. (1986) The souvenir: Messenger of the extraordinaory. *Journal of Popular Culture* 20, 135–146.

Hall Brierley, J. (1994) *Spices: The Story of Indonesia's Spice Trade*. Oxford: Oxford University Press.

Hall, C.M. and Page, S.J. (2003) *The Geography of Tourism and Recreation*. London: Routledge.

Jalleh, J. (2012) 'Hot and Spicy Penang' launched as part of island rebranding. *The Star*. http://thestar.com.my/news (accessed 30 May 2013).

Keay, J. (2005) *The Spice Route*. London: John Murray.

King, E. (1995) *Chile Fever A Celebration of Peppers*. Camel, California: Hampton-Brown Books.

Liu, Y. (2011) Evaluation of Sichuan food culture and construction of the gourmet city for Chengdu [J]. *Journal of Sichuan College of Education* 4, 014.

Long, L.M. (2003) *Culinary Tourism*. Lexington, Kentucky: University Press of Kentucky.

Milton, G. (1999) *Nathaniel's Nutmeg: How One Man's Courage Changed the Course of History*. London: Hodder and Stoughton.

Nelson, V. (2012) Tourism, agriculture, and identity: Comparing Grenada and Dominica. *Journal of Tourism Insights* 3 (1), 1–22.

Oxford English Dictionary (2008) Oxford: Oxford University Press.

Parry, J.W. (1955) The story of spices. *Economic Botany* 9 (2), 190–207.

Reunion Island Tourist Board (n.d.) http://www.reunion.fr (accessed 9 July 2013).

Scarpato, R. (2002) Gastronomy as a tourist product: The perspective of gastronomy studies. In A-M. Hjalager and G. Richards (eds) *Tourism and Gastronomy* (pp. 51–70). London: Routledge.

Sherman, P.W. and Billing, J. (1999) Darwinian gastronomy: Why we use spices. *BioScience* 49 (6), 453–463.

Smith, M. and Robinson, M. (2002) *Cultural Tourism in a Changing World: Politics, Participation and (Re)presentation*. Clevedon: Channel View Publications.

Smith, S.L.J. and Xiao, H. (2008) Culinary tourism supply chains: A preliminary examination. *Journal of Travel Research* 46 (3), 289–299.

Thampi, P.S.S. (1997) Spices and tourism. *Planters' Chronicle* 42 (6), 277–279.

The Sustainable Trade Initiative (2013) The sustainable spices initiative. http://www.sustainablespicesinitiative.com/en/downloads-1 (accessed 23 May 2013).

The Times of India (2013a) Corporation eyes warehouses to set up spice museum. http://articles.timesofindia.indiatimes.com/2013-04-19/kochi/38673948_1_kochi-corpora tion-french-team-lorient (accessed 13 April 2013).

The Times of India (2013b) The spice of Ooty's Summer Festival launched. http://articles.timesofindia.indiatimes.com/2013-05-07/coimbatore/39089655_1_spices-awareness-rally-horticulture-officer (accessed 15 April 2013).

Timothy, D.J. (2011) *Cultural Heritage Tourism: An Introduction*. Bristol: Channel View Publications.

Timothy, D.J. and Ron, A.S. (2013) Heritage cuisines, regional identity and sustainable tourism. *Sustainable Culinary Systems: Local Foods, Innovation, Tourism and Hospitality*, 275.

UNIDO and FAO (2005) *Herbs, Spices and Essential Oils, Post Harvest Production in Developing Countries*. Vienna, Austria: UNIDO and Rome, Italy: FAO.

Wang, N. (1999) Rethinking authenticity in tourism. *Annals of Tourism Research* 26 (1), 349–370.

World Spice Food Festival (n.d.) http://www.worldspicefoodfestival.com/ (accessed 20 May 2013).

Zanzibar Commission for Tourism (n.d.) About Zanzibar. Available at: http://www.zan zibartourism.net/ (accessed 21 May 2013).

# Part 1
# Spice Destination Studies

# 2 Spices and Agro-tourism on Grenada, Isle of Spice in the Caribbean

Kimberly Thomas-Francois and Aaron Francois

Grenada, also known as the Spice Isle of the West, is a 133 square miles volcanic island located in the low south of the Caribbean Sea just north (about 90 miles) of Trinidad and Tobago. The lush green tropical island, populated predominantly by descendants from the Africa-Caribbean slave trade, became a world-renowned trader of spices (mainly nutmegs and mace) and cocoa as early as the nineteen century following the abolition of the slave trade. Since the 1980s the Spice Isle had been the second largest nutmeg trader after Indonesia. Per square mile (the island being 133 square miles in total), Grenada has had the largest number of nutmeg trees, even after the devastating impact on the sector by Hurricane Janet in 1955. The nutmeg and other spices sectors, more recently succumbed to two second incidences of major Hurricanes Ivan and Emily in 2004 and 2005, respectively, resulting in the loss of its position as second largest spice trader in the world. However, demand for the island's spices continues to be high as Grenada is known to produce one of the best quality nutmegs in the world.

Despite the various challenges faced by the nutmeg and spice industry over the decades, the industry remains an engrained feature of the culture and tradition of the Grenadian people. The nutmeg, which became *the king spice*, was first introduced in Grenada in 1943 from Banda, a small island in the East Indies by Frank Gurney (Brizan, 1979). According to Brizan (1979), during the early years of its cultivation, nutmeg did not make any phenomenal expansion. It was not until 1860, coinciding with the crisis in the West Indian sugar industry and the search for alternative economic crops to replace sugar, that nutmeg was considered a major economic crop for Grenada (Brizan, 1979).

Today, although the nutmeg (*Myristica fragrans*) has maintained its preeminence, many other spices including clove (*Syzgium aromaticum*), turmeric (*Curcuma longa*), bayleaf (*Pimenta racemosa*), ginger (*Zingiber officinale*), cinnamon (*Cinnamomun verum*), pimento (*Pimenta diotica*), black pepper (*Piper nigrum*), vanilla (*Vanilla planifolia*) and cardamom (*Elettaria cardamomum*) have been introduced over the years, thus enhancing the island's national identity and more so its tourism brand as the Spice Isle.

Given such long and rich tradition in the growing of spices, the island's tourism industry has also seen a corresponding explosion in the uses of spices

**Figure 2.1** Warm spice welcome at the cruise ship terminal in St George's
*Source*: Lee Jolliffe

as part of the destination's products and services. The spices lend themselves as the piquancy in foods and cuisine, agro-tourism spice hideaways, scenting and ornamental crafts, healing and cosmetic products (such as the nutmeg pain spray and crèmes) and the overall national pride in nutmeg and spices is evident on the island's national flag and many Grenadian products – the emblem of the spectacular nutmeg symbol.

Undoubtedly, Grenada's *Isle of Spice* brand has significantly differentiated the islands from the usual sun, sea and sand neighbouring destinations (see Figure 2.1 which illustrates reinforcement of the spice brand through a warm spice welcome to cruiseship visitors). The ease of branding the destination as the Spice Isle of the Caribbean was innate. As stated by *The New Sunday Times* (2004) cited in Henderson (2007: 264), all countries can be branded as long as the essence of the nation can be found.

In an effort to assure the global community that Grenada firmly remains a 'Spicy' destination when doubts may have circulated following the severe devastation to the spice industry by the two successive major hurricanes in 2004 and 2005, the Government of Grenada, declared the year 2012 as the year of Nutmeg and Spices. The main activities during the year included a massive replanting programme which culminated with the hosting of an inaugural Grenada Nutmeg and Spice Festival. The festival was organized as a multi-sectoral event, which sought to reward and feature key stakeholders in the spice industry and strengthen the national pride and heritage of the spices which would contribute to reinforcing the destinations spice image and brand.

In addition, it is instructive to note that the festival not only occurred the same year when Grenada's first Olympic gold medal champion Kirani James proudly celebrated the nutmeg on his victory by kissing a nutmeg emblem, but was also coincided with the well-entrenched cruise ship season on the island. Certainly, the concerted efforts to rediscover and relive the nutmeg and spice heritage in Grenada would not only contribute to the authenticity of the tourism experiences, but subscribing to the view of MacDonald and Jolliffe (2003), this sort of heritage tourism is indeed a developmental tool.

This chapter examines the symbiotic relationship with spices and tourism as a tenant of agro-tourism in Grenada. Comparative case studies of agro-tourism experiences and development models are reviewed in the context of the heritage attraction experiences of the agriculture of spices and also the value creation for visitors after the experience. The cases of Belmont Estate, the Dougaldston Spice Estate and the La Grenade Industries are assessed. These cases were selected based on our foreknowledge of the businesses involvement in agro-tourism and international recognition of same.

Qualitative research methods were employed to gather data for the case studies presented. The main data collection instrument utilized was a semi-structured in depth interview which was conducted with the owners–managers. This type of interview allowed interviewees to be questioned systematically and in a consistent order but also allowing them the freedom to discuss further beyond the scope of the questions posed and as relevant to their business model (Berg & Lune, 2012). This in-depth interview also allowed interviewers whenever necessary to probe for more details from the interviewees. The interviews were supplemented with other secondary data and information packages provided by the owner managers which included business plans and other business records, promotional literature on the businesses, and business project documents.

# Understanding Agro-Tourism

The terms agri-tourism and agro-tourism are used synonymously in the literature. Sznajder *et al.* (2009) explained, however, that agri-tourism implies a style of vacation that is normally spent on farms, whereas agro-tourism denotes the management of an agricultural estate. The term tourism on the other hand is a form of active recreation away from one's place of residence. The conflicting views in the literature are similarly problematic when attempting to define agro-tourism. For consistency in this chapter, agro-tourism is used to generalize all related tourism activities occurring on farms and likewise the use of agricultural product for adding value to the tourism industry.

Phillip *et al.* (2010) reviewed several definitions in the literature to derive a typology for defining agro-tourism by identifying key characteristics. Phillip *et al.* (2010) therefore categorized the concept of agro-tourism into five types: non-working farm (NFW agro-tourism), for example, accommodation in ex-farm house property; working farm indirect contact (WFIC agro-tourism), for example farm produce served in tourist meals; working farm, director contact (WFDC agro-tourism) for example staged agro-tourism such as farming demonstrations; and working farm, direct contact authentic (WFDCA agro-tourism) that is visitors' participation in farm tasks.

In the context of the Caribbean, the Inter-American Institute for Cooperation on Agriculture (IICA) acknowledges a working definition of agro-tourism as 'any activity, enterprise or business that links agriculture with products, services and experiences in tourism' (IICA, 2006: 3). It recognizes six dimensions of agro-tourism, specifically including farm-based and agro-ecotourism, community tourism, health and wellness tourism, culinary tourism, agro-heritage tourism (forward linkages) and agro-trade (backward linkages).

Nonetheless, agro-tourism has been recognized as a means of sustainable tourism (Sims, 2009) and a precursor for sustainable rural development

(Akpinar *et al.*, 2005; Choo & Jamal, 2009). Theorists have therefore identified a myriad of agro-tourism benefits over decades. Some of the benefits identified are conservation of cultural heritage, preservation of family farms and communities, protection of cultural identity linked to agriculture, recycling of monies in the local economy (multiplier effect from tourism) and conservation of landscape and ecosystems (Choo & Jamal, 2009).

The following case studies include several dimensions of agro-tourism outlined in the literature. In addition, they illustrate how agro-tourism became fundamental to Grenada's spice industry and economy and vice versa.

# Belmont Estate – Case Study

## History of spices on the plantation

The 17th century plantation located in Belmont, St Patrick has positioned itself as one of the Caribbean's finest agro-tourism experiences and has been recognized locally and throughout the Caribbean for its best practices in agro-tourism development. The highly diversified agricultural and tourism product, was first a plantation estate obtained by an East Indian couple in 1944. The plantation was then operated as a major producer and trader of nutmeg and other spices but also cocoa and banana, the main export crops of the plantation era. Prior to the acquisition of the estate by the East Indians, in the late 1600s and early 1700s, the Belmont Estate was one of the 81 plantations established on the island with coffee being its major produce. Later in the late 1700s sugarcane was introduced.

Belmont Estate's connection with spices dates back over 200 years to the early 1800s when British merchants in the West Indies went to assist the East Indies to set up sugar processing and brought back nutmeg seeds to Grenada. Consistent with the period, the late 1800s, when the nutmeg was introduced to Grenada nationally, these crops thrived on the estates and became the estate's pinnacle, producing over 100,000 lbs of nutmeg annually placing it among the leading producers on island.

Currently, the 400-acre Estate of agricultural lands has allocated 150 acres to the production of spices including nutmeg, cinnamon, bay leaves, cloves, ginger and turmeric. The spices are not planted in pure stand but are intercropped with other fruits, vegetables and forest trees. The estate also remained a primary producer of cocoa with a 150 acres of cocoa established for the export market but also intricately linked to the agro-tourism business model with regards to chocolate making.

## Agro-tourism business model

The Belmont Estate, which is owned and operated by the grand-daughter of the East Indian migrants, a lawyer by profession, provides a diversified and authentic experience of agro-tourism for its visitors. The demise of plantation economy left most estates unprofitable including the devastating impacts of hurricane Janet in 1955 and later in 2004 and 2005 hurricanes Ivan and Emily respectively. The diversification efforts into the estate becoming an agro-tourism product started in 2002. The repositioning efforts included the preservation of the rich history of plantation life and the introduction of sustainable practices including fostering the development of an organic farm and the promotion of local foods in cuisine served at the restaurant.

The agro-tourism product development included the business entity offering tourist visits to a certified organic farm which includes spices, horticultural gardens, heritage museum, cocoa processing facilities, a goat dairy farm with demonstration of goat cheese production, petting farm, gift shop with locally produced craft, cultural entertainment, and a creole restaurant which uses local food and spices and epitomizing slow food cooked on traditional coal pots.

Business visitors have the opportunity of using the conference facilities while locals and visitors are invited to host their weddings at the attraction. Cultural entertainment and community activities festivals are also known features of the product. Some festivals hosted on the estate include Indian Arrival Day, African Heritage Day, Rhythms and Flavours which features ethnic foods (Nyack, 2009: 58 cited in Ministry of Agriculture, Forestry and Fisheries 2009) and more recently the culmination of the Nutmeg and Spice Festival, which included an award dinner for the farmers of nutmeg and other spices. The estate is also involved in the trading of nutmegs for export and fruits and vegetables to hotels and restaurants in the local market.

Thousands of stay-over and cruise ship tourists traverse the property annually as it is one of the 'must visit' destination attractions on island. The estate's financial records show that the tourism component of the business model comprising the restaurant and tours accounted for 70% of total income in 2011, whereas agriculture, which included the trading of spices, cocoa, fruits, vegetables, herbs, livestock, flowers and value added products to the European and local markets, accounted for 30% (personal communication, Belmont Estate).

## Importance of spices to the agro-tourism business model at Belmont Estate

Prior to the ravages of the two recent hurricanes in 2004 and 2005, the king spice, nutmeg and its mace were the number one agricultural products grown on the estate and contributed 20% to overall income of the business and 84% of agricultural farm income. That is, on average, 64,000 lbs of nutmeg and 1900 lbs of mace. However, the production of nutmeg experienced a 75% decrease, with production amounting to 17,000 lbs of nutmeg and 550 lbs of mace. Nutmeg and spices on the estate were therefore processed and packaged for direct sale to the visiting tourist and also used in the cuisine. With this established link the value of the limited spice produce resulted in tourism contributing 76% of overall income. This includes income for the restaurant but all fees paid by visitors to tour the estate. Tourists pay a fee of US$5 to visit and explore the estate's key attractions. (see Figure 2.2). Tour guides are trained by management and are provided with a thorough knowledge of the history of the estate. Subsequent to touring the facilities, visitors are encourage to purchase the spices merchandized at the estate shopping facility, which are presented both whole and ground, either in raw bulk form or packaged in clear plastic sacks packaging or bottles.

The estate has been actively replanting lost spices in an attempt to retain its income but also with cognizance of its critical role in contributing to the rehabilitation of the spice sector. In addition, at stake is the maintenance of

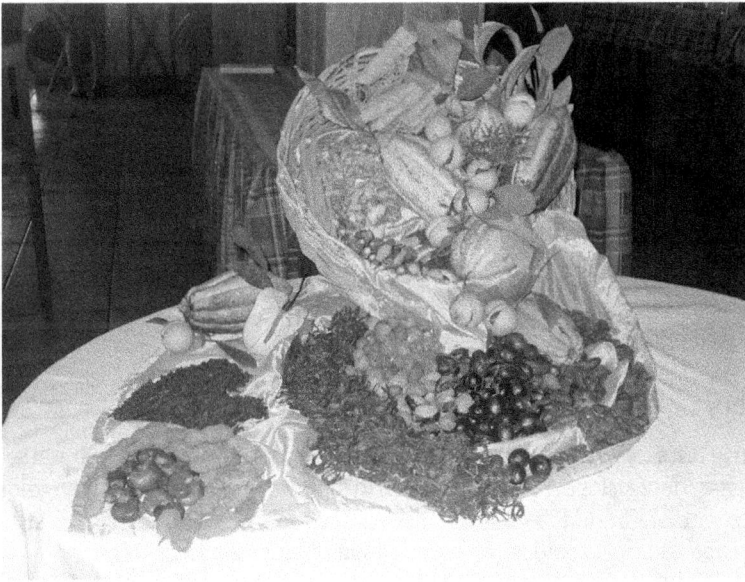

**Figure 2.2** Exotic spice display at Belmont Estate
*Source*: Belmont Estate

the estate's heritage, the quality of its tourism product and the contribution to sustaining the national image of Grenada as the island of spice and more so contributing to the national economy.

Over the last eight years, the estate has been strategically attempting to redirect the production, positioning and marketing of spices as an integral part of its product offering. In 2012, which was nationally declared the year of nutmeg and spices, in collaboration with the Ministry of Agriculture, the estate implemented a project with a group of scouts in the community to replant 300 nutmeg trees on the farm. The estate values the positive impacts of replanting nutmeg on the environment and the community and began the development of a farm plan for the full rehabilitation of nutmeg and spices on the plantation.

The innovative gastronomy at the estate restaurant is highly dependent on the use of spices as well. On average, over 16,000 visitors dine at the restaurants per year. Moreover, in an attempt to encourage visitors at the restaurant to practice the slow food cooking upon the return from vacation in the spice isle, the Belmont Estate Cookbook, co-authored with Wendy Hartland was printed in 2009 (Hartland, 2009), featuring the use of spices in cuisine. The promotional materials of the estate also advertise its emphasis on the use of organically grown herbs and spices used in its restaurant menu.

The decline in spices produced on the estate has significantly affected its income; however, the enterprise attempts to leverage the value of spices (intrinsic to the national brand) to strengthen its agro-tourism product. The authentic agri-tourism brand at Belmont Estate focuses on rewarding visitors with an exceptional experience in tasting, touching, smelling spices as well as educating them in agricultural production of spices, socio-cultural experiences, heritage and history of estate including role of nutmeg and spices in plantation life.

# Dougaldston Estate: Case Study

## History of spices on the plantation

Just outside the west coast fishing town of Gouyave, also famed as the city that never sleeps, is this beautiful 600 acre plus estate. Dougaldston Estate, one of Grenada's greatest historical monuments to its past, is still one of Grenada's largest, oldest and most-visited spice estates.

This well-known agro-tourism site located about one mile from the town and under the main mountain ranges on which Mt St Catherine, Grenada's highest mountain (2756 feet high) is found, offers the ideal environmental conditions that have afforded it to develop a strong historical tradition in the growing and processing of spices.

According to Mr John Branch, who is the manager, part-owner and incidentally a great-grandson of the first Grenadian owners of the estate, Dougaldston Estate, which was originally approximately 734 acres, was first own by the Duncan and De Freitas family from Europe. While under the ownership of European planters, Mr William Patrick Branch, a Grenadian, was overseer on the estate. Like most of the other 17th century estates on the island, sugar cane cultivation was one of the first major crops grown. However, one of the marked differences on Dougalston Estate was the significant quantity of other crops such as cocoa, banana, coffee, coconut, spices and citrus cultivated on the estate during the same period.

Following the abolition of the slave trade and consequently the demise of major sugar plantations in Grenada by the middle of the 1800s, Dougaldston Estate diversified its cultivation and increasingly focused on the production of cocoa, spices and bananas. Mr Branch indicated that with the change of the estate ownership in 1968 to Johnny and Willie Branch, greater emphasis was given to the growing of spices.

In addition to being at one time the largest banana producer on the island, Dougaldston Estate produced a large quantity of varying spice, with nutmegs being the predominant one. During the peak period, nutmeg production totalled 2000 to 3000 lbs per week, while banana production was estimated about 5000 boxes per week. Some of the other major spices cultivated included clove, cinnamon, pimento, bayleaf, tankerbean and turmeric. While turmeric was mainly used by the labourers on the estate, the other spice were sold on the commercial market. Dougaldston Estate was also on record as the first entity in Grenada to process nutmeg oil on a commercial basis for export. However, after 1968 nutmeg oil production ceased owing to demands for higher quality of oil that was free of impurities, which the estate processing facility was unable to meet.

## Agro-tourism business model at Dougaldston Estate

Dougaldston is nestled away from the city, almost hidden away in the bushes and is not so obvious by one plying the western main road under Mt St Catherine and Fedon Mountain range. Running adjacent to the south eastern end of Cuthbert Peters Park, the main playing field in the City of Gouyave, is a half mile road moving north east, which opens up into the stunningly picturesque and amazing historical Dougaldston Estate.

For as early as can be recalled, Dougaldston Estate has always been a major visitor centre. As one travels through the estate one can still find remains of 17th century architecture and artefacts which help to depict life on the estate back then. Remains of houses which were once the home of slaves and 'boucan', where the harvest of spices and other crops were stored when harvested can still be found. Drying trays for cocoa dating back to the colonial past still form part of the rich heritage of the estate, together with remains of furniture used in those times.

On a visit to the estate, tourists are given an experience that enables them to see actual spice cultivation, how the spices are harvested and processed and the chance to purchase samples of the different spices. Opportunities are given to also see the interior of the boucans and the buildings which were formerly the homes of slaves. Actual samples of tools, equipment, furniture and other accessories used by both the formers owners and workers of the estate can be seen and used.

Another famous and historical site of attraction on the estate is the area known as Maboya. Maboya, which is located on the estate's boundary with Belvidere Estate – once Grenada's largest nutmeg-producing estate, was the centre of major activities during the Fedon Rebellion of 1795.

During the period of the 1790s there was a great thirst for freedom among the Free Coloured and slave population in the Caribbean (Brizan, 1998). According to George Brizan (1998), the Fedon Rebellion, which was led by Julien Fedon, a Free Coloured Grenadian who used his estate as the meeting place and headquarters to plan a major insurgence to secure freedom from British rule, was one of the earliest and most famous rebellions in the history of Grenada. The insurgence, now popularly known in the literature as the Fedon Rebellion, is said to have been instigated by the principles of liberty, equality and fraternity as propounded by the French Revolution of 1789.

Today tourists can visit Maboya where they are reminded that during the Fedon Rebellion all of the island was captured, except St George's, and 48 of the 52 British citizens on the island were killed (Government of Grenada and Organization of American States, 1988).

Since the passage of Hurricane Ivan, which significantly devastated the estate's plantation, including about 90% of the most dominant spices – nutmeg – approximately 60% of the estate's revenue is derived from its tourism activities. In order to get a continuing flow of tourists on the estate, a strategic alliance has been established with one of the major tour operating companies. Between 65 to 70% of all tourists which sign up with George F. Huggins and Co Ltd, one of the major tour operators on the island, pass through Dougaldston Estate. All tourists are asked to pay an entrance fee to visit and sale of spices form the main source of revenue generation from the model.

## Importance of spices to the agro-tourism business model at Dougaldston

Tourist visitation has always been a major feature of Dougaldston Estate. For many years the estate preserved the buildings, which were once the homes of the slaves. Many tourists are extremely fascinated to be able to see the remains of these houses and 17th century artefacts. However, agricultural activities relating to the cultivation of spices over the years remain, even today, one of the most important features of its business model.

In fact, according to Mr Branch, Dougaldston Estate was once a main employer for the people of Gouyave, employing in excess of over 200 persons at one time. The significant production of spices and other agricultural commodities also contributed to Gouyave today being the city for the home of the largest nutmegs processing plant owned by the Grenada Cooperative Nutmeg Association (GCNA) – a farmers' cooperative, on the island.

Although the cultivation of spices on Dougaldston was drastically reduced due to Hurricanes Ivan and Emily of 2004 and 2005 respectively, the role of spices to sustain the business model there remains extremely important. On a daily basis the 15 workers that are now employed on the estate are largely involved in the harvesting and processing of spices and cocoa, samples of which are also sold to the tourists. Furthermore, 75% of the times that a group of tourists is seen heading up the west coast of Grenada, Dougaldston Estate is almost sure to be one of their main destinations. Visitors pay an entrance fee of US$1 (although the owner believes the tour is valued at least US$10) and are guaranteed a tour of the entire facilities, which includes the herb and spice garden, the fermentation houses where drying of spices are carried out and the 'boucan' where the history of the spices are told. Tour guides are provided with the requisite training (annually) by the manager but also by the tourism authorities and the Ministry of Agriculture, specifically in production and post-harvesting techniques. The training curriculum also includes primary health care and safety measures usually delivered by the Grenada Red Cross to ensure the safety of visitors. Tour guides are also taught some foreign language expressions for various spices such as German expression for nutmeg 'muskat', clove 'nelcan' and cinnamon 'cimpt'. The Italian words 'nocho muskata' for nutmeg, and 'alloda' for clove. This capability of the tour guides adds greater value to the visitors of different demographics, especially persons who do not speak English well.

Recently, although the owners of the estate have advertised it for sale because of financial constraints, the Government of Grenada has expressed strong interest in forging a private–public partnership to redevelop and keep Dougaldston Estate alive as a major spice producer, employer and more importantly one of the most important historical monuments to our past in the parish of St John.

# De La Grenade Industries: Case Study

## History of De La Grenade Industries

The De La Grenade Industries, which was commissioned in 1960, was formerly called De La Grenade Home Products. Originally, this cottage business was pioneered by Sybil De La Grenade who seized the opportunity to leverage a 200 year old family secret formula from the 'king spice' nutmeg as the main base. The legend and valued possession of the family is the recipe for a now world-renown nutmeg liquor. Captain Louis La Grenade, the discoverer of De La Grenade liquor, was a prestigious man of French descendants and one of the first 'free coloured' to acquire estate lands holdings in Grenada (Hilton, unknown).

Captain, who was once the commander of the St George's militia in Grenada, was the owner of schooners for shipping sugar and spices grown on his estates (Hilton, unknown). It is believed that in the 18th century, on a voyage to trade spices, Captain La Grenade received insights on the nutmeg liquor from a Dutch missionary who once worked in the Banda Islands, presently known as Indonesia, in appreciation of a favour he received from Captain La Grenade (Hughes, 1994). Since then, the formula was developed, modified and handed down, while meticulously protecting the secret, from generation to generation over the last 200 years (Hughes, 1994).

Captain La Grenade also experimented with the nutmeg syrup, made from the nutmeg pericarp (splits of the nutmeg fruit when ripened). He also included this syrup in the liquor as a secret ingredient. The family's policy requires only one family member in each generation to know the secret formula for the liquor, which was first used for home use and shared among family members and friends until the turnover of the formula to another generation.

Sybil La Grenade was granted stewardship of the formula, having gained access to it from her husband's uncle (Hilton, unknown). At the time, housewives in Grenada were already using the pericarp of the nutmeg (outer court), which is predominantly treated as waste by farmers, to make jams and jellies for their families. The seed or 'nut' and 'mace' of the nutmeg were the spices that are traded on the export markets. However, Sybil La Grenade, this cottage entrepreneur, decided to commercialize the jams, jellies, marmalades and nutmeg syrup while most importantly, leveraging the treasured secret family liquor for a competitive advantage. The spice-based products found favour locally and regionally with high demand.

In 1983 the American troops who came to rescue Grenada following the tragic end of the Grenada 1979 Revolution also acquired a taste for the product. In 1986, the De La Grenade home Products outgrew its status as a cottage industry and began trading as a limited liability company. By 1990, the company began to receive international recognition such as the Grand Gold Medal for its Morne Delice Nutmeg Syrup and a Gold medal for the La Grenade Liqueur from Monde Selection in Brussels. It was the first Caribbean food product to receive the grand gold medal (first prize) from Monde Selection (International Institute for Quality Selection).

Despite the tragic death of the company's founder Sybil La Grenade, the company was passed on, together with the family secret formula, to her daughter Cecil La Grenade, a food technologist and tourism and manufacturing business entrepreneur.

## Agro-tourism business model

The successor of the De La Grenade Industries Limited has continued the business as a manufacturing company, but has also diversified into agro-tourism business strategies. The company produces over 14 products with several others in the experimental stage. The majority of the product lines are spice based, mostly nutmeg. The company has been able to successfully establish backward linkages with local hotels and airlines. Nutmeg jams and jellies were served on breakfast trays of the British West Indian Airways (BWIA) and the British Caledonian Airlines, while the De La Grenade miniature rum punch is available in the flight bars of the Leeward Island Air Transport (LIAT) – the airline of the Caribbean. Both inbound and outbound tourists also have the opportunity to indulge in the spice products.

The construction of the modern factory house for commercial processing was built to accommodate tourists visiting the processing plant to view the various production processes together with a well furnished and decorated tasting and shopping area.

The most recent addition to the agro-tourism model is the De La Grenade Nutmeg Garden. This valuable business component further enhances the utility of the company's agro-process products as it allows visitors to connect with the spices used in the products they seek to purchase. The two-acre spice garden portrays the aromatic spices, indigenous fruits, herbs, a diversity of flowering plants together with the king spice. The garden is adequately landscaped with safe trails and labels on the various flora. Tourists (both stay-over and cruise visitors) are provided with tours guides who provide details on the history and various uses of spices and plants and fruits even as they can be found in the products. The company's strategic partnership with local island tour businesses generates the majority of visitors to the Spice Garden. The fees for the tours are therefore built into those of the tour company, who later compensates De La Grenade. The tour guides, however, are undertaken by the staff members of De La Grenade who are aptly trained by their manager.

## Importance of spices to the agro-tourism business model at De La Grenade Industries Ltd

The fortunes of the company came from its ability to use what was once considered the waste of the nutmeg (pericap) to create novelty foods and liqueurs. The ability to create an industry from a by-product has strengthened the value of the nutmeg to the country and extends its value towards tourism and the people of Grenada. The company has also received tremendous support from international development partners, having been identified as a sustainable business capable of multiplying benefits to grass roots people including workers and farmers. Nutmeg farmers are continually engaged to provide the company with the nutmeg pericap for which they are paid. These farmers are able to acquire value for the entire nutmeg (the seed, mace and pericap). This allows for the multiplier effect that is craved for in conventional tourism development by many tourism policy-makers.

Development partners, such as the CDI Partnership, herald the operation as a success having invested ECU$450,000 in the company to raise the production of agri-food products from nutmeg and spices from 3000 litres to 45,000 litres per year. Having reached this target, the partnership recorded a turnover of ECU $900,000 of which ECU $800,000 derived from export to other countries in the region for the consumption of tourist and national of these countries (CDI Partnership, 1993).

De La Grenade Industries continues to innovate with the local spices to further enhance the line of products offered to visitors. For the recently inaugurated Nutmeg and Spice Festival, the company launched two spice-based products (barbeque and dipping sauce) to commemorate Grenada as a national taste of spice country. The products, coined Spicy Nutmeg Ginger Barbecue Sauce and the Tangy Nutmeg Tamarind Dipping Sauce, are offered for sensory tasting and are sold to agro-tourist visiting the premise of the company and available in local tourist and national consumer shops.

## Discussion

The cases reviewed in this chapter capture the importance of the symbiotic link of the spices to the tourism destination, but more so the importance of agriculture and tourism linkages which is the backbone of the businesses in all three cases presented. It is evident that the Belmont Estate strategically engineered all of the six dimensions of agro-tourism in its business model: farm-based and agro-ecotourism, community tourism, health and wellness tourism, culinary tourism, agro-heritage tourism and agro-trade (IICA, 2006). Whereas, Dougaldston Estate focuses on agro-heritage tourism and farm-based and agro-ecotourism, and De La Grenade Industries pursues agro-trade of exotic processed spice products and farm-based agro-eco-tourism which allows visitors to connect with the processed products they purchase.

Consistent in all of the cases is the value of the heritage of spices to their agro-tourism businesses. The value proposition of their product offerings to visitors is coupled with the rich history of the spices, in the case of De La Grenade Industry a legendary story. As a result these businesses are able to sell agro-tourism experiences, which contribute to the overall destination image of the Isle of Spice. They therefore play a critical role in the destination branding process as they depict the essence of the destination (Henderson, 2007).

## Conclusion

As is evident in the case studies, agriculture has been intrinsically linked to Grenada's economy for centuries. The introduction of tourism as an economic pillar permitted a natural metamorphosis of agro-tourism in the destination. The island's comparative advantage in spices has not only provided a means of survival for its people, but also a strong culture and identity. This is then accentuated by the nature of tourism product development in agro-tourism and is clearly becoming the linchpin for further successes in tourism for the island. Grenada's spices are not only recognized as a primary or processed product that continues to be of high demand in the world markets, but also a deeply connected heritage that is rooted in the Grenadian people. This is the image translated in the marketing of Grenada as the Isle of Spice, together with the optimism that spices can lead the country and its people towards prosperity.

## References

Akpinar, N., Talay, I., Ceylan, C. and Gündüz, S. (2005) Rural women and agrotourism in the context of sustainable rural development: A case study from Turkey. *Environment, Development and Sustainability* 6 (4), 473–486.

Berg, B.L. and Lune, H. (2012) *Qualitative Research Methods for the Social Sciences*. NJ, USA: Pearson Publication.

Brizan, G. (1979) The nutmeg industry: Grenada's black gold. *Social Formation and People's Revolution: A Grenadian Study*. Published by Author.

Brizan, G. I. (1998) *Grenada, Island of Conflict*. London: Macmillan.

CDI Partnership (1993) Caribbean Agri-processing: Creating an Industry from a By Product. CDI Partnership Issue July–August No. 8.

Choo, H. and Jamal, T. (2009) Tourism on organic farms in South Korea: A new form of ecotourism? *Journal of Sustainable Tourism* 17 (4), 431–454.

Government of Grenada and Organization of American States (1988) *Plan and Policy for a System of National Parks and Protected Areas in Grenada and Carriacou*. Washington, DC: OAS Publication.

Hartland, W. (2009) *Great Caribbean Recipes*. Grenada: Belmont Estate Foundation.

Henderson, J.C. (2007) Uniquely Singapore? A case study in destination branding. *Journal of Vacation Marketing* 13 (3), 261–274.

Hilton, A. (unknown) *In the Discover Grenada Magazine*. Publication of the Discover Magazine Press.

Hughes, A. (1994) There is a secret in the nutmeg. In *Grenada, Carriacou, Petit Martinique: Spice Island of the Caribbean* (pp. 222–223). Hertford: Hansib Publications.

Inter-American Institute for Cooperation on Agriculture (IICA) (2006) 2006–2010 Medium-Term Plan – Promoting Prosperity in the Americas. San Jose, Costa Rica: IICA Publication.

MacDonald, R. and Jolliffe, L. (2003) Cultural rural tourism: Evidence from Canada. *Annals of Tourism Research* 30 (2), 307–322.

Nyack, S. (2009) Grenada's agrarian economy – exploiting the niche of agro-tourism. In *Grenada Annual Agriculture Review* (pp. 56–59). St George's: Ministry of Agriculture, Forestry and Fisheries.

Philip, S., Hunter, C. and Blackstock, K. (2010) A typology for defining agritourism. *Tourism Management* 31 (6), 754–758.

Sims, R. (2009) Food, place and authenticity: Local food and the sustainable tourism experience. *Journal of Sustainable Tourism* 17 (3), 321–336.

Sznajder, M., Przezborska, L. and Scrimgeour, F. (eds) (2009) *Agritourism*. Wallingford: CABI.

# 3 Spice Destination Case Study: Resident Perceptions of Tourism in Carriacou

## Stacy R. Tomas and Carol Kline

Carriacou, the second largest island of the tri-island country of Grenada, is approximately 13 square miles, and is home to around 6000 residents (see Figure 3.1). From the discovery of primitive pottery, it is believed that around 1000 AD, Arawaks settled the island, followed by Caribs, both of which were South American tribes. According to the Grenada Board of Tourism, the name Carriacou is derived from the earliest known written records (dating from 1656) which referred to the island as 'Kayryouacou', Carib for 'land surrounded by reef' (Grenada Board of Tourism, n.d.). Related to this derivation, Carriacouans often refer to themselves (and are called by other Grenadians) as Kayaks (Guerrón Montero, 2011). The geography of Carriacou is representative of its volcanic history, with an irregular coastline, high wooded hills, and sandy white beaches and coral reefs surrounding the island. A six-mile coral barrier reef resides on the eastern side of the island, and includes 'Kick 'em Jenny,' an active underwater volcano (Grenada Visitor Guide, 2006).

Carriacou was colonized first by the French in 1672, and then by the British in 1763. Although most residents are of African descent, influences from the French and British are still prevalent across the island, through town names and the use of patois (Government of Grenada, 2010). Additionally, Carriacou has a strong Scottish influence, evidenced by family names in the town of Windward (see Figure 3.2). Windward was settled in the 19th century by Scottish boat builders, and the tradition of wooden boatbuilding continues in the community. Carriacou has a reputation across the Caribbean for building quality wooden boats ranging from small fishing sloops to large trading schooners (Grenada Board of Tourism, n.d.).

Like many Caribbean islands, Carriacou had a history of agriculture as the dominant economic activity. As production of sugar declined in the

**Figure 3.1** Overlook

**Figure 3.2** Windward

mid-1800s, other agricultural crops began to appear, including bananas, cocoa, nutmeg, cinnamon, ginger and allspice (Nelson, 2012). Nelson (2012) posited that the unique agricultural production of the different Caribbean islands became the differentiator for each island and thus the main market-ing and promotional message of each of the island nations. Nelson (2012: 10) documents Grenada's claim as 'The Spice Island of the West' was first used by travel writers as early as 1901. By the mid-20th century, nutmeg and cocoa accounted for 90% of Grenada's exports (Brierley, 1998, cited in Nelson, 2012). However, between 1987 and 1991, the export value of nutmeg fell by over 75%, and Hurricane Ivan in 2004 had devastated much of the remaining nutmeg industry (Nelson, 2012). According to the Food and Agriculture Organization (FAO) of the United Nations, nutmeg, mace and cardamoms were still rated as the number one commodity in production value for Grenada in 2011 (FAO, 2012). Although production is less than its historic levels, Grenada still brands itself as 'The Spice Island,' using slogans such as 'The Spice of the Caribbean' and encourages visitors to explore the 'Rhythms of Spice' (Grenada Board of Tourism, n.d.). This strategy creates product dif-ferentiation for Grenada among the other Caribbean islands.

Carriacou does not enjoy the abundance of spices similar to the main-land, and as such does not have as many spice-related products for tourists to enjoy. However, the natural and human heritage of Carriacou helps to distinguish it from mainland Grenada. Although spices are still important to Carriacou, and their influence is prevalent across the island, Carriacou accen-tuates its unique cultural identity to entice tourists from mainland Grenada to make the trek to the island for an authentically different experience. Carriacou is largely undeveloped, and as a result, the island is steeped in natural beauty and tourism development is limited to relatively small-scale, burgeoning attractions. Thus, as Carriacou strives to expand its own brand of tourist experiences, while still maintaining its connection to Grenada, an examination of residents' attitudes about tourism development can provide insights into potential future directions. This chapter will (1) highlight Carriacou's unique tourism attractions; (2) provide insights gleaned from residents during research trips made to the island in 2005 and 2007; and (3) outline appropriate research and development directions for the future.

## Tourism Inventory and Activities on Carriacou

The unique heritage and culture of Carriacou is celebrated through several key festivals, particularly those related to dancing and drumming traditions. These include the Shakespeare Mas festival during Carnival

(February), the Carriacou Maroon and String Band Music Festival (April), the Carriacou Regatta Festival (July–August) and the Parang Festival (December). One of the most famous festivals is the Carriacou Maroon and String Band Festival, which highlights the island's African heritage with drumming, singing, dance performances, and elaborate costumes. Central to the Maroon Festival is the Big Drum Dance (brought to the island from Africa during the slave trade) and quadrille dances, as a reflection of their French heritage. According to the official festival website, it 'epitomizes food, music and culture by bringing people together' (Carriacou Maroon & String Band Festival, 2013). Ancestral meals of various smoked food are prepared with local, traditional spices and enjoyed throughout the three-day festival. The Carriacou Regatta Festival began in 1965 to celebrate the island's rich history in boat building. The Parang Festival started in 1977 and is a competition for village string bands (Grenada Visitor Guide, 2006).

Additionally, Carriacou is known for its beautiful beaches and barrier reef ecosystem making it an ideal dive tourism locale for those wishing to be off the main route of Caribbean tourism. As Carriacou is accessible only by water taxi and small aircraft from Grenada, its natural resources have remained pristine. Because the tourism infrastructure is underdeveloped, and Caribbean hospitality and culture is strong, a key facet of the tourism 'product' is socializing with local residents, often over a casual meal or beverage.

The Grenada Tourism Board highlights 'soft adventure' attractions including scuba diving, ecotours, hiking, sport fishing, snorkeling and boating/sailing as the main attractions for Carriacou. There is only one hiking site featured on Carriacou, High North, the highest point on the island (Grenada Board of Tourism, n.d.). The KIDO Ecological Research Station (KERS) is located on the northwest side of Carriacou. The mission of the research station and sanctuary is 'To preserve the natural ecosystems, arts, heritage, and encourage sustainable development of the Southern Grenadines through environmental education, social development' (KERS, 2008). According to the KERS website, 'The area is considered to be one of the most bio-diverse in the Caribbean' (KERS, 2008). There are three accommodation sites that can sleep up to 22; the primary market are researcher and student groups, and meal plans of Italian/West Indian vegetarian dishes made from local produce are offered onsite from the KERS kitchen.

On the official Grenada website, 16 lodging properties on Carriacou are listed, most of which are located near the island's main street. Dining options are casual – grills, take out and street food. The cuisine found on Carriacou is locally harvested and produced and has been influenced by its French, African, Spanish and British history, infused with local and traditional spices. Carriacouan food includes local meats (predominantly fish, conch, goat and chicken), starchy local vegetables, rice, stews and soups. Popular dishes include traditional Caribbean Roti and Callaloo. Caribbean Roti is often thought of as fast food and can be purchased both in restaurants and from street vendors. Roti consists of a flour wrap, filled with curried meat, chick-peas and vegetables. Callaloo is a West African side dish with a stew-like consistency, usually prepared with callaloo leaves, onions, spices, and coconut milk. Most of the meats are locally produced, with fish and conch (referred to as lambi) harvested just off the island shores. Plantains, jicama and sweet potatoes are common vegetables. Grenada's famous spices of nutmeg, cloves, allspice, bay leaf, scotch bonnet peppers, ginger, black pepper, cinnamon, sapote, tonka beans, turmeric and vanilla can all be tasted in the delicious food on Carriacou (see Figure 3.3).

Handmade crafts are the most common type of souvenir found on Carriacou. These include artwork, jewelry, t-shirts, scarves and trinkets. Keeping true to the spice history of the country, spice-related souvenirs are common. These include spice necklaces, carved and painted calabash shells, and spices sold in painted jars (see Figure 3.4). While there are a few tourist shops on the island, many souvenirs are sold by street vendors who gather on the main street near the center of Hillsborough.

## Current visitor activity levels and spending

Over 106,000 fly-tourists and 333,500 cruise tourists visit Grenada each year (Caribbean Tourism Organization (CTO), 2010). Nearly one-quarter (24.3%) of tourists are from the United Kingdom, another 18.9% from the United States, and 12.6% from Grenadians who live abroad. The peak visitation months are December through March, July and August (CTO, 2010). While the Grenada Board of Tourism collects data on visitors coming to Grenada, specific tourism numbers for Carriacou could not be found.

The organization RARE (2005) conducted a survey of visitors to Carriacou and to Grenada and while both samples were small (57 and 55 respectively), their results indicated that:

- over 40% of visitors to Carriacou learn of it after arriving in Grenada, while another 17% learn about it in a guidebook;
- the largest category of visitors to Carriacou (46%) are day-trippers, but over one-third (36%) stayed between 2–6 days, and another 18% stayed beyond one week;
- the attractions most visited are Sandy Island (57%), High North (21%), Harvey Vale, the community where the Big Drum Festival is held (13%),

**Figure 3.3** Food

**Figure 3.4** Cinnamon jars

and Belair, a plantation resort (8%), and most of the attraction to Carriacou is due to the beaches and snorkeling;
- visitors to Carriacou do not spend much more than US $150 a week on recreational activities; over half of expenditures on Carriacou go toward lodging and food. RARE notes that potential financial gain that small businesses have to access is relatively small;
- visitors are less likely to hire guides on Carriacou than on Grenada, and instead use public transportation or rent a car.

A brief discussion of sustainable development and the nuances of island tourism are outlined below to provide a context for discussion of tourism development on Carriacou.

# Sustainable Tourism

Owing to the rapid growth of tourism worldwide, many countries regard tourism as a critical component of their economic development and progress. Many governments, including those in the Caribbean, view tourism as a means to diversify local economies, particularly in rural areas where few industries exist. However, as tourism grows in less developed economies, the influence of foreign interests and ownership can create significant problems. Not only does foreign investment lead to economic leakage out of the local economy but foreign ownership can lead to a loss of local control over a destination's resources and a loss of autonomy. Moreover, the sense of place can change to meet expectations of foreign developers and tourists, which violates the principles of social equity inherent in sustainable tourism (Mbaiwa & Stronza, 2012).

Island destinations serve as a unique laboratory to examine sustainable tourism given their bounded tourism systems. As Hall (2010) noted, islands may be more sensitive to environmental impacts such as waste disposal and conservation of biodiversity than other tourism destinations. He suggested 'islands typically have limited resources, and increased visitor arrivals and temporary workers along with tourism-induced increases in permanent population may strain the use of these beyond sustainable levels' (Hall, 2010: 245). Additionally, the alluring and exotic imagery highlighting the unspoiled natural resources and unique local culture used in promoting these small, relatively secluded islands can attract tourists, and they, along with the accompanying development, may change the nature of the physical and cultural resources on which tourism was based.

While this has happened in island destinations around the world, tourism development in these regions does not necessarily need to be viewed with pessimism. Several researchers have suggested these islands can act strategically to maximize benefits of tourism and minimize economic, sociocultural and environmental costs. Wilkinson (1989: 153) posited two key fronts in which islands must act: 'First, they must decide on the degree in which they will become involved in tourism decision making in order that priority can be placed on their own goals, rather than those of external actors. Second, they have to examine alternative forms of tourism development to avoid many of the problems which have plagued some destinations.'

Grenada, and particularly Carriacou, has remained relatively undeveloped, compared to other Caribbean islands. Part of this is attributable to the topography of steep rainforest mountains which have prohibited the clearing of large tracts of land. Additionally, Grenada has put in place some of the strictest building and zoning laws in the Caribbean. For example, 'hotels cannot be higher than a coconut tree and must be set back 165 feet from the high watermark' (Sharpe, 1993: 53). Additionally, Grenadians own approximately 90% of all hotels, ensuring local ownership and control (Nelson, 2005). Furthermore, as outlined in Grenada's Master Plan, almost 90% of all approved development projects were for the tourism industry (Government of Grenada, 2000).

Grenada's Tourism Master Plan (Government of Grenada, 2000) focused on product diversification and sustainable development. The policy objectives were outlined as follows:

- 'to ensure that tourism development is consistent with the protection and conservation of the country's natural and cultural resources, built environment and the nation's moral values;
- to foster the most appropriate form and scale of tourism development in harmony with the resource endowment of the islands and the aspiration of the people;
- to ensure that tourism plant (sic) and essential infrastructure services keep pace with the demand of the sector within the context of the established carrying capacity' (Government of Grenada, 2000: 9).

This plan suggests Grenada policy makers understand the importance of self-determination and the protection of natural, cultural, social and historical resources. Grenada's governmental policies have created the institutional and regulatory framework to ensure sustainable development. This policy extends to Carriacou.

While the governmental policies, coupled with Carriacou's topography, have created a more 'authentic' touristic experience, Carriacou struggles economically with a limited industry base. As such, many Carriacouans see tourism as a catalyst for economic prosperity. Other issues facing the island include environmental degradation and public health. As tourism increases, the concern for the other issues has become amplified. Nature-based tourism is a relatively new industry to Carriacou. As a result, the local communities lack proper tools and resources to make educated decisions on the best strategies to insure that tourism development coincides with community development, environmental protection, local economic diversification and public health.

Aside from agricultural practices, tourism is the only sustainable industry on the island. In addition, there is the strong desire to preserve a number of sites on Carriacou associated with both the island's prehistory and historic periods. However, the tourism infrastructure is in its infancy, general educational facilities are lacking and there is considerable threat by outside parties to develop and control the direction of development as well as gaining the significant portion of benefits. Because tourism is a non-traditional industry, community acceptance of the industry is vital and attitudes towards tourism development must be assessed prior to investment of additional resources from private or public sectors.

# Resident Research

During research trips to Carriacou in 2005 and 2007, the authors: (1) developed an inventory of tourism assets on Carriacou; (2) conducted an exploratory assessment of stakeholder attitudes of tourism; and (3) gained an insight into current and past visitor activity. These were accomplished through observation, secondary data collection, surveys and in-depth discussions with stakeholder groups including Grenada tourism officials, Carriacou elected officials, business owners, cultural and natural resource managers, street vendors, 'unofficial' community leaders, and visitors.

## Interview-surveys

A total of 12 interviews were conducted with nine men and three women. At the end of the interview, informants were asked to complete a short survey about the impacts of tourism on Carriacou. Data were collected in this manner to establish rapport with the informant, and to gain a mix of qualitative and quantitative data. The ages of the informants ranged from 24 to 62; however, half were in their 20s. Most informants finished formal schooling in middle school or high school. One quarter had completed college. Ten informants were native Grenadian; one was from Trinidad and one did not answer. The majority of informants (eight) had lived in Carriacou all of their life. Nine of the 12 informants owned a business related to the tourism industry or worked in the tourism industry.

Interview questions were general in nature regarding tourists who come to the island, what activities and amenities are available for tourists, and how local residents viewed their impacts. Litter seemed to be a problem associated with visitors, but the economic gain from tourists far outweighted this issue. A few resondents wished for Carriacouans to sell property to foreigners so that new owners would bring their money to the island.

Overall, the majority of respondents wanted more tourists in Carriacou to see and experience their island and culture. They were proud of their island and its rich heritage and wanted more people to experience and appreciate the uniqueness of Carriacou. Several respondents indicated that if more tourists had positive experiences they could, through word-of-mouth advertising, influence other travelers to visit. All respondents indicated how important it was to be hospitable to visitors as a way of creating meaningful, engaging experiences. Respondents also repeatedly indicated how safe Carriacou was to visit, as opposed to other places in the Caribbean.

A survey was given to the informant at the end of the interview, in an attempt to capture more specific information about his/her perspective on tourism impacts. Survey items were derived from tourism impact and tourism development literature (Andereck & Vogt, 2000; Gutierrez *et al.,* 2005). Possible responses were recorded on a 5-point Likert scale ranging from *Strongly Disagree (1)* to *Strongly Agree (5)* (Table 3.1). Statements in the questionnaire reflected both positive and negative opinions regarding tourism development. A notable finding was that all positive statements had higher ratings than negative statements. Additionally, responses to the negative statements were either neutral or disconfirming, suggesting that local residents did not perceive any serious negative impacts associated with tourism development. This finding supports conversations had with local residents, who looked forward to increased tourism development, without many concerns for negative impacts.

**Table 3.1** Respondent assessment of tourism impacts (*n* = 12)

| Questionnaire item | Average response |
| --- | --- |
| *Positive impacts* | |
| I am happy and proud to see tourists coming to see what my community has to offer | 4.8 |
| The tourism organization of my community's government should do more to promote tourism | 4.8 |
| Tourism can be one of the most important industries for a community | 4.6 |
| My community should (actively) plan and manage the growth of tourism | 4.4 |
| I favor building new tourism facilities which will attract more tourists | 4.4 |
| The quality of public services in my community has improved due to tourism | 4.4 |
| Increasing the number of tourists to a community improves the local economy | 4.3 |
| I would personally benefit from more tourism development in my community | 4.3 |
| The tourism industry provides worthwhile job opportunity community residents | 4.3 |
| Tourism provides incentives for restoration of historic buildings | 4.3 |
| Tourism encourages a variety of cultural activities by local residents | 4.3 |

*(Continued)*

**Table 3.1** (*Continued*)

| Questionnaire item | Average response |
|---|---|
| The tourism industry will continue to (or could) pay a major economic role in this community | 4.3 |
| I support tourism having a vital role in this community | 4.3 |
| Tourism development improves the appearance of an area | 4.3 |
| Tourism holds great promise for my community's future | 4.3 |
| Shopping opportunities are better in communities as a result of tourism | 4.3 |
| I feel I benefit personally from tourism in my community | 4.2 |
| Tourism provides cultural exchange and education | 4.2 |
| Tourism improves understanding/image of my community and culture | 4.2 |
| Tourism helps preserve the cultural identity of my community | 4.2 |
| Because of tourism, communities develop more park and recreational areas that local residents can use | 4.0 |
| Additional tourism would help this community grow in the right direction | 3.5 |
| Tourism increases a community's tax revenue | 3.4 |
| *Negative impacts* | |
| Tourism causes change in traditional culture | 3.1 |
| Tourism development increases the traffic problems of an area | 3.0 |
| Tourism results in an increase in the cost of living | 2.9 |
| An increase in tourists in my community will lead to friction between local residents and tourists | 2.9 |
| Tourism results in more vandalism in a community | 2.8 |
| Tourists negatively affect a community's way of life | 2.3 |
| Tourism results in more litter in an area | 2.1 |
| In recent years, my community has become overcrowded because of tourists | 2.1 |
| Tourism development increases the amount of crime in an area | 2.0 |
| Tourists are a burden on a community's services | 2.0 |
| Native people are being exploited by tourism | 1.8 |

## Street surveys

Additionally, a variation of Nominal Group Technique (NGT) was employed to gain wider input (Doick *et al.*, 2009). This approach was used to encourage participation, and was culturally appropriate in a setting where local residents prefer to engage in conversation rather than to take a survey. Near the center of the main town, Hillsborough, two large easel pads were set up. Each easel pad contained one question. Round orange stickers were given to residents, and they were asked to place a sticker next to the item to mark their response. The goal was to learn more about what types of amenities residents would like to see developed for tourists as well as what concerns or negative impacts might be associated with tourists. Responses are presented in ranked order below (Table 3.2 and Table 3.3); respondents were only allowed to select one response.

**Table 3.2** The important thing that should be developed for tourists (*n* = 32)

| Item | Number of responses |
| --- | --- |
| Historical and archaeological sites | 11 |
| Arts and music | 6 |
| Hiking and recreation | 5 |
| Shopping | 5 |
| Other | 3 |
| Restaurants | 1 |
| Diving and boating | 1 |
| Lodging | 0 |
| Nightlife | 0 |

**Table 3.3** Most common problem with tourists (*n* = 32)

| Item | Number of responses |
| --- | --- |
| Litter | 11 |
| Traffic | 8 |
| Health risks | 3 |
| Damage to environment | 3 |
| Other | 3 |
| Drugs | 2 |
| Rudeness | 2 |
| Taking artifacts away | 0 |
| Crime | 0 |

Respondents felt more historical and archaeological sites should be developed for tourists. This was likely related to recent archeological digs conducted in conjunction with an ongoing archeological research program and related annual study abroad program. The work of the study abroad program and the results of their archeological digs have increased the awareness and interest of residents in preserving and displaying their cultural history; and the annual influx of student groups was well known in Hillsborough as a source of tourism revenue. Additionally, respondents felt arts and music, a strong part of Carriacou culture, should be developed further to enhance tourists' experiences. There was also interest in increasing hiking and recreation to capitalize on natural resources and opportunities already available on the island. Several respondents also felt more shopping opportunities with locally produced crafts would encourage tourists to visit.

While many respondents did not feel tourists would bring serious problems to the island, several respondents did agree that increased tourists would lead to increased litter and traffic. Both of these problems could be managed effectively to help decrease the negative potential.

However, one respondent noted large sailing boats regularly dropped anchor off one of Carriacou's main tourist attractions, Sandy Island, a popular site for snorkeling and scuba diving. This repeated behavior was destroying the nearby reef and causing devastating erosion to Sandy Island. Much of the vegetation was already gone from Sandy Island as a result. According to the respondent, it is likely people dropping their anchors were unaware of what they were doing, and there are no educational signs to prevent the behavior. These boating tourists seldom came ashore to interact with Carriacouans and thus created limited educational opportunities to try to reverse this negative behavior.

Beyond these instances, the findings suggest the majority of stakeholders viewed tourism positively; when asked about negative impacts of tourism, most informants indicated neutral or disconfirming statements. The general consensus was that tourism development (in any form) provided opportunities for economic enrichment and most Carriacouans welcomed new businesses, even from outsiders.

Results of this research are similar to findings from another ethnographic study conducted during the same general time frame. Guerrón Montero (2011) noted Carriacouans accepted but had not wholly embraced tourism. She also found that Carriacouans emphasized the importance of maintaining family networks and generally distrusted foreign influence:

Kayaks accentuate the importance of controlling tourism development with regard to the numbers of tourists, activities offered to tourists, and the management and ownership of facilities. (Guerrón Montero, 2011: 28)

# Implications

Island destinations have been the topic of much discussion regarding sustainable tourism. Many islands have developed with large-scale and foreign investment; however, Grenada and particularly Carriacou have not. While most research on island tourism highlights potential negative externalities, tourism can be developed sustainably, appropriately, and uniquely, offering opportunities to highlight and preserve local resources and culture and maintain social equity. Scheyvens and Momsen (2008) argued against the narrow and frequently negative conceptualizations of small island states as vulnerable and demonstrated how the distinctive features of small islands can work as strengths in developing tourism in a sustainable manner. They identified six areas of strength common in many small island states:

(1)  small is beautiful;
(2)  small islands are good economic performers;
(3)  high levels of cultural, social and natural capital;
(4)  respect for traditional, holistic approaches to development;
(5)  strong international linkages; and
(6)  political strength.

Several of these strengths will be used as the framework to guide discussion of Carriacou's tourism development.

## Small is beautiful and unique

According to Scheyvens and Momsen (2008), small islands were historically relatively isolated from larger, more global development. This isolation now serves as an enticing element of the tourism product that often makes the destination more attractive, less developed and more exotic than other locations. As compared to Grenada, Carriacou is less developed and as such offers Grenadian tourists a unique opportunity for a more nature-based and cultural experience as an attractive side trip to their Grenadian holiday. Carriacouan respondents indicated their desire for more development of historical and archeological sites for tourists as well as more arts and music attractions. Tourism products such as this will continue to help highlight the uniqueness of Carriacou and create differentiated tourism products as compared to mainland Grenada.

Additionally, because Carriacou is a small, closed island system, development of these products (as well as related research programs examining their efficacy) can yield straightforward results. Given the small microcosm environment of Carriacou, the phenomena can be easily studied due to few confounding factors. The scale of the economy and society in Carriacou provides a setting where research about island tourism could yield valuable lessons.

## Small islands are good economic performers

The small size of Carriacou and close-knit community of residents helps easily facilitate tourism development, through small-scale entrepreneurs who can quickly adapt and change according to tourist needs (Scheyvens & Momsen, 2008). The presence of street craft vendors, street food vendors and taxi drivers/tour guides on Carriacou illustrate the ability of these entrepreneurs to innovate and adapt to meet fluctuations in tourist numbers as well as requests. However, the entrepreneurial ecosystems forming the supporting framework within the entrepreneur's environment, is composed of many elements – physical, financial, legal, political, institutional, and cultural (Kline et al., 2012). The organization RARE (2005) noted that the barriers to entry for most small-scale tourism enterprises are low; however, in Grenada the barriers ranged from low to moderately high. Assessment of the entrepreneurial ecosystem in Carriacou, as well as research into the motivations and processes of the entrepreneurs themselves would be a fertile topic for future research.

As noted by Guerrón Montero (2011), most of the larger tourism businesses, including lodging, eateries and craft stores on Carriacou are owned by Carriacouans. There are three scuba diving facilities on the island owned by non-Carriacouans, but the owners have lived on the island for several years. Additionally, the low-scale tourism development opportunities outlined by RARE (2005) include opportunities that could easily be capitalized on by Carriacouans, with the assistance of training.

## High levels of cultural, social and natural capital that lead to respect for traditional, holistic approaches to development

The cultural, social and natural capital of islands can boost the economy, not just by attracting tourists and providing unique experiences, but these types of capital can provide a controlling force to guide the way in which tourism develops on the island as well as drive 'holistic development outcomes for the local population' (Scheyvens & Momsen, 2008: 500). The strong cultural heritage of Carriacou (as evidenced through its numerous festivals and events) provides a glue that holds the residents together and a sense of belongingness and social capital. These cultural events can help to encourage Carriacouans to work together for common interests and maintain their unique cultural and historical identity.

Guerrón Montero (2011) noted 'rootedness' and a sense of belonging were strong themes expressed by Carriacouans. She posited that much of this was due to the slave history of Carriacou. Citing Fayer (2003), she described the historically high number of slaves proportionate to the while population of Carriacou. 'In 1833, just before emancipation, there were 3200 slaves in a population of about 4000 people. Plantation owners and managers were often absent from their estates, and this enabled the enslaved workers to express, create and re-create cultural manifestations with a relatively higher degree of freedom than elsewhere, a legacy that continued after emancipation' (Fayer, 2003, cited in Guerrón Montero, 2011: 28).

This distinct local culture and pride keeps Carriacouans connected and rooted to their community, creating the strong sense of place and desire for locally owned and controlled interests, and as such constitutes effective social capital. A comparison of the visual arts, craft, performing arts, and cultural festivals of Carriacou with other areas of Grenada or the Caribbean could yield insight into the nature of bridging and bonding social capital, and its effect on cultural capital evolution within a small island setting (McGehee et al., 2010).

## Strong international linkages

Carriacou, like many other small islands, loses a large percentage of its population to migration. Carriacouans tend to migrate to Trinidad, Aruba, the UK, Canada and the US (Guerrón Montero, 2011). However, they tend to maintain strong links with 'home,' sending money, investing in businesses, providing innovative ideas for entrepreneurship, and serving as agents of change on the island. As such, Scheyvens and Momsen (2008) discuss how these strong international linkages help tie small islands to a larger society, transferring skills, knowledge, money, and technology with 'home.' Additionally, these expatriates maintain strong ties and visit 'home' often, contributing to the tourism market.

Carriacou, like many remote and rural settings, must rely on niche tourists who are comfortable undergoing many 'legs' of a journey to reach the destination and who are seeking an experience in more rustic surrounds. Especially because Carriacou does not have a port for cruise ships, it seems destined to develop by courting a broad portfolio of niche tourist markets including the expatriate/migrant market mentioned above. A market that is beginning to be explored in rural outposts is the Scientific, Academic, Volunteer and Educational (SAVE) market. Many individual travelers and groups of tourists engaging in scientific research, study abroad courses,

volunteerism and intensive educational tours are willing to forego the amenities of an established destination to gain a more authentic, intimate, and
connective travel experience – Carriacou offers that experience and has
become well-versed in hosting archeologists, biologists, social science
researchers, and study abroad groups to its shores. Each of these niche markets provide fodder for future tourism development on Carriacou.

# Conclusion

While Carriacou is a dependent island of Grenada, 'The Spice of the
Caribbean,' it has managed to distinguish itself from the main island by
focusing on its unique history, culture, natural resources, and intimate scale
of the society and its activities. The rustic accommodations, traditional local
foods, and handmade crafts are part of the appeal of Carriacou that helps to
further differentiate it as a unique destination. Carriacou does not share the
same strong spice history as Grenada, and as such has found its tourism niche
through nature-based tourism, both in its forest and beaches, as well as cultural and heritage tourism. Despite the limited tourism infrastructure that is
usually considered as a necessary precursor to tourism growth, Carriacou
appears to be developing rather sustainably. Perhaps the lack of traditional
tourism infrastructure has provided unique opportunities for tourism on
Carriacou to develop in a more holistic and fluid manner, allowing for more
local interaction and control.

Future tourism development directions could certainly connect with
the theme of spice without relinquishing the 'genuine' and 'casual' qualities of Carriacou's current tourism brand. Development of agritourism
centered on spice and native vegetables could complement other nature-
based activities offered. Additional inclusion of spice interpretation in festivals, heritage tours, printed materials, and souvenirs could be done
without diluting Carriacou's authenticity or positioning Carriacou as too
similar to Grenada. However with any of these development directions,
caution would need to be taken to ensure the presence of 'spice' themes is
not overdone and as a result, becomes meaningless. As such, Carriacou is
on a path to craft its tourism product in an unhurried manner; given that
measures of purposeful action and management are taken to preserve the
island's personality and heritage.

## References

Andereck, K. and Vogt, C. (2000) The relationship between residents' attitudes toward
    tourism and tourism development options. *Journal of Travel Research* 39 (1), 27–36.

Brierley, J.S. (1998) Changing farm systems: From estate holdings to model farms, gleanings from Grenada, 1940–92. In D.F.M. McGregor, D. Barker and S.L. Evans (eds) *Resource Sustainability and Caribbean Development* (pp. 253–272). Barbados: The Press University of the West Indies.

Caribbean Tourism Organization (2010) Individual country statistics. http://www.onecaribbean.org/statistics/countrystats/ (accessed 22 February 2013).

Carriacou Maroon and String Band Festival (2013) About the event. http://www.carriacoumaroon.com/index.php (accessed 27 April 2013).

Doick, K.J., Pediaditi, K., Moffat, A.J. and Hutchings, T.R. (2009) Defining the sustainability objectives of brownfield regeneration to greenspace. *International Journal of Management and Decision Making* 10 (3), 282–302.

Fayer, J.M. (2003) 'The Carriacou Shakespeare Mas': Linguistic creativity in a Creole Community. In M. Aceto and J.P. Williams (eds) *Contact Englishes of the Eastern Caribbean* (pp. 211–226). Amsterdam and Philadelphia: John Benjamins PF.

Food and Agriculture Organization of the United Nations (2012) FAO country profiles: Grenada. http://www.fao.org/countryprofiles/index/en/?iso3=GRD&subject=30 (accessed 16 February 2013).

Government of Grenada (2000) Biodiversity strategy and action plan. http://www.cbd.int/doc/world/gd/gd-nbsap-01-en.pdf (accessed 24 February 2013).

Government of Grenada (2010) About Grenada. http://www.gov.gd/index.html (accessed 16 February 2013).

Grenada Board of Tourism (no date) Carriacou history. http://www.grenadagrenadines.com/ (accessed 16 February 2013).

Grenada Visitors Guide (2006) Welcome to Carriacou and Petite Martinique. In Concepts Advertising In (ed.) *Truly Discover Grenada, Carriacou and Petite Martinique* 3, 100–101.

Guerrón Montero, C. (2011) On tourism and the constructions of 'Paradise Islands' in Central America and the Caribbean. *Bulletin Of Latin American Research* 30 (1), 21–34.

Gutierrez, E., Lamoureux, K., Matus, S. and Sebunya, K. (2005) *Linking Communities, Tourism and Conservation*. Prepared for Conservation International.

Hall, C.M. (2010) Island destinations: A natural laboratory for tourism: Introduction. *Asia Pacific Journal of Tourism Research* 15 (3), 245–250.

KIDO Ecological Research Station Sanctuary (2008) http://www.kido-projects.com/ (accessed 23 February 2013).

Kline, C., McGehee, N., Paterson, S. and Tsao, J. (2012) Using ecological systems theory and density of acquaintance to explore resident perception of entrepreneurial climate. *Journal of Travel Research* 52 (3), 294–309.

Mbaiwa, J.E. and Stronza, A.L. (2012) The challenges and prospects for sustainable tourism and ecotourism in developing countries. In T. Jamal and M. Robinson (eds) *The SAGE Handbook of Tourism Studies* (pp. 333–353). London: SAGE Publications, Ltd.

McGehee, N.G., Lee, S., O'Bannon, T.L. and Perdue, R.R. (2010) Tourism-related social capital and its relationship with other forms of capital: An exploratory study. *Journal of Travel Research* 49 (4), 486–500.

Nelson, V. (2005) Representation and images of people, place and nature in Grenada's tourism. *Geografiska Annaler Series B: Human Geography* 87 (2), 131–143.

Nelson, V. (2012) Tourism, agriculture, and identity: Comparing Grenada and Dominica. *Journal of Tourism Insights* 3 (1), 1–22.

RARE (2005) *Assessing the Potential for Small-scale Tourism Development in Grenada and Carriacou* [report]. Published by RARE in association with The Nature Conservancy and USAID.

Scheyvens, R. and Momsen, J. (2008) Tourism in small island states: From vulnerability to strengths. *Journal of Sustainable Tourism* 16 (5), 491–510.

Sharpe, J. (1993) 'The original paradise' Grenada ten years after the US invasion. *Transition* 62, 48–57.

Wilkinson, P.F. (1989) Strategies for tourism in island microstates. *Annals of Tourism Research* 16, 153–177.

# 4 Paprika: The Spice of Life in Hungary

## Melanie Smith and Márta Jusztin

*'What spice do you associate with Hungary?' The answer to this question is unlikely to tax competitors in gastronomic quizzes anywhere in the world.*

Mirko, 2012

This chapter analyses the role of paprika in the development and promotion of Hungarian tourism, as well as in the construction of national cultural identity. Paprika has something of an iconic status in Hungary, not only as part of the national gastronomy or cuisine, but also as a symbol of Hungarian identity. A recent exhibition entitled 'Mi a Magyar' or 'What is Hungarian?' in Budapest used the image of a green and red pepper for the promotional poster (Figure 4.1). This suggests that the notion of 'Hungarian-ness' is somehow inextricably linked to the pepper or paprika. According to Hofer (1999) the stereotypes that Hungarians have about themselves are closely connected to national symbols. The national 'image bank' tends to be based on history, myths, memories and legends, and paprika became a part of this over time. Paprika is so important in Hungary that two museums in Kalocsa and Szeged have been devoted to its history and usage.

The first question asked by many visitors to the two Paprika museums in Hungary is about the meaning of the word 'paprika', because in Hungarian it refers to both the vegetable (the pepper) and the spice (paprika). Paprika is used extensively in Hungarian cuisine and is the key ingredient for many of Hungary's most renowned and popular dishes such as goulash. Hungarian paprika is deemed to have the greatest range of flavour in the world, ranging from sweet to hot. The spice is regularly used in Hungarian cooking but the image of the (red) vegetable is also commonly used as a cultural icon, not only in the tourism souvenir industry, but also in traditional arts and crafts (e.g. tablecloths, regional costumes, home decorations). Dried red peppers can

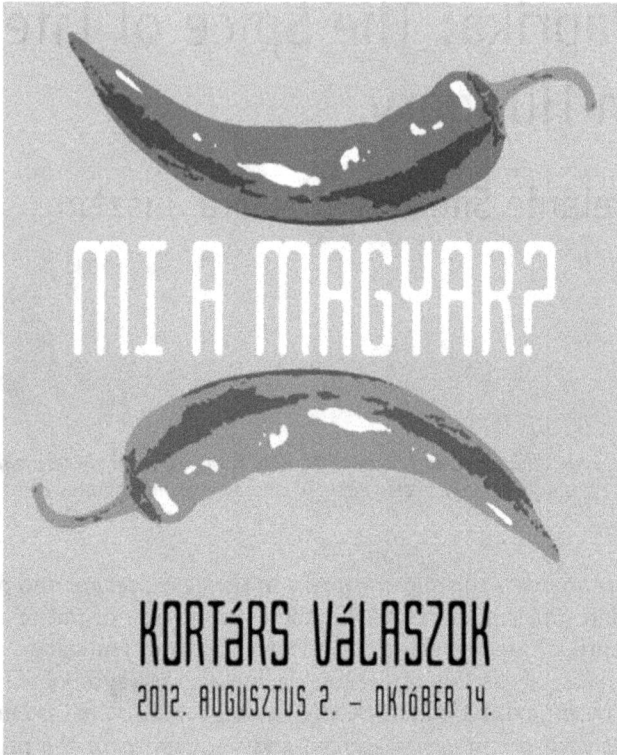

**Figure 4.1** Mi a Magyar – What is Hungarian？ Exhibition poster
*Source*: Palace of Art, 2012

be seen hanging as decorations and is ubiquitous in the souvenir industry in the form of keyrings, fridge magnets, etc.

This chapter therefore considers not only the gastronomic use of paprika, but also its cultural and symbolic significance, such as its importance for commercial activities such as tourism marketing and branding. The chapter will first trace the history of paprika with its culinary origins, moving on to an analysis of the role of paprika in the construction of Hungarian national cultural identity and will finally focus on the iconic and symbolic role of paprika in tourism. Two case studies of the Paprika Museums in Kalocsa and Szeged will be given, based on the researchers' guided tours, participant observation and interviews with the Museum Directors. Archival sources were used for the historical research such as newspapers and journals in the Hungarian, German and English languages.

# History of Paprika in Hungary

*If you have salt and paprika you have all spices.*

Hungarian proverb

The Hungarian word 'paprika' is a diminutive version of the Slavic expression 'papar' – originally meaning 'pepper'. An unknown author, presumably a companion of Cortés, in his printed Relazione di alcune cose della Nuova Spagna, 1556 (A Description of a Few Things from the New Spain) refers to paprika as some kind of 'pepper' possibly because of its extraordinary hot and spicy nature (Montanari, 1996).

Paprika, originating in Meso- and South America, was first brought to Spain by Christopher Columbus before it quickly spread to Europe in the same way as many foods did from the New World. First, it became an exotic luxury plant in the gardens of the nobility, later appearing in the kitchen gardens of the common people before it appeared in agricultural cultivation.

Paprika was brought to Hungary by the Greek, Turkish and Slavic people via the Balkans firstly called 'Turkish pepper' or 'red Turkish pepper' after the Turks who invaded Hungary in the 16th century. A noble lady (Margit Széchy) widely known for her special collection of rare plants is reported to have ordered 'red Turkish pepper' for her garden in 1569. A decade later paprika was transported to the ornamental garden of Lord Boldizsár Batthiány with the help of the famous French botanist Clusius.

Paprika was a rare species in the 16th century ornamental gardens of the Hungarian aristocracy and is mentioned as 'Turkish pepper' in the famous Latin-Hungarian dictionary of Albert Szenczi Molnár a protestant priest and translator as well as in the basic book on gardening 'Posoni kert' (the Garden of Pozsony – the Hungarian name for Bratislava now in Slovakia) by the scholar and Jesuit monk János Lippay. The author of the geographic and historic description of Hungary in 1723, Mátyás Bél refers to paprika no longer as Turkish pepper, but as Hungarian pepper which is – as he says – so hot that it can blind anyone if it gets into the eye.

The term 'paprika' appears first in a Slavic dictionary in 1742. Definite evidence of a relatively wide usage of the spice in the 18th century is the appearance of the term 'paprika' in a monastery inventory in Szeged in 1758. It is not clear when and how the rare species became a widely used spice among ordinary people, but it seems certain that Slavic people migrating to Hungary from the Balkans settled down in the favourable climatic region surrounding Szeged and Kalocsa and domesticated the paprika.

In the church register of Érsekcsanád, a town near Kalocsa many families were listed as having the name 'Paprika' in 1770, and in the same period a shepherd is listed in the shepherd list of Szeged with the same family name. This seems to support the idea of a widespread growth of the spice. In a book about research on flora by József Csapó in 1775 edited in Pozsony it is mentioned that Turkish pepper-paprika is grown in peasant gardens and is ground to sprinkle on meals in powder form. The place of publication proves that paprika in the 18th century was grown beyond the surroundings of Szeged and Kalocsa and even reached the western counties of Hungary. During this period, paprika was mainly grown in family gardens. During the 19th century it was already grown for markets, for example in 1807 paprika was documented to have been weighed in quintal (around 100 kg) and to have been sold in markets (Finály, 1955)

In spite of a widespread growth and use of paprika throughout the country the two emblematic centres remained Szeged and Kalocsa. By the middle of the 19th century garden cultivation transitioned to industrial production resulting in significant changes. A kind of family-run plantation remained and still remains the basis of industrial production. The preparation, drying and grinding of paprika was a domestic activity of women, and often even of children. When the capacity of simple tools of manufacturing (such as the manual grinder called 'külü', and water and dry mills) were no longer enough to meet the demand, the invention of the Pálfy bothers revolutionised the process by separating the pulp, the vein and the seeds thus regulating its spiciness or hotness. One of the conditions of export was to moderate the spiciness. 'Szegedi paprika' appeared at the Vienna World Exhibition in 1874 (Bálint, 1962), and Grossmann Paprika Company exported paprika from Kalocsa in 1886 (Horváth, 1936). János Kotányi, a paprika producer from Szeged operated a paprika mill in Vienna to make fresh paprika available in Viennese markets. He was successful enough to become the royal transporter for the imperial court of Franz Joseph during the time of the Austro-Hungarian monarchy. The paprika of Szeged and Kalocsa even reached America eventually, and it is thought that the French chef Escoffier introduced the spice to western European cuisine around 1879 (Russell, 2012).

In 1917 the Paprika Research and Chemical Plant Kalocsa was established, to control paprika production and to develop new varieties of paprika. During World War I paprika often became a substitute for pepper. In order to preempt an over-production crisis, and to protect the quality of the paprika, a statutory order was released in 1934, establishing the Kalocsa and Szeged closed paprika district (*zárt fűszerpaprika körzet*). Centralised, large-scale production of paprika started in the middle of the 1950s, with the foundation of the Kalocsa Region Paprika Company (*Kalocsavidéki Fűszerpaprika Vállalat*) (Puszta.com, 2012a).

Paprika has been used as a medicine since the 17th century and the first Hungarian document to be regarded as scientific comes from 1813 (Diószegi, 1813) Meals spiced with paprika are suggested for those with a weak stomach, for those who cannot recover from a cold, and for those, who have breathing difficulties. Some people also consider paprika to be a home remedy for so-called 'trembling fever'. Fishermen in Szeged put paprika into boiled wine to cure themselves of fever, and it was used as a medicine during the cholera epidemics of 1831. Drinking paprika seed in *pálinka* (a type of Hungarian brandy) or taking nine seeds per day for nine days are docu-mented to have been used even in the early twentieth century.

Everyday observation was then proved by scientific research: paprika became world famous after Albert Szent Györgyi won the Nobel prize for his work which researched the health giving properties of paprika, including its vitamin C content. After Szent Györgyi proved the high vitamin C con-tent, further scientific research by others proved that paprika was efficient in regulating blood pressure, and is rich in antibacterial properties and anti-oxidants that help the immune system. It is an energiser and a stimulant, it can help the heart and reduce cancer because of the capsaicin content, it can help circulation by preventing and controlling cholesterol, and it can aid digestion. However, the unique popularity of paprika in Hungarian gastron-omy is not attributed to its medical effectiveness, but to its beautiful colour and aroma.

# The Use of Paprika in Hungarian Gastronomy

*The spice of their food is some red beast, and they call it paprika, and it burns like the devil.*
Ubaldus, 18th century

In 2003, when asked to name three traditionally Hungarian food items in marketing surveys, 52% of respondents mentioned paprika first (Popovics & Pallóné, 2003). Nobody eats more paprika-spiced food than the Hungarians said Mátyás Bél in the 18th century. The first description of the usage of paprika is to be found in the hand-written recipe collection by Kristós Simai roughly of the same period (Simai, 2011). This is only true for the eating habits of simple people – aristocratic people ate it only in pickled form (Kisbán, 1989). Hungarian horsemen in the 18th century substituted expensive pepper with paprika by simply slicing it into their so-called 'paprika-meat' cooked outdoors on the pastures. This dish 'goulash' was named after those who first prepared it, as one meaning of 'goulash' was 'horseman'. This simple but tasty meal spread first to the army then to roadsides. Half a century later it was being served in Szeged restaurants for civilians and the recipe can even be found in a Viennese cookery book. In Hungarian cuisine it is known as 'pörkölt' (stew) and then if more liquid is added as 'goulash'. The latter is a soup whereas the dish usually thought to be goulash by foreigners is the original 'pörkölt'. Neither of the two can be prepared without paprika. Indeed, most Hungarian traditional dishes contain paprika, such as paprika chicken, stuffed cabbage, fish soup, and letcho (a mixture of tomatoes, onions and peppers). Paprika can be used both as a flavouring and a garnish to give colour to dishes. It must be heated to release the flavour, but it is relatively easy to over-heat and burn because of its high sugar content. Paprika paste is also put into or served with Hungarian-style dishes. It comes either in small bottles under the brands Erös Pista (hot) and Édes Anna (sweet), or in tubes under the name Piros Arany (meaning Red Gold).

Gille (2004: 2) explores what makes paprika Hungarian, as its origins are clearly not purely Hungarian. She describes paprika as:

A one-of-a-kind product, one that enjoys worldwide brand name recognition, and thus it contributes positively to the image of Hungarian products. Second, it is used in many other products Hungary exports such as (.........) Pick salami and Gyulai sausage. Third, as a national symbol, it is an asset in promoting tourism. In a sense, we can call paprika the Hungaricum of Hungaricums.

A 'Hungaricum' refers to a unique product marketed and protected as originating in a particular geographical location. Michalkó (2002) discussed the importance of Hungaricums for the external image of Hungary. Within this analysis he included Tokaji wine, Herendi porcelain, Gyula sausage, as well as emphasising the importance of Hungarian paprika, which he compares to Scottish whisky, Cuban cigars, French perfume or Chinese tea. The research he discusses shows that around 40% of foreign visitors tend to buy as souvenirs paprika-related products such as ground paprika, paprika spread and pickled paprika. Szeged and Kalocsa paprika were patented by EU law in 2010 and 2011 respectively (European Commission, 2010, 2011). In 1999 a Hungaricum Club was founded in Hungary launched by Herend Porcelain, Pick Szeged Co., Tokaj Trading House and Zwack Unicum. These and other products are supposed to represent the 'pure essence of Hungary' (Ministry of Foreign Affairs, 2012). Paprika is mentioned as an essential ingredient in Hungarian stews (especially Goulash), fish soup ('no true Hungarian fish soup omits the paprika', p. 8), as well as Paprika Sausage made from Mangalica (a type of pig). However, changing tastes and globalisation have resulted in new and different uses for paprika, including in Tabasco sauce or Bloody Mary cocktails.

Hudgins (2010) describes each kind of paprika:

- *Különleges* (Special): the brightest red paprika of all, with a good aroma and very mild, sweet flavor;
- *Édesnemes* (Noble Sweet): bright red in colour but with only a mildly spicy flavour. Most of the paprika exported to the rest of the world is this type;
- *Csípmentes Csemege* (Delicate): mild-tasting, richly flavored, light- to bright-red paprika;
- *Csemege* (Exquisite Delicate): similar in colour and aroma to 'Delicate,' but with a slightly spicier taste;
- *Csípős Csmege* (Pungent Exquisite Delicate): similar in colour and aroma to Delicate and Exquisite Delicate, but a bit spicier in flavor; oneof the most popular of the hotter varieties of paprika in Hungary;
- *Félédes* (Semi-Sweet): medium-hot paprika;
- *Rozsa* (Rose): paler-red in colour, with a strong aroma and hot-spicy taste;
- *Erös* (Hot): the hottest variety, pale rust-red to light brownish-yellow in colour.

## Paprika as Icon: Hungarian Cultural and National Identity

> *In Hungary, paprika has become a symbol of national identity.*
> Katz, 2009: 13

Frew and White (2011: 1) provide an analysis of the intersection between tourism and national identity, stating that:

> The tourist may develop a deeper appreciation of a destination by understanding it through the lens of national identity, and in the same way tourism marketers and planners might be better equipped to promote and manage it.

Promoting a national identity through tourism is one way in which a country can project a particular self-image to the international community and create unique and distinctive selling propositions. The strategic development of tourism products relating to national identity can help to enhance regions economically or socially (as seen later in the case of Szeged and Kalocsa in Hungary).

Smith and Puczkó (in Frew & White, 2011) suggest that Hungary has struggled to establish its national identity, simultaneously trying to cast off the shadow of its socialist heritage, whilst highlighting pre-socialist 'Golden Ages' and promoting post-EU-accession cosmopolitanism. The authors do not mention paprika specifically, but they emphasise the fact that national tourism promotion has almost exclusively been based on cultural tourism and heritage for the past 20 years. It is also suggested that gastronomy, wines, festivals and 'Hungaricums' (of which paprika is one, as mentioned earlier) are all becoming increasingly important.

Themes explored in Frew and White's (2011) book include identity and image; culture and community; and heritage and history. This section will discuss further the role paprika has played in the history and heritage of Hungary, including its emergence as a national symbol of identity for peasant and noble communities alike. References in national cultural sources such as literature, poetry and song are also considered. The icon or image of the paprika is also associated with political struggles for identity, for example, on websites or blogs and in contemporary exhibitions.

There is no other spice in Hungarian gastronomy that is as culturally significant as paprika. It appears in both language and literature. A 'paprikás hangulat' (paprika atmosphere) means a tense atmosphere or mood, whereas 'paprika piros' (as red as paprika) is used for people who blush. 'Paprika Jancsi' is used to mean a fool. The great Hungarian author Sandor Peföfi compares the colour of the setting sun to the red colour of paprika, whereas a 20th century lyric poet Dezsö Kosztolányi associates the atmosphere of autumn with drying strings of paprika. In a children's poem Tündérek szakácskönyve (Fairy Cookbook) by Géza Páskándi paprika is described as a red-nosed clown. Paprika is often mentioned in songs, and after Szent Györgyi's discovery, in an Operetta tune, the so called paprika 'czardas' (authors' own translation):

> Paprika, you are C Vitamin
> Your problem is, you are stronger than gin
> Your nose has a blue and purple sheen
> Paprika, you are C Vitamin

The motif of paprika appeared in both applied arts and in folk art. Strings of paprika have been and are still used to decorate verandahs or the sides of houses in Kalocsa and Szeged and in the surrounding villages. The motif of the paprika flower and that of the paprika itself often feature in the embroideries of table cloths, blouses and dresses originally containing mostly flower patterns and to a lesser extent human and animal figurative elements. The walls of interiors are also painted with these motifs by the so-called painting-women (pingáló asszonyok) and the paprika pattern can be seen on the porcelain products of the Kalocsa porcelain factory founded in 1971.

The fact that paprika has become an element of national identity is partly attributable to the 'paprika meat' dish of the horsemen in the 18th century mentioned earlier and partly because of history itself. Hungarian aristocracy in their protest against the centralisation and modernisation politics of the Habsburg dynasty from the late 18th century chose two symbols: national costume and gastronomy. Gastronomy meant above all the simple dishes of simple people. Goulash thus became a national symbol as a result of the 'romantic' search for national roots. Foreigners have therefore long associated goulash with Hungarianness.

Count Hoffmannsegg, a traveler from Saxony ate 'paprika meat' in the surroundings of Szeged and called it a Hungarian national food, although he also calls it Turkish pepper (Kisbán, 1989) After the compromise of 1867 between Austria and Hungary the dish lost its protest character, but it continued to be the symbol of Hungarian national gastronomy and the subject of national pride.

The term 'Goulash Communism' was sometimes used when referring to Hungary during the socialist era (1962–1989). It represented a departure from Stalinism and embraced elements of free-market economics and social welfare. This metaphor was used to refer to the mixed ideology of Hungarian communism, presumably considered as mixed as the ingredients in a goulash!

Bako (2012) writes on a website called 'Paprika Politik' about Hungarian identity. This article has nothing much to do with paprika, but is about the cultivation of a healthy national identity. A group calling themselves 'Planet Paprika' organised seminars in April 2012 which looked at challenging stereotpes of Roma people and racism against them (Phiren Amenca, 2012). Another Blogspot by an English resident about Hungarian identity is entitled 'PaprikaTown'. He discusses the exhibition about Hungarian identity mentioned earlier 'What is Hungarian', describing 'One witty exhibit, juxtaposing traditional with contemporary pleasures, has a shot of palinka in a small glass beside two "lines" of finely ground red powder – which is, of course, paprika' (Paprika Town, 2012). The researchers' own interpretation of this exhibit was that paprika along with *pálinka* somehow represented the Hungarian 'drug' of choice! There is also a quotation in the 'What is a Hungarian' exhibition which suggests that the motif of paprika can also refer to Hungarians' 'spicy', poignant language.

# The Role of Paprika in Hungarian Tourism

> *Brazilian and Spanish peppers could never win against the*
> *paprika from Szeged and Kalocsa.*
> Gille, 2004: 6

As mentioned above the main areas for growing paprika have always been and still are two towns on the Hungarian Alföld (Hungarian Great Plain) Szeged and Kalocsa together with the surrounding areas and villages. When looking at the relationship between paprika and tourism in this area, it should be focused on in the inter-war period which was the birth and the first golden age of Hungarian tourism. The professional newspapers of the period help us understand the role of paprika in the tourism industry.

Szeged was the bigger, more significant town and easier to reach by railway. Szeged was and is a university town on the banks of the river Tisza, a cultural centre with open-air performances in summer time, where direct trains were organised to transport visitors. The water found near Szeged was considered equal in value to the Vichy water in France (A Szálloda, 1937).

A newspaper called *'Fremdenverkehr in Ungarn'* (Tourism in Hungary) mentions the university clinic as a place to visit because of its 'fame that has reached five continents'. This was the place where Albert Szent Györgyi succeeded in extracting a large amount of vitamin C from the Szeged paprika. The text calls Szeged the world centre of vitamin C because the best Turkish pepper is grown around the town in an amount that could (it claims) cover the vitamin C needs of the whole world (Fremdenverkehr in Ungarn, 1934). The unknown author of the article places the town on the world map because of a scientific discovery based on paprika.

Three years later the *Budapester Fremdenzeitung* (Budapest Foreign Gazette) published an article on Szeged. A special feature was an organised tour for tourists to Röszke, the 'paprika village' very close to Szeged where a paprika mill could be visited and the grinding could be seen. In this case the visiting of the paprika mill functions as an independent touristic activity designed to extend the stay in Szeged.

According to the articles of the Kalocsi Újság (Kalocsa Newspaper) the town worked hard to develop tourism. Originally it was very difficult to reach the place as it was five hours by railway. A more convenient way for tourists with more time was by ship. From the little harbour horse-drawn trains took the tourists into the town. (The railway station building is now owned by the Kalocsa Rowing Club.) Folk art and the characteristic Kalocsa wall paintings (pingálás) were considered the biggest attraction. The Népművészeti Ház (folklore house), the railway station house and some private houses were used to demonstrate the special painting style and patterns. Further cultural programs included visiting the cathedral and a short trip outside the town to see the stud-farm. From 1938 the visit to the paprika mill was also documented (Kalocsai Újság, 1938), but it did not lengthen the stay. A Swiss ship on its way to the Black Sea is reported to have stopped for one day in Kalocsa on 10 April, 1936. The first information about bags advertising paprika being given to visitors is documented here (Kalocsai Újság, 1936).

Paprika seems to have played a very similar role in the tourism of Kalocsa compared to Szeged but to a lesser extent. The paprika mill was an exotic site as well as paprika being given as a gift. They were part of 'local colour' or an early Hungaricum. The idea of selling paprika as a souvenir had not yet been thought of. Only embroideries were considered worth selling.

Tourists' attention was drawn not only to paprika in its homeland, but also in the capital Budapest. Brochures were placed in the rooms of elegant hotels and the Budapester Fremdenzeitung in a 1936 issue published an article with the title: 'Spezialitäten der ungarischen Küche' (Hungarian Gastronomic Specialities). The introduction is very telling 'The main spice in Hungarian cuisine is paprika. Do not forget this means real Hungarian rose-paprika, not to be confused with pepperoni, which is usually considered paprika abroad.' The article finishes by saying 'Take home Szeged paprika as a gift' (Kalocsai Újság, 1936: 11) proving that in Budapest paprika was quite consciously used as souvenir in the same period.

Historical examples of the two main paprika centres clearly shows the various functions of paprika in tourism: an activity or programme, a site (e.g. visiting a paprika mill), a gift or souvenir, as well as a marketing tool used to promote the towns. Today, the website for the Kalocsa Paprika Museum (Puszta.com, 2012b) urges:

> Don't miss this once in a life-time opportunity. You will never look at a bag or box of paprika the same way again. ... And you'll never buy any that don't have the Hungarian flag on them, and they don't say Kalocsa or Szeged.

Ripe peppers are harvested in September. Kalocsa, Szeged and the neighbouring villages are adorned with bright red, threaded strings of paprika, hung from the fences and porches. These have also become a common sight in other parts of Hungary, and are often seen for sale in markets or at cultural and gastronomic festivals. The Great Market or *Vásárcsarnok* tends to be a major tourist attraction in Budapest, and is one of the main places where tourists can purchase a wide range of paprika. Metro-Roland

(2008: 171) describes how 'one of the most obvious signs of the tourist nature of the site are stalls which turn paprika into an aestheticised folk item through the inclusion of decorative bags and wooden spoons'. However, she notes that it is actually the same paprika that is available in local grocers' shops in Hungary!

## Case Studies: Kalocsa and Szeged Museums

There are two museums in Hungary focusing on paprika. One of these is in a small picturesque town called Kalocsa which is about 120 km south of Budapest. It has a 1000 year old religious and folk history, an important cultural museum and pretty buildings, but Kalocsa is not on the typical tourist trail in Hungary, indeed, it is somewhat remote and not that easy to access except by car or possibly river boat. Szeged in the south-east of Hungary is a larger University town which attracts a reasonable numbers of tourists because of its wider range of cultural attractions and events. Interestingly, however, the Paprika Museum in Kalocsa seems to play a more important role in tourism. Indeed, an employee of the Szeged Tourist Information Office stated during an interview that Szeged is more famous for Pick Salami, fish soup and Szeged folk slippers than paprika. Szeged is perhaps more famous for Pick Salami, as there is a factory there (established in 1869, but which is not open to visitors) and the Paprika Museum shares the same space as the Pick Salami Museum. From the 1960s the Szeged Paprika Corporation operated a small history of paprika collection but it was discontinued. In 1975 Pick Salami established a company history collection, which was moved in 1987 to the location where it can still be found today. In 1999 to commemorate the 130th anniversary of the factory, the museum was opened where some of the aforementioned paprika collection was exhibited.

The museums are arguably not typical of many of the museums in Hungary, which tend to be very traditional and focus mainly on collections. There are some tangible artefacts such as industrial and agricultural tools and machines, some costumes and examples of embroidery, paprika boxes and containers, but the exhibitions also include histories, stories, definitions, quotations and illustrations. They operate more according to Simpson's (1996: 5) idea that museums must become focused increasingly on people rather than collections if they are to evolve and to become 'exciting, lively and entertaining'. Engaging the audience becomes as important as the artefacts themselves. Here, that includes Hungarian school groups, elderly excursionists as well as domestic and international tourists. As advocated by Urry

(1990) they emphasise 'plural histories', such as that of the peasants or folk culture, as well as industrial heritage (e.g. factory production of paprika). Ross (2004) suggests that audience awareness makes museums more accessible, which may explain the relatively high visitation levels for these 'niche' museums. They are more like the 'post-museums' described by Hooper-Greenhill (2000) where the use of objects is as important as their contemplation, and intangible culture and its interpretation counts as much as tangible objects. (Post)-museums and heritage sites need to provide engaging, interactive experiences (Ferrari, 2012; Puczkó, 2012). The senses can be engaged through music or films (e.g. the Kalocsa Museum shows a film about the making of paprika) or tasting and sampling (e.g. the Szeged Museum offers salami tasting and gives sachets of paprika as souvenirs to take home).

In September 2012 the researchers visited both the Kalocsa and Szeged Paprika Museums. They were given a guided tour and were granted an in-depth interview with each of the Museum Directors. They also undertook participant observation while in the Museums. The Museum Directors were asked the following questions:

- Approximately how many visitors do you have per year?
- What is the typical profile of your visitors?
- Is the main interest in paprika connected to gastronomy or other products/usages too?
- Do you think Hungarian and foreign visitors have a different knowledge of and interest in paprika and its associated products?
- Do you think that interest in paprika and museum is growing or declining?
- How important is the role of the museum in attracting tourists to Kalocsa/Szeged?
- What have been the impacts of globalisation (e.g. technology, media, transport) on paprika production and promotion?
- Has there been a change over the years in the way that paprika has been used in cuisine, culture and crafts (i.e. adaptation to tourists' tastes; loss of authenticity)?
- How important is paprika in the development of Hungarian identity in your view?

## Kalocsa

The Paprika Museum in Kalocsa was established in 1977 supported by the Kalocsa Paprika Factory and the Hungarian Museum of Agriculture. It is open from Tuesday to Sunday from 9.00–17.00 but only between 1 April and 31 October. Group visits are possible at other times, but only by pre-arrangement. The seasonal opening times suggest that its main markets are tourists and excursionists. Almost all tourists to Kalocsa come to the Paprika Museum especially as there is a boat cruise which stops there and the Paprika Museum is on the itinerary as a 'must see' attraction. It is therefore probably true to say that many visitors come to Kalocsa with the primary motivation of visiting the Paprika Museum, but it is also because it features on most tour itineraries for groups. There are about 15,000–18,000 visitors per year. At present, the temporary home of the Paprika Museum is not really big enough to accommodate the number of visitors (it moved from another building shortly before the researchers' visit as the former building was being repaired). While the authors were interviewing the Director, a large English-speaking tour group arrived. One of the researchers questioned the Guide who said that the Paprika Museum was on the tour for new international students to a nearby Music School as part of their cultural orientation. The profile of the visitors varies considerably, but tends to be 24–40 year olds during long weekends, but also 50–70 year olds from boat trips or on wellness holidays. Most of them visit the Museum in groups. The main interest seems to be in gastronomy, especially Hungarian Goulash. Foreign visitors need more information and explanation, especially about the different types of paprika, whereas Hungarians have a better knowledge (most know what 'édes nemes' or 'noble sweet' is, for example).

Information in the exhibition is available in English, French and German and is attractively presented in laminated books which serve as an addition to the trilingual panels of explanation and description. The exhibition starts with definitions of paprika, as according to the Museum Director, this is always the first question of visitors. They are sometimes surprised that there is only one word in Hungarian for both the vegetable and the spice. Translations of the word paprika are also given in many languages. This is followed by the history of paprika as outlined earlier in this chapter. There is then a film about how paprika is grown, harvested and processed once picked, but this is only in Hungarian. On the floor there is an educational trail showing how a paprika seed is planted and what happens next. This is especially useful for school children or those who enjoy visual more than verbal representations. There is also information about the health benefits of paprika as discovered by Hungarian scientists. There are cabinets showing the different beauty products that have been developed from paprika, including massage oil, weight loss and cellulite treatments, even face creams. However, the Director pointed out that these were not necessarily Hungarian products.

Thus, the spice more than the vegetable is closely associated with Hungary, although the vegetable seems to have developed an iconic status too. This is evident in the motifs used to decorate the walls of houses or the clothes and costumes of Kalocsa. Sometimes the paprika flower rather than the actual pepper is used as decoration, especially for embroidery. According to the exhibition, red peppers were not used in folk art until the 1920s and 1930s, including for wall and furniture paintings.

The Paprika Days Festival has also been organised in Kalocsa for the past 23 years and coincides with the harvest in September. The festival consists of two main parts: the Paprika Days and a cooking competition of foods containing paprika, which became part of the festival 16 years ago. The festival attracts around 10,000 people who are mainly locals and their family members or friends, as well as visitors from several of the twin cities of Kalocsa. The event is financed by Kalocsa City Marketing Ltd. and the Municipality and is supported by bids and sponsorships.

## Szeged

The Szeged Museum has limited opening hours from Tuesday–Saturday 15.00–18.00 which the Director deemed adequate for the number and nature of the visitors. It does not have seasonal opening hours like Kalocsa, however, and only closes during major holidays. Groups are also welcome at other times if a pre-booking is made. There is an informative website (Szeged Paprika Museum, 2013). The exhibition has information in Hungarian, English and German, but downloadable information is available in a further eight languages. There is an exhibition about the internationally famous Pick Salami in the same Museum. It is therefore difficult to research how many visitors come specifically for the Paprika exhibition, but the Director noted that visitors tend to buy more salami fridge magnets from the shop! On the other hand, visitors are attracted by the paprika in decorative boxes. There is also the added complication of Szeged being a larger town than Kalocsa with many more cultural attractions. The Museum does not necessarily feature as a 'must-see' sight of Szeged in the same way as the one in Kalocsa. Nevertheless, if visitors are already in Szeged, they tend to visit the Museum, especially as the Tourist Office gives out a map on which the Museum is featured prominantly. There are between 8000–17,000 visitors per year (the latter being an unusually good year when tour operators sent several bus tour groups per day). The State does not support the Museum, but statistics have to be collected about visitor numbers anyway. There have been many adverts and media promoting the Museum. In the first few years after the Museum opened, the numbers grew surprisingly rapidly. However, there has been a slight decrease in numbers recently. There are many foreigners as well as Hungarians from Germany especially, but even Kenya and Saudi Arabia. While the researchers were in the Museum in September, at least 6–7 visitors came and at least two of them were English-speaking (i.e. non-Hungarian). There are varied age groups because school groups are very common at certain times of the year (e.g. April onwards). The summer is generally quite mixed. Every visitor receives a sachet of paprika on leaving. The shop sells posters, puzzles, fridge magnets, postcards, bags and decorative tins of paprika.

The actual exhibition is of a similar size to that of Kalocsa, but focuses a little bit more on the process of growth, harvesting and production, including some of the more technical details. There is more emphasis on gastronomy than culture, whereas Kalocsa represents the wider significance of paprika more fully. The focus on gastronomy and production is not surprising given that the factory is nearby and it gives the visitor insight into the 'biology' of the paprika itself and its transformation from vegetable to spice. This information is available in Kalocsa too, but it is not quite as prominent.

'Paprika Days' were also organised in Szeged from the end of the 1990s until 2006, but since 2008 there has been an annual 3-day Paprika Festival in late September or early October. The focus is mainly on gastronomy, but includes concerts, folk dancing, puppet theatre and other cultural activities. Each year so-called 'Ambassadors of Paprika' are elected. In 2012 however, there was no festival. In comparison, the Szeged Open Air Festival in summer based on music, opera and musicals has existed for 70 years and attracts 55,000–70,000 visitors of whom 1–2% come from abroad.

# Conclusions

*Once you've tasted true Hungarian paprika – and mastered the simple technique of cooking with it – you'll never again think of paprika as just a pretty spice.*
Hudgins, 2010

This chapter demonstrates how one humble red vegetable can be elevated to the status of a national symbol and icon as well as a tourist attraction through its conversion to a spice. Ferenc Temesi claimed that 'Milling pepper is a Hungarian invention' (Kalocsa Museum, 2012) and Gille (2004: 3) states that 'Obviously, what made it Hungarian were various practices surrounding this plant and spice'. She refers to genetic modification, processing peppers into a spice, and integrating them into the culinary repertoire. Paprika clearly has many associations in Hungary, some are practical, others cultural and a few are symbolic. As discussed earlier from its origins as an exotic foreign houseplant, via the ornamental gardens of the nobility, paprika has become an indigenised, EU-patented 'Hungaricum' known all over the world. It was used as an ingredient for stews and soups by horsemen and peasants; as a symbol of protest against the Habsburgs and a romanticised icon of folk life by the aristocracy; as a medicine and a health food scientifically proven to be extremely rich in vitamin C; as a motif for decorating the walls of houses, tablecloths, folk costumes and porcelain; it appears figuratively and metaphorically in Hungarian literature, music, poetry and proverbs, as a tourist attraction, gift and ubiquitous souvenir in markets and shops; and as a symbol of Hungarian identity, from the late 18th century right up until a 2012 exhibition.

Although spice-related paprika activities do not usually serve as a primary motivation for tourists to visit Hungary, the paprika production in and around Szeged and Kalocsa have been relatively popular tourist attractions since the 1930s. Today the paprika museums are sometimes even a must-see attraction on tour group itineraries (especially boat tour groups to Kalocsa). Paprika is a rich and vibrant icon symbolising both the past and present identity of Hungary and no doubt its future too. As stated by Éva Marton, the famous Hungarian opera singer (Operanews, 1983): 'Paprika is our national spice, we cannot exist without it'.

## Acknowledgements

Special thanks to Dr Andrea Hübner for translating the Hungarian parts of this chapter into English. Thank you to Adél Lakatos from the Treasury of the Archbishop of Kalocsa, Gyula Végh, Director of the Pick Salami and Szeged Paprika Museum, and Ferenc Stadler, the Director of Kalocsa City Marketing Ltd for their help with the research.

Thank you also to Gábor Gulyás, the Director of the Palace of Art for permission to use the exhibition photo (Figure 4.1).

## References

Bako, T. (2012) 'Xenophobia or National Self-Preservation', *Paprika Politik*. http://www.paprikapolitik.com/2012/09/xenophobia-or-national-self-preservation (accessed 15 September 2012).

Bálint, S. (1962) *A szegedi paprika*. Budapest: Akadémiai Könyvkiadó.

Budapester Fremdenzeitung (1936) IV, p. 11.

Diószegi, S. (1813) *Magyar Füvészkönyv*, Debrecen.

European Commission (2010) Szegedi Paprika. http://eur-lex.europa.eu/LexUriServ/LexUriServ.do?uri=OJ:C:2010:044:0008:0012:EN:PDF (accessed 15 December 2012).

European Commission (2011) Kalocsai Fűszerpaprika-Őrlemény. http://eur-lex.europa.eu/LexUriServ/LexUriServ.do?uri=OJ:C:2011:303:0016:0020:EN:PDF (accessed 15 December 2012).

Ferrari, S. (2012) An experiential approach to differentiating tourism offers in cultural heritage. In M.K. Smith and G. Richards (eds) *The Routledge Handbook of Cultural Tourism*. London: Routledge. Chapter 47.

Finály, I. (1955) *A Magyar Pirospaprika*. Budapest: Müvelt Nép.

Fremdenverkehr in Ungarn (1934) May, p. 5.

Frew, E. and White, L. (eds) *Tourism and National Identities*. London: Routledge.

Gille, Z. (2004) European Union food and environmental standards: A Polanyian self-protection of society. http://www.michaelmbell.net/suscon-papers/gille-paper.doc (accessed 15 September 2012).

Hofer, T. (1999) *A nemzettudat változó jelképei*. In *Magyarságkép és történeti változásai* (pp. 133–141). Budapest: MTA.

Hooper-Greenhill, E. (2000) *Museums and the Interpretation of Visual Culture*. London: Routledge.

Horváth, F. (1936) *A fűszerpaprika feldolgozása*. Budapest.

Hudgins, S. (2010) Paprika: Hungary's 'Red Gold'. http://europeantraveler.net/archives/taste-of-europe/paprika.php (accessed 12 June 2012).

Kalocsai Újság (1936) 10 April, p. 3.

Kalocsai Újság (1938) 23 August, p. 4.

Katz, E. (1989) 'Chili pepper from Mexico to Europe. Food, imaginary and cultural identity'. In F.X. Medina, R. Avila and I. De Garine (eds) *Food, Imaginaries and Cultural Frontiers: Essays in Honour of Helen Macbeth*, Guadalajara: Universidad de Guadalajara. http://www.documentation.ird.fr/hor/fdi:010052105 (accessed 15 September 2012).

Kisbán, E. (1989) Társadalmi rendszerváltozáson átívelve 1780–1880. In M. Flórián (ed.) *Magyar Néprajz I.2. A magyar népi műveltség korszakai* (pp. 418–420), Budapest: Akadémia Kiadó.

Michalkó, G. (2002) *Országkép és kiskereskedelem: A külföldi turisták szabadidős vásárlásai a magyarországi idegenvezetők szemével*, Turizmus Bulletin, VI (3). http://www.itthon.hu/site/upload/mtrt/Turizmus_Bulletin/02_03/P22.htm (accessed 5 January 2013).

Metro-Roland, M.M. (2008) Reading signs, interpreting meaning and placing culture in the Budapest Landscape. PhD thesis. http://gradworks.umi.com/3331272.pdf (accessed 24 September 2012).

Ministry of Foreign Affairs (2012) Hungaricum: All that is inimitable, unique, distinct – and Hungarian. http://www.mfa.gov.hu/NR/rdonlyres/56997B6D-A939-4ED6-91A7-5075718B6B61/0/Hungaricum_en.pdf (accessed 15 September 2012).

Mirko (2012) A taste of Europe: Hungary. http://www.mirkostasteofeurope.com/hungary.htm (accessed 15 September 2012).

Montanari, M. (1996) *The Culture of Food*. London: Blackwell.

Operanews (1983) *Marton Éva: Különleges étkezési és utazási szám*, April. http://www.martoneva.hu/hu/kulonleges-etkezesi-es-utazasi-szam (accessed 15 January 2013).

Paprika Town (2012) What is Hungarian? 5 August. http://paprikatown.blogspot.hu/2012/08/what-is-hungarian.html (accessed 24 September).

Phiren Amenca (2012) Welcome to Planet Paprika. http://www.rgdts.net/wp-content/uploads/2012/08/Welcome-to-Planet-Paprika-Seminar-Description.pdf (accessed 15 September 2012).

Popovics, A. and Pallóné, I.K. (2003) *Hagyományos és tájjellegű élelmiszerek ismertségének vizsgálata [Survey of the knowledge of traditional and characteristic regional food]*. Budapest: Élelmiszeri Közlemények.

Puczkó, L. (2012) Visitor experiences in cultural spaces. In M.K. Smith and G. Richards (eds) *The Routledge Handbook of Cultural Tourism* (Chapter 48). London: Routledge.

Puszta.com (2012a) History and Dispersal of Paprika in Hungary. http://puszta.com/eng/hungary/cikk/paprika_tortenete_elterjedese (accessed 15 September 2012).

Puszta.com (2012b) Paprika Museum Kalocsa. http://puszta.com/eng/programs/cikk/paprika_muzeum_kalocsa (accessed 24 September 2012).

Ross, M. (2004) Interpreting the new museology. *Museum and Society* 2 (2), 84–103.

Russell, J. (2012) Paprika. http://www.foodreference.com/html/artpaprika.html (accessed 24 September 2012).

Simai K. (2011) *Némely étkek elkészítési módja*. Budapest: Alinea Kiadó.

Smith, M.K and Puczkó, L. (2011) National identity construction and tourism in Hungary: a multi-level approach. In E. Frew and L. White (eds) *Tourism and National Identities* (pp. 38–51). London: Routledge.

Simpson, M. (1996) *Making Representations: Museums in the Post-Colonial Era*. London: Routledge.

A Szálloda (1937) I, October, p. 11.

Szegedi paprika cco. (2012) http://www.szegedipaprika.hu/english/frame (accessed 24 September 2012).

Szeged Paprika Museum (2013) http://www.pickmuzeum.hu/index-en.html (accessed 24 January 2013).

Urry, J. (1990) *The Tourist Gaze: Leisure and Travel in Contemporary Societies*. London: Sage.

# 5 Agriculture and Ecotourism in India's Goa Province: A Taste of Spices

Ana Firmino

> *You are now in India, with its various*
> *Peoples who prosper and grow rich*
> *From gold and sweet perfumes and peppercorns,*
> *Cardamoms, hot chilies, and precious stones.*
> Camoens, Luis (1524/5–1580)
> The Lusiads, translated by White (1997: 145)

Spices have long dictated the destiny of Goa. The local population and the Vaidyas, practitioners of Ayurvedic medicine, were familiar with their therapeutic uses. The arrival of the Portuguese boosted local production and introduced other species that were acclimatized here and later exported to different parts of the world. The trade of these valuable goods contributed to an era of wealth with economic, social, technical and scientific repercussions, mainly during the 16th and 17th centuries. In spite of all the wars and conflicts that were registered during the history of this Indian province, spices remained one of its main products and are still an asset today.

During the 1990s some Indian farmers decided to diversify their activities, taking advantage of the international flow of tourists to Goa. This gave rise to a set of interesting rural thematic parks [established on spice plantations], where leisure and pedagogical activities are offered together with accommodation. The potential of these plantations to integrate spices into tourism goes far beyond this activity since the farmers also work with schools, contributing through the diversification of their activities to the maintenance of this important historical and cultural heritage. They show a global consciousness of the environmental problems by framing their activities in a sustainable mode of production, while responding to present societal challenges of food security, clean water supply, biodiversity and ecosystem services.

The region of Ponda in Goa, India, where the majority of these spice plantations are located, may thus be considered in the future as a 'Globally Important Agricultural Heritage System' (GIAHS) as a recognition for its cultural system, dynamic conservation and adaptive management, as well as agricultural biodiversity, knowledge systems, food and livelihood security (FAO, n.d.).

This chapter will tackle the relevance of a common past to sustainable development in Goa, with positive ecological, social and economic repercussions, based on a concept of ecotourism on spice plantations, examining how this historical and cultural patrimony has been preserved as one of the most valuable touristic resources.

# In the Dawn of History

The majority of the inhabitants in the world, when strolling around their own lands, are not aware that most of the species that are today familiar to them in their environments were brought from distant and exotic places.

Spices were one of the most valuable products traded that today are commonly used in our gastronomy.

Trade in the ancient world included the use of caravans with as many as 4000 camels carrying the treasures from the east, namely, spices. We can imagine the caravans trudging along from Calicut, Goa and Orient to the spice markets in Babylon, Carthage, Alexandria, and Rome. For hundreds of years, traders also used ships which sailed along the Indian coast, past the Persian Gulf, along the coast of South Arabia, and finally through the Red Sea into Egypt. Trade in antiquity was subject to constant robberies, storms and shipwrecks, and piracy. (Cornillez, 2012: 1–2)

The plants with capacity to acclimatize in different geographic locations participated in an epopee, such as the one described in the opening rhyme by Camoens, in the 16th century in his book 'Lusiads', about the discoveries undertaken by the Portuguese and their endeavour to globalize a world not yet known. As a result, in some South East Indo-European languages sweet oranges are named after Portugal, because they were brought from India to Europe in the 15th century by Portuguese traders. Examples are Bulgarian *portokal*, Greek *portokali*, Persian *porteghal*, and Romanian *portocala*. Also in South Italian dialects (Napolitan), orange is named *portogallo* or *purtualle*, literally 'the Portuguese ones'. Related names can also be found in other languages: Turkish *Portakal*, Arabic *al-burtukal*, Amharic *birtukan* and Georgian *phortokhali*.

Singh (1998: 2) mentions that 'some of the common fruits, which we take for granted in this country [India], have been introduced from the tropical parts of America, probably by Portuguese settlers. These include guava, papaya, sapota or chikoo, custardapple and pineapple'. Russell-Wood (in Correia, 2006: 355) explains that 'the Portuguese were the carriers of plants and vegetables from temperate to tropical climes and vice-versa through the relocation of seeds and cuttings or even through transporting the whole plant'. Therefore 'a great variety of flora is known to have been carried by the Portuguese between tropical India, South-East-Asia, China, Oceania, Africa, the Atlantic Islands and Brazil'.

Goa is rich in fruits, for instance bananas, jackfruit, pineapple, papaya. chikoo, litchi, cashew nuts, lemon, etc. Mangos are present 'in different varieties, unique taste, with Portuguese names: Afonso, Monserrate, Fernandino, malcorado, etc. that probably were taken from those persons who isolated the variety and spread via the "grafting" of plants' (Monteiro, 2012: 102). Goan gastronomy reflects the intensive contacts that were deepened through miscegenation and missionary work combining Indian spices (Figure 5.1) with Portuguese techniques and recipes. Sen (2010: 2) wrote that 'gastronomically, the Portuguese legacy was widespread, profound, and enduring'. In 'The Portuguese Influence on Bengali Cuisine' (Sen, 2010: 11–12) presents some Goan recipes that she collected from Das Gupta et al. (1995) and Limond (n.d.) where this influence is clear, although spices have been added to the original recipe. Sorpotel, for instance (sarapatel, a traditional Portuguese dish prepared with pieces of pork, ox tongue, beef heart, vinegar and onions) garlic, ginger, cumin seeds, cloves, green cardamoms, cinnamon, black pepper and dry red chilies were added; vindaloo (vinha de alho, pork originally marinated in wine or vinegar and garlic) is prepared with red chilies, coriander, cumin, cloves, green cardamoms and cinnamon. Similarly many of the traditional Goan desserts (such as bebinca, Christmas cake and custards) are inspired by Portuguese conventional monastic recipes. Reciprocally a large variety of spices are common in the Portuguese cuisine, namely cinnamon used to decorate rice pudding or 'pastel de nata' (small custard tart) often sprinkled with cinnamon; in some coffee shops you will even get a stick of cinnamon to stir your coffee! Cloves flavor baked apples with an exotic taste. Pepper and nutmeg are appreciated in codfish cakes and potato purée.

A wide range of plants, fruits and spices participated in one of the most marvelous and at the same time painful and thrilling acts of humanity. They brought food to the people, wealth to the merchants and power to the sovereigns.

**Figure 5.1** Spices in a street market – Mapusa, Goa
*Source*: Author's photograph

The main product brought back to Lisbon was black pepper. Pipernigrum was as valuable as gold in the age of discovery. In the 16th century, over half of Portugal's state revenue came from West African gold and Indian pepper and others spices. The proportion of the spices greatly outweighed the gold. (Cornillez, 2012: 2)

Furthermore Monteiro (2012: 100) writes that 'Goa, naturally attracted them [Vasco da Gama and his companions] for the well established wide-range commerce and quality of its people, used to produce and/or trade silk, spices, color pigments and other luxury items not yet dreamt of in larger European cities'.

The discovery of the maritime route to India by Vasco da Gama in 1498 marked the beginning of a story of the suffering due to famine and disease during dreadful journeys in miniscule vessels that crossed the oceans. Today plants, fruits, herbs and spices are a living testimony to an historic past that culturally links the Goan and Portuguese people, whose ancestors participated in this adventure, blending their gastronomies and thus contributing as an added value to different economic activities.

## Let us Discover Goa

Goa is the smallest State of India with an area of only 3702 sq. km and it is located between the Western Ghats and the Arabian Sea. It lies between latitude 14°53' to 15°40'N and between longitude 73°40' to 74°21'E (Figure 5.2). The mean temperature in the state ranges from 16.2°C to 36.7°C. The average annual rainfall is 3000 mm. According to the 2001 census the total population of the state is 1.35 million with a density of 363 persons per sq. km. In addition 'The State of Goa encompasses the rich biological diversity of

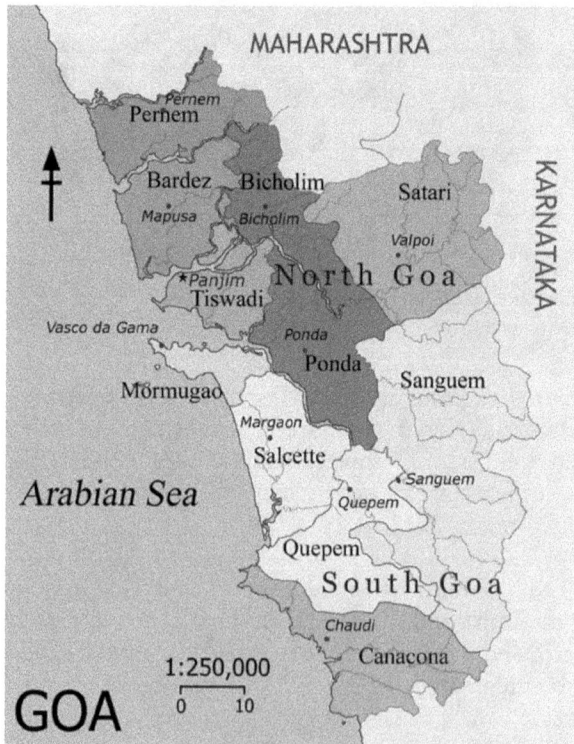

**Figure 5.2** Map of Goa with Ponda, where the study spice plantations are located
*Source*: http://upload.wikimedia.org/wikipedia/commons/c/cf/Goamap.png

Western Ghats on the eastern part and coastal Ecosystem all along the western side with humid and per humid climate' (Government of Goa, 2011: 3). According to the tourism board of Goa 'a poet once described the physical shape of Goa as one half of a heart, the other half being carried in the very heart of every Goan' (Goa Tourism, n.d.).

It is indeed with affection that people usually describe Goa, also known as 'Pearl of the Orient'. Elsa dos Santos (2012: 234) for instance, portrays Goa as a territory different from the rest of India in cultural and linguistic aspects; a little corner of paradisiacal landscapes. In the book coordinated by Santos and Dias (2012) other authors refer to this territory showing a tender feeling but also some concern about the drastic changes that have been occurring in the last decades. Kamat (2012: 203) writes that 'Goa is a small state by area and population but it is a beautiful state'. Nevertheless the four major environmental drivers of mining (post-1945), urbanization (post-1961), industrialization (post-1971) and tourism (post-1972) have strongly impacted its ecology and economy over the past 60 years. Kamat (2012: 203) indicates that 'Goa is on the verge of a serious environmental crisis' enumerating the following issues:

> destruction of the rich watersheds, pollution of traditional ponds and lakes, deforestation, removal of urban tree cover, cutting of the lush green hills, reclamation of the eco-fragile flood plains of the major estuaries, destruction of the low lying Khazan ecosystem, leveling of the coastal sand dunes, fragmentation of the natural habitats, interference in the natural migratory corridors of the wild animals, overuse of chemical fertilizers, air pollution, dust pollution, impact of mining and quarrying, alluvial sand excavation, plastic waste, mountains of municipal solid waste, human-wild animal (elephants, monkeys, panthers) conflicts, erosion of wild and agrobiodiversity, gene pools and the most dangerous of all – the ecological and cultural simplification.

On the other hand Xavier (2012: 131), emphasizes the emergence of the identity of the Goan society, after 451 years of Portuguese colonialism and 52 years of integration into the Indian territory (it became a Federal State in 1987). This has occurred as a consequence of a mutation forced by the influence of both Western and Indian cultures, which has contributed to the cohesion of the civil society.

Nevertheless old architecture and street names, religious monuments and a certain lifestyle still denote the influence of the Portuguese who ruled the territory until 1961, although most of the population does not speak the language anymore. As Jackson (1993: 142) stated, the Portuguese presence in Asia can now only be perceived through its absence represented by the relicts and vestiges of a past society that transform history into archeology and culture into semiotic. The religious festivities for instance, are one of these relicts of the past that can bring together thousands of people, as it is the case every five years to view the body of St Francis Xavier at the Basilica of Bom Jesus in Old Goa, which constitutes an important tourist attraction. An impressive array of baroque churches attest to one of the motivations evoked by the Portuguese conquerors 'to evangelize according to the Christian religion' a process which was often brutal.

Rapid urbanization, namely in the old conquest 'talukas' (Tiswadi, Salcete, Bardez, Mormugao) place Goa at the top of the list of highly urbanized Indian states, according to the 2002 National Census. 'In 1950 Goa had only 13% urban population. There was a marginal rise in 1960. But in 1971 the urban population showed a quantum jump from 14.80 to 25.56%. Again in 1981 it went up to 32.03, followed by 41.01 in 1991 and 49.77 in 2001. The latest estimate shows the urban population to reach 54% by March 2005' (Kamat, 2012: 211). This urban sprawl has had a considerable impact on the agricultural lands and in the consumption patterns as well, boosted by the mass tourism that contrasts with the panorama lived in Goa by the end of the sixties, when it was 'discovered' by the Beatles.

Although tourism raises environmental problems it also contributes to the foreign exchange earnings. Indeed 'tourism brings about Rs. 2500 crores [25,000,000,000 Rupees] to the foreign exchange kitty of the Government of India. The tourists spend annually about Rs. 5000 crores [50,000,000,000 Rupees] in Goa. But for strategic reasons the Goa government has been projecting only Rs. 650 crores [6,500,000,000 Rupees] as income from tourism. More than two lakh [200.000] people derive their employment from tourism during the tourist season and hence the stakes are very high' (Kamat, 2012: 212). Monteiro (2012: 102) informs that 'in the high season of tourism in 2010/11 Goa received more than 900 charter flights mostly from Russia'. Other origins of the foreign tourists registered in the period of Oct/May between 2008/09 and 2010/11 are reported as being mainly Britain, Norway and Germany (Figure 5.3).

Kamat (2012: 212) classifies the cultural, social and environmental concerns caused by tourism as shown in Table 5.1. However he complains that 'there seems to be a fair degree of social sanctification and an economic trade-off by the local people which has resulted in the movements against mass tourism and its ill impacts getting very limited grass roots level support. . . . As long as there is support for tourism at local level the environmental and social concerns may be side tracked in Goa' (Kamat, 2012: 211). This view contrasts with a prior definition of the Goan people by Gadgil and Guha (1993) that presented them as 'ecosystem people', corroborated by

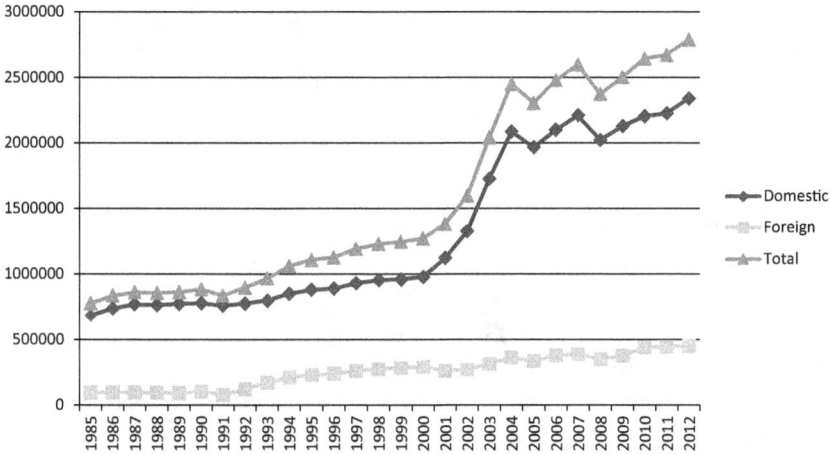

**Figure 5.3** Tourist arrivals 1985–2012 (Year Wise, 2012 – Provisional Figures)
*Source*: Department of Tourism, Government of Goa, India

Kamat, who wrote that 'it is difficult to identify a distinctly Goan set of environmental ethics but the tradition of worshipping sacred groves and sacred trees proves that ecotheologically and ecospiritually the people were quite advanced (Kamat, 2012: 206). The Goa State Forest Policy of 2009 pinpoints that 'Goa has a rich tradition of maintaining the "Sacred Groves"'

**Table 5.1** Concerns regarding tourism in Goa (according to Kamat)

| | | | |
|---|---|---|---|
| (1) | Change of land use for tourism purpose | (9) | Entry of HIV/AIDS |
| (2) | Labor shift from primary sector | (10) | Rise in alcoholism, gambling and crimes |
| (3) | Depletion of the ground water table | (11) | The menace of narcotic trade |
| (4) | Pollution of water resources | (12) | Real estate speculation driving up the land prices |
| (5) | Destruction of the mangroves, Khazans and salt pans | (13) | Incessant noise pollution owing to trance parties |
| (6) | Shift of traditional fishermen to water sports business | (14) | Entry of international crime syndicates |
| (7) | Solid waste pollution | (15) | Paedophilia and other sex-related deviant lifestyle |
| (8) | Emergence of mosquito borne diseases | (16) | Growth of peripheral slums |

mainly because of beliefs and tradition attached with these places' (Government of Goa, 2011: 11) and emphasizes the need to document and protect them, in what can be good news for the future here. In the next section of the chapter the importance of forest and farming to secure the rural sustainable development of Goa and support ecotourism will be discussed.

## Forest and farming

In a moment of human history when so many afforested areas are being rapidly destroyed it is important to remind that 'Forests are home to approximately 50–90% of all the world's terrestrial (land-living) biodiversity – including the pollinators and wild relatives of many agricultural crops' (WWF, 2010). However 'twenty to thirty percent of the world's forest areas have been converted to agriculture, resulting in extensive species and habitat loss' (Wood *et al.*, 2000). The situation is summed up by the following:

> Trees once covered early all of Earth's land mass, today they cover about 3.9 billion hectares or just over 9.6 billion acres, which is only about 29.6% of Earth's total land area ... Nature has supported, fed, clothed and sheltered humanity for 95% of its existence – agriculture only first emerged 10,000 years ago. (Eliades, 2011: 4)

Taking into consideration the nature of the spice plantations, which is the main object of this study combined with agriculture and ecotourism, it is pertinent to introduce the concept of food forests or forest gardens (also known as edible forests). These form, according to McConnell (2003), probably the world's oldest and most resilient agroecosystem. They comprise seven layers: (1) Canopy (large fruits and nut trees); (2) Low Tree Layer (Dwarf Fruit Trees); (3) Shrub Layer (Currants and Berries); (4) Herbaceous Layer; (5) Rhizosphere (Root Crops); (6) Soil Surface (ground Cover Crops); (7) Vertical Layer (Climbers, Vines). The most frequent crops in these edible forests include: fruits, nuts, edible leaves, spices, medicinal plant products, poles, fibers for tying, basketry materials, honey, fuelwood, fodder, mulches, game and sap products. An example is Martin Crawford's forest garden at Dartington (Crawford, 2013).

McConnell (2003: 1–2) goes on to identify four relevant systems in the concept of forest gardens, considering their broad social value much greater than their value as private farms:

> As production systems: they produce foods, fibers, materials, medicinal, industrial inputs and probably do this more efficiently (per ha of land

or other units of input) than any other tropical farming system. As conservation systems (highly efficient in preserving soil, water, biodiversity, human culture and knowledge (notably of medicinal plants and their uses). As rehabilitation systems (probably the most efficient and least cost method of reclaiming eroded or otherwise degraded lands and catchments, after this degradation has been caused by exploitive unsustainable forms of agriculture. As strategical environmental systems they offer one least cost land use strategy for countering such emerging universal problems as greenhouse gas emissions, ozone depletion, broad climate change.

This type of agroforestry system described by McConnell (2003) is presently quite 'fashionable' among the followers of permaculture, a mode of production that became a life's philosophy for many, mainly young people, and was introduced in the seventies by Bill Mollison and David Holmgren (Mollison, 1999).

For those familiar with the spice plantations, these are quite similar to a food forest/forest garden. They may not always have the seven layers (that is also not indispensable) but just like the forest garden they can be seen as an agronomic system that is based on trees, shrubs and perennial plants. These are mixed in such a way as to mimic the structure in a natural forest. The primary aims for such a system are:

- to be biologically sustainable, able to cope with disturbances such as climate change;
- to be productive, yielding a number (often large) of different products;
- to require low maintenance, i.e. tend to be a virtually a self-sustaining living eco-system. (Crawford, 2013)

According to the Goa State Forest Policy of 2009 (Government of Goa, 2011: 3):

the State's total Government forest area is spread over 1224 sq. km which constitutes 33.06% of the total geographical area. There are forest areas and also other tree vegetation including horticulture crops/plantations on private land is 2432 sq.km, which is 65.69% of the geographical area of the State (SFR-2005). ...Out of the total Government forest area (1224 sq. km) about 755 sq. km area constitutes protected area network covering about 62% of the total forest area.

The policy furthermore indicates that 'in order to facilitate the Western Ghats to fulfill their ecological functions and to preserve/conserve the biological diversity, the soil and moisture, it is essential to maintain a protective clothing of tree cover in this region. Soil fertility and high water regime are the foremost of the intangible benefits to result from such a measure and this in turn, helps sustain economic growth and development especially in an ecologically sensitive State such as Goa' (Government of Goa, 2011: 7). In the next sub-chapter of the policy the need to encourage the planting of trees on the available private lands as well as to create awareness among the local people in general and particularly children and women is emphasized. Moreover, it is argued within this policy document that 'lot of fallow lands are available in Goa which can be brought under tree vegetation' and that 'local farmers should be encouraged to go for agro-forestry and farm forestry', (Government of Goa, 2011: 7). Also see Figure 5.4 regarding the agro-forest concept envisaged by the government.

Thus the concept of food forest or forest gardens would perfectly suit the purpose that the Government of Goa advises, since it would contribute to protect the soils and watersheds, feed families, produce some marketable products, create jobs and, in what concerns the trees, offer ecosystem services and wellbeing as summarized by the Forest Department Goa (2012) in Why Grow More Trees?

**Figure 5.4** Agro-forest concept in Ponda Region
*Source*: Author's photograph

(1)  Shade trees can make buildings up to 20° cooler in the summer.
(2)  An average size tree produces enough oxygen in one year to keep a family of four breathing.
(3)  By cooling the air and ground around them, the shade from trees helps cool the Earth's temperature.
(4)  Three trees planted in the right place around buildings can cut air-conditioning costs up to 50%.
(5)  Over one given year one hectare of mature forest will absorb the carbon emissions of 100 average family cars.
(6)  Trees improve water quality by slowing and filtering rainwater, as well as protecting aquifers and watersheds.
(7)  One acre of trees removes up to 2.6 tons of carbon dioxide each year.
(8)  Trees increase the value of property. Houses surrounded by trees sell for 18–25 percent higher than houses with no trees.
(9)  Trees provide shelter and food for wildlife such as mammals, birds, reptiles, frogs, insects and spiders.
(10)  Trees make people feel good. Workers are more productive when they see trees along their commute routes and from their office windows.
(11)  Hospital patients who have a view of trees heal faster, use fewer pain medications, and leave the hospital sooner.
(12)  Trees in the landscape relax us, lower heart rates, and reduce stress.
(13)  Trees located along streets act as a glare and reflection control.

## Ecotourism in spice plantations in Ponda

Goa has much more to offer than just beaches, delicious food and monuments. It has beautiful scenic landscapes, agriculture and forests that can back up activities such as ecotourism. In this part of the chapter it will be discussed how spice plantations can contribute to diversify the touristic offer and create an added value to an agricultural production that supports many other activities, such as food markets (vegetables, nuts, fruits, spices, herbs, fibres), handcraft (cocoa shell and wood) and medicinal products (Ayurvedic medicine, diet products, teas, massage products, beauty care and wellness, so fashionable in spa's today).

The fieldwork to get acquainted with the spice plantations and collect the data about the ecotourism units was carried out in December 2008 in the Ponda region (see Figure 5.2). The studied units were selected for being the most important in the region and, if the oral sources consulted are reliable, correspond to 75% of this kind of farms in Ponda. Although the three plantations visited differ, among them they all have similar plants: Pepper, Cardamom, Nutmeg, Vanilla, Cinnamon, Cloves, Chillies, Coriander, and tropical trees such as Cashew, Arecanut, Palm trees and tropical fruit trees (Star fruit, Jack fruit, Custardapple, Bananas, Papayas and Pineapples). In two of these farms (Tropical Spice Plantation and Sahakari Spice farm) a list is available of spices and herbs used in the Ayurvedic medicine with the indication of their use.

The Ayurvedic medicine, as explained in an earlier publication (Firmino, 2009) is the Hindu system of medicine, also known as Veda or Knowledge of Ayur or life (Figure 5.5). The ancient Hindus achieved a considerable perfection in the sciences of medicine and surgery, due to their capacity to observe, generalize and analyze supported by the large diversity of herbs and plants existent in their territory.

Deepak Chopra wrote that Ayurveda is one of the most important contributions of India to humanity. It is a prevention system that can cure diseases, but it is also a guideline for a healthier and happier life, which is being rediscovered all over the world (Luca & Barros, 2007). In India there are families that still pass the Ayurvedic knowledge from parents to children and it is among these that masseurs are usually recruited. There is today a particular interest in Ayurvedic medicine worldwide probably as a response to the need for a different approach 'that considers the unique nature of the individual as the

**Figure 5.5** Ingredients for 'Special Ayurvedic Medicine', spontaneous street market, Old Goa
*Source*: Author's photograph

primary factor in health, not disease as an entity in itself' (Frawley & Ranade, 2007: 5). These authors believe that Ayurveda has an important role to play in the West and that 'this trend is bound to continue for decades to come as we enter a new era in which natural healing will supplement, if not begin to surmount, modern biochemical medicine' (Frawley & Ranade, 2007: xiii).

## The Tropical Spice Plantation

This is located at Keri, Ponda region, it occupies 150 acres (1 acre is equivalent to 4046.84 m$^2$) and is a 350 year old mixed plantation (spices, fruits, nuts and herbs) owned by the third generation of a Goan family. They integrate a joint-venture of three farms, including this one, in a total of 250 acres and nearly 120 workers. Four years ago they started the conversion into organic in order to get certified in this mode of production. They sell their spices to cooperatives in Goa and most of the raw material will be used in medicines. The family took the initiative to build facilities for tourists in 1995, aiming at diversifying the activity and taking advantage of the touristic flows to Goa. They offer a wide range of services, such as the guided tour of the plantation, during which tourists are given the possibility to get acquainted with the different spices, herbs and fruits that they produce, or watch birds from a row boat, watch the 'Goan Tarzan' climbing the trees and swinging from tree to tree, or purchase handicrafts made from coconut shell and wood, and fresh oils extracted from different herbs and spices grown in situ (Figure 5.6). During the visit a traditional Goan meal will be served on a banana frond and a cashew Feni liquor (produced from the juice of cashew apples) offered (Tropical Spice Plantation, n.d.).

Initially they only intended to offer traditional Goan food and show how the herbs are used. But in the last 10 years they introduced some tourist attractions such as the elephant bath (Figure 5.7) and a demonstration of how the spices are ground with old instruments. This farm is visited annually by nearly 50,000 tourists, mainly foreigners transported in buses. Since the area is inhabited by about 75 species of birds that are sighted in the plantation, the owner do not wish to receive more than 100/150 tourists per day, in order not to disturb the animals. They also offer cottages for those who wish to stay at the plantation and be in contact with Nature.

## Pascoal Spice Village

This next plantation is located near the Khandepar village, Ponda, 50 acres in size, was the first ecotourism unit in Goa, in 1993, established with 11 cottages (Figure 5.8). The farm belonged to a Portuguese family who

**Figure 5.6** The 'Goan Tarzan' in the Tropical Spice Plantation
*Source*: Author's photograph

abandoned it after the independence in 1961. In 1992 it was considered to be the best farm in Goa. This farm does not receive groups of tourists for visits. They produce flowers, spices and herbs that are sold in Goa (Pascoal Farm, n.d.).

## Sahakari Spice Farm

This plantation located in Curti, Ponda, has existed for more than 300 years, occupies 130 acres and employs 70 workers (Figure 5.9). They started with visits to the spice plantation 15 years ago and for seven years they have been certified as organic. Several medicines, oils, spices and herbs, as well as handicrafts are available for sale. It is also possible to get an appointment with an Ayurvedic doctor for consultation or have a massage. During the visit a traditional Goan meal will be served. Tourists also partake in activities

**Figure 5.7** 'Elephant Wash' in the Tropical Spice Plantation
*Source*: Author's photograph

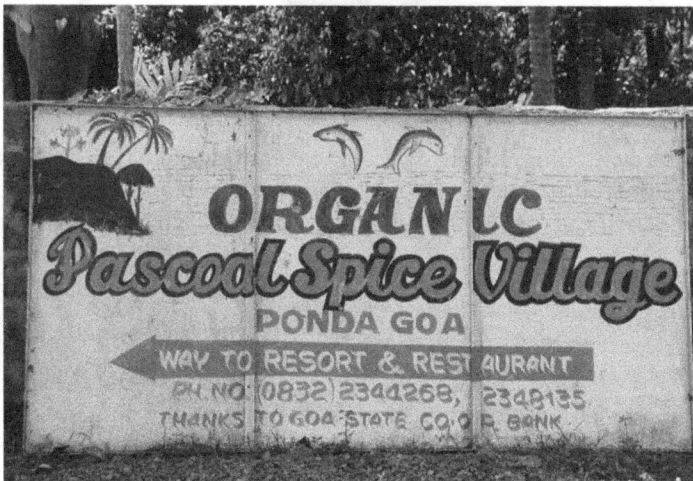

**Figure 5.8** Entrance to the Pascoal spice village
*Source*: Author's photograph

**Figure 5.9** Sahakari spice farm: 'In Nature we Trust'!
*Source*: Author's photograph

such as birdwatching, elephant feeding, washing and riding. This farm accepts many tourist buses, which contributes to a higher concentration of tourists than in the case of the two previous farms (Sahakari Farms, n.d.).

## Conclusions

The farms studied in the Ponda region of Goa, show how the spice plantations, combined with ecotourism, complemented with tourist attractions and eventually services such as Ayurvedic medicine, are an added value to the farm activity, contributing to its multi-functionality and rationality in the use of resources. Besides they create jobs, protect nature by adopting sustainable modes of production such as organic farming and keeping the tree cover that constitutes habitat for the many birds and other animals in the area, offer ecological services, preserving simultaneously gastronomy, cultural and historical traditions, namely the sacred groves.

The spice plantations here correspond to the forest garden concept, which may release from famine the poor families who live in the growing peripheral slums, if programs are created to give them access to the land where they will be able to produce their own food and make some money with the marketable products. The spice plantations also match the strategy recommended in the 'Goa State Forest Policy of 2009' by the Government of Goa (2011) in terms of soil and water conservation, wildlife and biodiversity enhancers, sources of medicinal plants and development of ecotourism among others. As it is acknowledged in this document (2011: Section 6.4) 'Eco-tourism has tremendous opportunities of meeting the market require-ments within the framework of sound eco-system management on one hand and offering good employment and livelihood opportunities for the poor communities on the other'. They furthermore recommend that ecotourism initiatives taken in Ponda, Collem and Hathipal 'may be further strength-ened to meet the requirement of tourists and also efforts may be initiated to identify more sites suitable for promoting eco-tourism and other related activities'. Certainly some work must be done in order to provide suitable training in hospitality, bird watching, botanization and nature guides and thus develop the skills and confidence of the local people and encourage them to start such initiatives in their own holdings, as stated in Section 6.4.3. of the policy.

The Goa State Forest Policy of 2009 (Section 6.7.2) refers to demonstration plots and herbal parks that should be 'set up to educate people about the use of medicinal plants in the traditional Indian systems of medicine', among which is Ayurvedic medicine. Further on the policy recommends (Section 6.10), 'perfecting the technology of composting and manuring with the avail-able waste to enhance the organic cultivation and employment/income gen-eration to rural people', which backs up sustainable modes of production such as organic farming that will certainly enhance an added value, especially in the external market.

Last but not least the characteristics of the spice plantations in Ponda make them eligible for a GIAHS (Globally Important Ingenious Agricultural Heritage System) site, 'building on local knowledge and experience, these ingenious agricultural systems reflect the evolution of humankind, the diversity of its knowledge, and its profound relationship with nature. Those systems have resulted not only in outstanding landscapes, maintenance and adaptation of globally significant agricultural biodiversity, indigenous knowledge systems and resilient ecosystems, but, above all, in the sustained provision of multiple goods and services, food and livelihood security and quality of life' (FAO, n.d.).

However, as previously warned (Firmino, 2010: 470) this idyllic scenery may be threatened by the rapid transformation in the Indian society, which is visible in the vicinity of Ponda, namely the shopping mall at Patto Plaza in Panjim, which introduces Western life styles (supermarkets and fast-food restaurants) (Figure 5.10). Besides, especially in a society that has a rather high income if compared to the rest of India, it will be difficult to moderate this change, which may be seen by the local population as a sign of progress and modernization. According to Rostow (1960) 'in surveying now the broad contours of each stage-of-growth, we are examining, then, not merely the sectoral structure of economies, as they transformed themselves for growth, and grew; we are also examining a succession of strategic choices made by various societies concerning the disposition of their resources, which include but transcend the income- and price-elasticities of demand'.

In the Western societies people are getting more and more concerned with their consumption patterns and how they can contribute to reduce the ecological footprint preferring the short cycle sales and the local food to avoid the food miles and safeguard the food security. But first many vital resources were destroyed before people started realizing that we were losing

**Figure 5.10** Shopping malls at Patto Plaza, Panjim. Globalization at work!
Source: Author's photograph

more than we were benefiting from that model. Rostow (1960) questions: 'what to do when the increase in real income itself loses its charm? Babies, boredom, three-day weekends, the moon, or the creation of new inner, human frontiers in substitution for the imperatives of scarcity?'

Harrison (1982, cited in Bunce 2003: 15) speaks of 'a profound and universal human need for connection with land, nature and community, a psychology which, as people have increasingly separated from these experiences, reflects the literal meaning of nostalgia; the sense of loss of home, of homesickness'. Latouche (2011: 50) advocates an autonomous society of decrease represented in eight interdependent changes, as follows: reevaluation, re-conceptualization, restructuration, redistribution, re-localization, reduction, reuse and recycling, in order to unleash what he calls a process of quiet decrease, sustainability and conviviality. Finally Lamberton (2005: 61) appeals for 'the need for the (economically) developed world to reduce consumption levels as a prerequisite to the transition to a sustainable society' and suggests that 'sustainability is achievable if the typical neoclassical economic perspective that dominates modern conceptions of sustainable development is replaced with a Buddhist version of economics. This alternative version of sustainability is referred to as *sustainable* sufficiency'. Today will this kind of discourse make sense to the Goan population or will they need, as we did, to destroy much of what they have to realize that it was all an illusion, as Stiglitz describes in his book *Globalization and its Discontents* (2004: 319):

'So that globalization works, many things must be changed'.

## Acknowledgement

The author would like to especially thank Graham Reed for reading and commenting on the draft chapter.

## References

Bunce, M. (2003) Reproducing rural idylls. In P. Cloke (ed.) *Country Visions* (pp. 14–30). Essex: Pearson Educational Limited, Prentice Hall.

Camoens, L.V. (1997) *The Lusiads*, Translated by Landeg White, from Cidade, H. (ed.) (1947) Luis de Camões: Obras Completas: Lisboa, Vols. IV and V, Oxford: Oxford University Press.

Cornillez, L. (2012) *Spice Trade in India*, Postcolonial Studies@Emory. http://postcolonialstudies.emory.edu/the-history-of-the-spice-trade-in-india (accessed 4 April 2013).

Correia, L.A. (2006) *Goa – Through the Mists of History From 10 000 BC – AD 1958 – A Select Compilation on Goa's Genesis*. Panjim: Maureen Publishers.

Crawford, M. (2013) (Video) Martin Crawford's forest garden at Dartington. http://www.agroforestry.co.uk/forgndg.html (accessed 4 April 2013).

Das Gupta, M. *et al.* (1995) *The Calcutta Cookbook*. New Delhi: Penguin.

Eliades, A. (2011) *Why Food Forests?* Permaculture Research Institute. http://permaculture.org.au/2011/10/21/why-food-forests/ (accessed 4 April 2013).

FAO (n.d.) http://www.fao.org/nr/giahs/en/ (accessed 6 April 2013).

Firmino, A. (2009) The awakening of ayurvedic wisdom: Lessons from India. In A. Mendes (org.) *Garcia de Orta and Alexander von Humboldt – across the East and the West* (pp. 105–117). Lisboa: Universidade Católica Editora.

Firmino, A. (2010) New challenges for the organic farmers in India – tourism, spices and herbs. *Revija Za Geografijo [Journal for Geography]* 5 (1), 101–113.

Forest Department Goa (2012) Why grow more trees? http://www.goaforest.com/ForestNews/July%202012.pdf (accessed 9 April 2013).

Frawley, D. and Ranade, S. (2007) *Ayurveda Nature's Medicine*. Reprint. Delhi: Lotus Press.

Gadgil, M. and Guha, R. (1993) *This Fissured Land, An Ecological History of India*. Delhi: Oxford University Press.

GIAHS (Globally Important Ingenious Agricultural Heritage System). http://www.fao.org/nr/giahs/en/ (accessed 4 April 2013).

Goa Tourism (n.d.) http://www.goa-tourism.com (accessed 10 April 2013).

Government of Goa (2011) *Goa State Forest Policy 2009*. Porvorim, Goa: Forest Department.

Harrison, F. (1982) *Strange Land*. London: Sidgwick and Jackson.

Jackson, K. (1993) Sinkings, Sailors, Soldiers, Spice: O corpo encoberto do português na Índia. In *Revista História*, São Paulo, n° 127–128 (pp. 141–162). August–December/92 to January/July 1993. São Paulo: Universidade de São Paulo. (www.revistas.usp.br/revhistoria/article/view/18695)

Kamat, N.M. (2012) Wild panther in Miramar? How Goa is on the verge of an environmental Hara-Kiri. In E. Santos and J. Dias (eds) *Goa – Passado, Que Futuro?* (pp. 203–219). Lisboa: Calçada das Letras.

Lamberton, G. (2005) Sustainable sufficiency an internally consistent version of sustainability. *Sustainable Development* 13, 53–68.

Latouche, S. (2011) Pequeno Tratado do Decrescimento Sereno, in the original *Petit Traité de la Décroissance Sereine*, Arthème Fayard, 2007. Lisboa: Edições 70.

Limond, D. (n.d.) *Anglo-Indian and Portuguese Dishes*. Calcutta: L. O. H. de Silva.

Luca, M. and Barros, L. (2007) *Ayurveda – Cultura de Bem Viver*. S. Paulo: Editora de Cultura.

McConnell, D.J. (2003) *The Forest Farms of Kandy and other Gardens of Complete Design*. Hampshire, England: Ashgate Publishing Limited.

Mollison, B. (1999) *Permaculture – A Designer's Manual*. Tyalgum: Tagari Publications

Monteiro, E. (2012) Evolução Económica de Goa Pós-1961. In E. Santos and J. Dias (eds) *Goa - Passado, Que Futuro?* (pp. 89–106). Lisboa: Calçada das Letras.

Pascoal Spice Plantation (n.d.) http://www.pascoalfarm.com (accessed 4 April 2013).

Portuguese Cuisine (n.d.) http://en.wikipedia.org/wiki/Portuguese_cuisine (accessed 4 April 2013).

Rostow, W.W. (1960) *The Stages of Economic Growth: A Non-Communist Manifesto*. Cambridge: Cambridge University Press.

Russel-Wood, A.J.R. (1992) *World on the Move – the Portuguese in Africa, Asia and America in 1415–1808*. Baltimore, Maryland: JHU Press.

Sahakari Spice Plantation. http//www.sahakarifarms.com (accessed 30 May 2013).

Santos, E. (2012) A Gastronomia Goesa. In E. Santos and J. Dias (eds) *Goa – Passado, Que Futuro?* (pp. 233–237). Lisboa: Calçada das Letras.

Santos, E. and Dias, J. (2012) *Goa – Passado, Que Futuro?* Lisboa: Calçada das Letras.

Sen, C.T. (2010) *The Portuguese Influence on Bengali Cuisine.* www.colleensen.com/pdf/portuguese_influence.pdf (accessed 4 April 2013).

Singh, R. (1998) *Fruits.* India: National Book Trust.

Stiglitz, J.E. (2004) Globalização – a grande desilusão *[Globalization and its Discontents]* (3rd edn). Lisboa: Terra Mar.

Tropical Spice Plantation (n.d.) http://www.tropicalspiceplantation.com) (accessed 4 April 2013).

Wood, S. *et al.* (2000) *Pilot Analysis of Global Ecosystems: Agroecosystems,* International Food Policy Research Institute and World Resources Institute. http://www.wri.org/publication/pilot-analysis-global-ecosystems) (accessed 5 April 2013).

WWF (2010) *Living Planet Report.* http://wwf.panda.org/about_our_earth/all_publications/living_planet_report/ (accessed 4 April 2013).

Xavier, C.H. (2012) Goa contemporânea: entre o legado português e o contexto indiano. In E. Santos and J. Dias (eds) *Goa – Passado, Que Futuro¿* (pp. 123–134). Lisboa: Calçada das Letras.

# Part 2

# Spice Attraction Studies

# 6 Rediscovering Spice Farms as Tourism Attractions in Zanzibar, a Spice Archipelago

Obeid Mahenya and M.S.M. Aslam

Growing interest in the use of spices is related to tourism in some countries including Sri Lanka, India, Malaysia and China (Chomchalow, 1996). The word spice generally refers to 'pungent or aromatic seasonings, often extracted from the bark, buds, fruit, roots, seeds or stems of various plants and trees' (Chomchalow, 1996; Herbst & Herbst, 1995). In many places in the world spices have been used to flavour food and drink throughout the eons, they have also been favoured for a plethora of other uses including making medicines and perfumes, religious ceremonies and as burial accoutrements for the wealthy (Herbst & Herbst, 1995). Examples of some popular spices include: cardamom, cinnamon, cloves, ginger, mace, nutmeg, paprika, pepper, saffron and turmeric. Spices are also sold in blends, such as curry powder and spice parisienne (Herbst & Herbst, 1995; Sherriff, 1995). Therefore, reflecting such a myriad of uses, spices have become one of the important tourist attractions and a source of income in many spice producing developing nations, such as Zanzibar.

Zanzibar is a part of the United Republic of Tanzania consisting of the two main spice producing islands of Unguja and Pemba and about 50 other small islets. The archipelago is located 40 km off the mainland coast of East Africa in the Indian Ocean between latitude 5 and 6 degrees South and longitudes 39.5 and 40 degrees East. The two main islands are 50 km apart, separated by the 700 m deep Pemba Channel. The total surface area of the islands of Zanzibar is 2654 square kilometres; Unguja, the larger of the two main islands has an area of 1666 square kilometres, whereas the smaller Pemba has an area of 988 square kilometres. The 1988 census indicated that the total population of Zanzibar was 640,685. The population had risen to

984,531 by 2002 with a growth rate between 1988 and 2002 of 3.1% (Revolutionary Government of Zanzibar, 2012).

The cultural formation of Zanzibar is a melding of traditions between foreign nationalities and the natives from various parts of Tanzania. Through trade relations, Zanzibar has integrated African cultures with those of Asia and Europe (Revolutionary Government of Zanzibar, 2012). This is attributable to the different cultures that have settled on the islands at various points in time. The island has been home to many cultures, such as those of the Sumerians, Assyrians, Egyptians, Phoenicians, Indians, Chinese, Persians, Portuguese and also the Omanis, who were the last occupiers before Zanzibar became a British Protectorate in the late 1890s (ZTC, 2011). Kiswahili is a lingua franca of the Island; other languages spoken include English, Arabic, Italian and French (Revolutionary Government of Zanzibar, 2012).

# Spices in Zanzibar

Historically in Zanzibar, spice plantations had once attracted the Sultans of Oman for their rich production, which eventually led to the beginnings of the slave trade (Hitchcock, 2002). The slave trade arose as a result of demand for cheap labour from various regions of the world; from Arabia where there they intensively cultivated dates; from India for sugar and tea plantations; from Central Asia where they cultivated cotton on a large scale; from Zanzibar itself where manual labourers were needed to work on the plantations. This prompted the resident Omanis to initiate the slave trade (Hitchcock, 2002). Seyyid Said bin Sultan made Zanzibar the capital of the Omani empire and moved his court and palaces to the island in 1832. In 1818, he had introduced cloves to the islands, and they flourished in the sunshine and fertile soil on the west coasts of both Unguja and Pemba. During the 19th century, clove mania hit the islands and the archipelago became the largest producer of cloves in the world (Hitchcock, 2002). Coconuts, cloves, ivory and slaves powered Zanzibar's economy, making it a centre for trade. In 1860, cloves made up 22% of Zanzibar's exports, with the royal family receiving a hefty 25% export tax on all clove exports (Hitchcock, 2002; Martin, 1991; World Bank, 2010). The royal family owned several plantations, manned by slaves, picking, drying and sorting cloves in the baking sun. Over time, other spices were introduced from Asia and South America, including cinnamon, ginger and cardamom, which have become an ingrained part of Zanzibar life. The archipelago became known as the Spice Islands and it was said that visitors were greeted by the scent of cloves on the wind as they moved into port in Zanzibar (ZTC, 2001a).

Today, Zanzibar is known throughout the world as the Spice Island. In 2000 the Stone Town of Zanzibar was inscribed as a World Heritage site due to its cultural and physical significance to the common heritage of humanity (Hitchcock, 2002; UNESCO, 2012). Following this designation, today the tourism and agriculture sectors are the main pillars of the economy of Zanzibar. The declaration by UNESCO of Stone Town as a World Heritage site facilitated an increase of visitors by 80% and a rapid increase in tourism investment to accommodate increasing visitor numbers. The contribution of tourism to Zanzibar's gross domestic product (GDP) was approximately 14%, employing about 37,000 people (CHL, 2003). Visitors may be attracted to and choose destinations with excellent attractions and it can be argued that the introduction of spice farms in Zanzibar has indeed attracted many visitors in recent years.

Zanzibar is home to numerous spice farms run by small-scale farmers, the majority of which are not more than one acre (Akyoo & Lazaro, 2007) and one large government-owned spice plantation (Agriculture Experiment Station) that yield cloves, nutmeg, cinnamon, pepper and other delightful spices. Farmers who own and farm the cloves on a small scale sell the cloves to the Government at a fixed price (personal communication, Said Ally, 2012). However, recently, the spice export trade has declined, and thus the majority of farmers and government increasingly depend on tourist visits as an alternative source of income (Anderson & Juma, 2011). This has led to the establishment of spice farms not as working farms but as demonstration sites for tourism or to the transition of producing farms to tourist attractions.

## Methodology

Inadequate facts and figures resulted in this study carrying out an empirical investigation (Yin, 2009) on tourism and spice farms of Zanzibar. An explanatory case study was carried out to bring forth the interpretations from the natural setting (Merriam, 2009) of Kizimbani Village in Zanzibar between April and July of 2012. In order to ensure the empirical validity the study incorporated multiple methods of data collection (Yin, 2009). Semi-structured in-depth interviews were conducted to understand the interpretation (Esterberg, 2002) of key informants, who are owners, operators or employees of spice farms. Direct observations were carried out to illuminate the naturalistic interpretations and authenticity

(Tjora, 2006) of tourism in spice farms. In addition, a documentary analysis was done through published and unpublished documents either in printed or electronic forms. The data collected from multiple sources were descriptively analyzed and triangulated to derive clear themes on tourism in spice farms of Zanzibar.

## Spices of Zanzibar

Spice farms in Zanzibar are now for the most part owned and administered by small holders. Most of the work is still done by hand, with young boys climbing trees on these farms, harvesting, drying and sorting manually. Chase and Burch (1998) claim the name 'Spice Island' as a synonym for Zanzibar owing to the production of spices such as clove, cumin, ginger, cardamom and pepper over time. A number of types of spices grown on these farms are discussed below.

Before 1770 cloves from the Maluku Islands (now Indonesia) were not grown elsewhere. The French brought seedlings and established them in Mauritius and from there plants or seeds were distributed to other French colonies in the Indian Ocean including Zanzibar (Martin, 1991). Studies indicated that by 1835 the ruler of Zanzibar, Seyyid Said bin Sultan, had about 4000 trees on his plantation at Kizimbani which were yielding an average of 2.7 kg of cloves a year (Martin, 1991). The best time to harvest them is when the buds are green, with the cap covering them intact. Cloves are pressed into oil, used in perfume, dental products and cigarettes, and can act as an antiseptic.

Cardamom is considered to be one of the three most expensive plants in the world; green cardamom is also grown in Zanzibar. The pods house sticky aromatic black seeds, with a sweet taste. Cardamom loses its essential oil and flavour quickly and is best used fresh. It can be used as a digestive, breath freshener or to treat stomach aches and heartburn, although in Zanzibar it is used to flavour *pilau* (a seasoned rice dish) and *chai* (tea).

Cinnamon is indigenous to Sri Lanka; it is peeled in strips from the bark of the cinnamon tree. Fresh cinnamon has an almost lemony scent and drying releases the warm woody scent we are accustomed to. An ingredient in garam masala, cinnamon can be ground into a powder and used in desserts or whole to flavour *pilau*, curries, meat dishes and *chai*.

Vanilla beans grow in an orchid, filled with tiny seeds with a rich fragrant scent. The beans are picked when they are immature and still yellow and left to dry in the sun to ferment and become dark brown, moist and sticky inside. Zanzibar vanilla originally came from Madagascar and is used to flavour desserts and custards.

Saffron, the most expensive spice in the world, is handpicked from purple crocus flowers, taking 20,000 stems to make just 125 g of saffron. As well as its medical properties, saffron is used to flavour rice and Indian desserts, giving foods a rich golden yellow hue. It was believed to induce sleep, act as a heart tonic, a cure for flatulence and as an aphrodisiac.

When the apricot-like fruit of a nutmeg tree is split open a shiny brown nut is found, wrapped in a scarlet red lattice. Nutmeg only grows in equatorial regions, originating from the Moluccas and is used to flavour desserts. Taken in high quantities, it has narcotic and hallucinogenic effects. In Zanzibar, the red lace is dried and made into a tea to cure bridal shyness on a woman's wedding night. Elsewhere the red lace is known as another spice, mace.

Ginger generally thrives in warm climates and has a sweet lemony flavour if it is cut when fresh. As ginger ages, it becomes more fibrous and tougher to peel. It's a base flavour for many Chinese and Indian dishes and can be used to help digestion and improve blood circulation.

Tourists to Zanzibar may experience the rich spice heritage of this destination through shopping in Stone Town, which was built by Indian and Arab traders and merchants (Middleton, 2000). In this historic town the spice market sells clove, black peppercorn, cardamom, nutmeg, turmeric, pilau mix and curry powder packed into handmade banana leaf baskets and wrapped in plastic. The souvenir shops sell a variety of arts and crafts. A visitor can enjoy spices in the local cuisine and experience the spice cultivation and processing at spice farms. Spice-incorporated tourism allows the tourists to gain an insight into rural life and the traditional livelihood of local people based on spice agriculture.

# Tourism in Spice Islands

*In Zanzibar, spices have played a role in tourism development through organized spice tours.*
ZTC, 2001a; Anderson, 2010

*The lure of the legendary spice islands (Zanzibar) have drawn tens of thousands of foreigners a year to these exotic climes throughout the 1990s.*
Middleton, 2000: 46

It is argued that the clove industry and marine resources are unique features that make Zanzibar viable as a tourist destination (ZTC, 2001b). In 2010, tourism contributed to almost 51% of Zanzibar's GDP (Steck *et al.*, 2010). Tourist arrivals to Zanzibar increased from 86,918 in 1999 to 134,919 in 2009, with

75% of the visitors coming from Europe (ZTC, 2011). Today tourism is the second largest income generator after the agriculture in Zanzibar (Middleton, 2000). Emerging tourism in spice farms is recognized as an ideal alternative for tourists, who are not interested in diving, snorkelling or fishing. This has also been a rejuvenating strategy for traditional spice cultivation and trading of Zanzibar, since the country's traditional export crops face several vulnerable conditions related to prices in the global market (Akyoo & Lazaro, 2007).

The case study site, Kizimbani Village, is located about 30 miles northeast of Stone Town, and includes a 200-acre agricultural research farm run by the Zanzibar government for leisure and educational tourism. The village farm displays a wide range of aromatic plants such as cinnamon, pepper, ginger, lemon grass, iodine, cocoa, nutmeg, clove, ginger and turmeric. At the farm (Kizimbani Village) visitors are provided with opportunities to experience and learn medicinal and dietary uses of spices and discover how to cook and heal with them. In a personal interview with a farm manager, he reported that visitors enjoyed food that was prepared and seasoned by cooks from local communities and in some restaurants which serve local indigenous foods (personal communication, 2012). Further, he noted that visitors who had experienced the beauties of spices during their trip felt they had received good value. In the smaller spice farms in this area visitors may also smell and taste varieties of fresh spices such as coriander, cardamom, black pepper, cinnamon, cloves, ginger, vanilla sticks and nutmeg together with other tropical fruits such as pineapple, mango, banana and apple, fresh from the farms. For the purpose of enhancing visitor satisfaction, private spice farms provide free local caps made from coconut palm leaves for tourists. In an interview, Said Ally, a tour guide states 'visitors may see a farm staff member climbing a coconut tree and plucking the fruit' (personal communication, 2012). This is a popular activity included in the spice tour. The usual package of spice tours, which are sold by tour companies, may be 1.5–3 hours in duration depending on the interest of the visitors. A tour package may include or exclude lunch but the researchers observed that most of the visitors were taken to nearby restaurants in Stone Town. Hamada (n.d.) observes 'the Zanzibar spice tours are pretty good value for money and offer the chance to see some of the world's most aromatic and mythical spices and fruits'. Several tour operators, such as Zan Tours, Fisherman Tours and Travels organize and operate their excursions to spice farms. However, there are visitors who come directly from the airport, from their hotels or from Zanzibar port to the plantations.

As indicated in Table 6.1 the tour operators are able to differentiate their products by offering spice experiences in differing settings, for example serving an authentic lunch either on a farm or in a local house. Longer tours

**Table 6.1** Zanzibar spice tours

| Title | Duration/ Price | Activities | Company/Source |
|---|---|---|---|
| Zanzibar Spice Tour | Half day – $40 US | Tour to factory making essential oils and a spice farm, includes lunch on the farm. | PureZanziabr. com http://www. purezanzibar.com |
| Spice Tour | Half day – $55 US | Guided walk through villages and spice farms culminating in a Swahili lunch served in a local home. | Ecoculture Zanzibar http://www.ecoculture-zanzibar.org/day-tours/spice-tour |
| Princess Saleme Spice Tour | Whole day – $85 US | Tour includes visits to local historical properties associated with the spice trade, boat trip, ride in a donkey cart through clove groves to a spice garden. Traditional lunch served at historic Bubu House. Portion of tour profits to the Mtoni Palace Conservation Fund. | Ecoculture Zanzibar http://www.ecoculture-zanzibar.org/princes-salme-spice-tour |

(day versus half day) are able to accommodate different forms of transportation such as walking, riding on a traditional donkey cart and a boat tour. Some tour operators also include cooking lessons using local spices in their packages. Pricing for the organized tours is dependent on the number of visitors participating and the number of activities and stops selected. It is also possible for budget tourists such as backpackers to travel to the spice gardens by public transportation and negotiate their own tours at a much reduced price (Hamada, n.d.).

At Kizimbani Village visitors are required to pay 2 dollars (US) to enter the government spice plantation, but for private farms entrance is free although tips are required for guides. Currently, private spice farms obtain about an average of 40 visitors in the low season per day compared to 20 visitors at government-owned plantation. The observable reason for this is lack of interest and less service priority of the government staff in anticipating tourist expectations. Although the government spice farm is purpose-built and visited by students in large groups for educational purposes, the private-sector-owned spice farms' tourism performance is highly admirable. The empirical investigation through interview and observation elucidates some challenges such as inadequately qualified and skilled guides, poor capacity of owners, operators and employees, poor awareness and understanding of local stakeholders on tourism in general. In addition, Anderson and Juma (2011) identify language barriers as one of the major challenges for the tourism sector in Zanzibar. Economic instability and poor infrastructure facilities are also recognized as challenges for development of tourism in Zanzibar (World Bank, 2010). As Zanzibar's majority community is under the faith of Islam, negative impacts of tourism on society and culture, especially drugs and sex abuse is a frequently addressed challenge for further expansion of tourism in Zanzibar (Middleton, 2000).

Shopping for spices as souvenirs is a distinctive activity included in the organized spice tours. Middleton (2000) notes that buying souvenirs during day trips is the only contribution to the local economy. Visitors are provided with the opportunity to witness spice-scented bazaars (Chase & Burch, 1998), where selling various spice products made locally by crushing freshly flowers and herbs. Other products include perfumes and soaps (clove soap is popular), palm woven products, woven hand bags, beaded sandals and kikoi garments. These spice souvenirs are reasonably cheap and interestingly visitors are allowed to bargain to get lower price. Visitors are not cornered to buy but rather kindly invited to view the local souvenirs. As tourism is familiar to Stone Town dwellers, many of them make their livelihood through providing services to visitors (Chase & Burch, 1998).

The emerging spice tours in Zanzibar have attracted the attention of a number of small spice farm holders. For example, the Zanzibar Organic Spice Growers, a non-governmental organization (NGO), consists of 22 farmers with six farms each having only three acres of land area. The objective of the NGO is to elevate the spice farms as tourist attractions while enhancing the production (Zanzibar Organic Spice Growers, n.d.). One of the challenges faced by the NGO is to integrate commercial production of spices while maintaining it for tourism purposes. On the one hand only a few spice productions yield good return through trading, on the other hand maintaining spice farms for tourism demands a wide variety of spice cultivation on the farms. Further, the NGO verifies that 99% of the spice farms in Unguja are operated exclusively for tourism but 100% of spice farms in Pemba are working farms (Zanzibar Organic Spice Growers, n.d.). This is to ensure a balanced proportion of production farms versus tourist farms. These objectives tally with the sustainable tourism objectives that the Government of Tanzania has established (CHL Consulting Group, 2003).

# Discussion

Although Zanzibar is traditionally popular as a spice island, booming tourism is the latest chapter in the long historical link with the outside world (Middleton, 2000). Zanzibar has been a world-renowned source of spices (Akyoo & Lazaro, 2007). Historically well known for spice farming, trading and livelihood activities encounter an alternative avenue to integrate tourism. Fleischer and Tchetchik (2005) argue that adding tourism to agricultural farms generates auxiliary funding for farming activities and utilizes human and physical capital more efficiently. Introducing tourism in spice farms helps the country to regenerate the declining agriculture sector, which is the primary source of livelihood. Emerging tourism enables the farmers, community and tourism developers to rediscover the spice plantations and farms as a tourist attraction and enhance the tourist satisfaction through diversified tourist products. The Indicative Tourism Master Plan for Zanzibar and Pemba 2003 indicates that 'At present, the available tours to spice plantations are of variable quality, and depend on the degree of knowledge of the tour guide or taxi driver. If the guide or driver is knowledgeable, the experience can be both enjoyable and educational' (CHL Consulting Group, 2003: 23). Both the Indicative Tourism Master Plan for Zanzibar and Pemba 2003 and the Tourism Policy Statement (n.d.) are two significant documents for Zanzibar tourism. The trend for incorporation of spice and tourism in both documents is negligible. The Tourism Policy Statement includes various aspects of tourism development in Zanzibar, but it mentions nothing about spice tourism or spice tours (Tourism Policy Statement, n.d.).

Although spice tourism in Zanzibar is more popular than the spice garden tourism in Sri Lanka, both destinations face similar issues related to sustainability. Common identifiable issues in both countries are: lack of time allocation for spice tours as part of tour itineraries, inadequate capacity building through training for guides and operators, poor monitoring of quality and pricing standards, absence of holistic integration, poor infrastructure facilities, domination of tour operating companies or travel agencies. Unlike in Sri Lanka, holding a government-owned spice plantation in Zanzibar would be an opportunity to develop an ideal model site for spice tourism. However, increasing demand for visitors to spice farms and plantations induced the establishment of privately owned spice farms. Developing spice gardens purposively for short tourist visits could ruin the authenticity and attributes of spice tourism. This trend also tends to employ more unqualified and poor-skilled labour and diminishes visitor satisfaction. Observation elucidated another consequence of tourist-centered spice farms without production: overdependence on tourism income and seasonal loss of employment. This is a result of the switching of livelihood from traditional sources to an attractive and easy source of tourism. Changing the objective of spice farms from production to attraction may therefore harm spice heritage and production, on which spice tourism depends. This can be against the tourism policy criteria on contribution for sustainable agricultural development of Zanzibar (Tourism Policy Statement, ZTC, 2001b). In contrast, observation of tourism in a traditional production-centred spice farm verifies that the tourist visits improve their earnings and strengthen production, even though employees are not qualified in tourism services.

Organizing very short duration spice tours does not allow tourists to gain sufficient knowledge or broader experience of spice cultivation, processing and diverse utility. Although spice farms and plantations are capable of providing a wide experience and enjoyment for visitors, spice tourism has not been segmented or branded as a separate tourism product from Zanzibar as well as from Sri Lanka. As Zanzibar aspires to develop environmentally and culturally friendly sustainable tourism (Middleton, 2000), diversifying tourism products into spice plantation and farms could be identified as a significant strategy. In addition, the potential for community-based tourism, an alternative for sustainable tourism in and around spice farms underpinning the socio-cultural fabric of Zanzibar's community also could be observed prevalently. The Tourism Policy Statement (ZTC, 2001b) indicates that any tourism should help to conserve and improve the welfare of the local people as responsible tourism. The present growth trend of spice tourism in Zanzibar substantiates the possibilities of bridging tourism potentials with sustainable or responsible tourism policy.

## Conclusion

The historic archipelago of Zanzibar stands out, with its mesmerising natural and human geography. Spices of Zanzibar are one of the primary factors bridging the country with the rest of the world historically. Although spices contribute to the national economy as traditional export crops, price and demand elasticity led to decline the export earnings of traditional crops. However, the rapid growth of tourism in Zanzibar boosted agriculture, small-scale industries and fishing and tourism-related art and craft manufacturing (Middleton, 2000). Rediscovering spice farms and plantations as tourist attractions enabled the country to regenerate declining agriculture and empower the local development. Increasing visitor numbers and their interest in spice farms and plantations caused many traditional and new spice farms to incorporate tourism. At present it seems spice farms and plantations are more popular as tourist attractions than for production of spices.

Rising demand and an increasing number of spice farms encounters a number of issues and challenges in the execution of spice tourism in Zanzibar. This encompasses variability in quality and price, poorly skilled and qualified labour, less priority in the tourism development context, poor infrastructure and capacity building, prevailing negative impacts of tourism, economic instability and domination of conventional tourism organizations. Together with these dilemmas, operating only short excursions to spice farms and plantations prevents a holistic experience and shrinks the broader spectrum of spice tourism. On the other hand building and diverging spice farms purely for tourism purposes may lead to staged authenticity and threaten sustainable development of agriculture. However, introducing tourism into traditional production centred spice farms and plantations, as supplementary or complementary activities, improves the income and strengthens production. This requires additional tourism awareness and human and physical capacity building programmes inevitably.

Integration of history, traditional livelihood, anthropology, ethnography and rural context of local people in and around spice farms and plantations presents sound potential for community-based tourism. The tangible and intangible resources can be reconceptualized as countryside capital for tourism development (Garrod et al., 2006). This enables the authorities to enforce the responsible tourism approach as emphasized by the Indicative Tourism Master Plan 2003 and the Tourism Policy Statement of Zanzibar.

This study envisages that sustainable tourism through appropriate incorporation of traditional livelihood, socio-culture, anthropology, ethnography and environment of any destination. This would be supported through well-integrated tourism planning and policy development and prioritized implementation, human and physical capacity building, and segmented and branded marketing as a niche tourism product of spice-related tourism.

## References

Akyoo, A. and Lazaro, E. (2007) *The Spice Industry in Tanzania: General Profile, Supply Chain Structure, and Safety Standards Compliance Issues.* DIIS working Paper no 2007/8, Copenhagen: Danish Institute for International Studies.

Anderson, W. (2010) Determinants of all-inclusive travel and expenditure. *Tourism Review* 65 (3), 4–15.

Anderson, W. and Juma, S. (2011) Linkages at tourism destinations: Challenges in Zanzibar. http://www.arajournal.net/files/pdf/article/ca_ES/44.pdf (accessed 10 December 2012).

Chase, H. and Burch, B. (1998) Zanzibar: The Spice Island in The Sun. *Crisis: Travel and Leisure* 105 (3), 68–69.

Chomchalow, N. (1996) Spice production in Asia: An overview. Unpublished, Paper presented at the IBC's Asia Spice Markets '96 Conference, Singapore.

CHL Consulting Group (2003) *The United Republic of Tanzania: Indicative Tourism Master Plan for Zanzibar and Pemba*, Final Report. http://www.zanzibartourism.net/docs/masterplan.pdf (accessed 29 May 2013).

Esterberg, K.G. (2002) *Qualitative Methods in Social Research*. Boston, MA: McGraw-Hill.

Fleischer, A. and Tchetchik, A. (2005) Does rural tourism benefit from agriculture? *Tourism Management* 26 (4), 493–501.

Garrod, B., Wornell, R. and Youell, R. (2006) Re-conceptualising rural resources as countryside capital: The case of rural tourism. *Journal of Rural Studies* 22 (1), 117–128.

Hamada, R. (n.d.) Spice up your life. Mango magazine. http://www.mambomagazine.com/in-deep/activities/spice-up-your-life (accessed 10 January 2013).

Herbst, S.T. and Herbst, R. (1995) *The Food Lover's Companion* (2nd edn). New York: Barron's Educational Services Inc.

Hitchcock, M. (2002) Zanzibar Stone Town joins the imagined community of World Heritage Sites. *International Journal of Heritage Studies* 8 (2), 153–166.

Martin, P. (1991) The Zanzibar clove industry economic botany. *New York Botanical Garden* 45 (4), 450–459.

Merriam, S.B. (2009) *Qualitative Research: A Guide to Design and Implementation*. San Francisco: Jossey-Bass.

Middleton, N. (2000) Totally tropical. *Geographical* 72 (2), 46–53.

Revolutionary Government of Zanzibar (2012) Zanzibar investment policy. http://www.zanzibarinvest.org/investment_policy.pdf (accessed 10 December 2012).

Sheriff, A. (1995) *Mosques, Merchants and Landowners in Zanzibar Stone Town in The History and Conservation of Zanzibar Stone Town*. Ohio, USA: Department of Archives, Museums and Antiquities, Ohio University Press.

Steck, B., Wood, K. and Bishop, J. (2010) *Tourism more Value for Zanzibar: Value Chain Analysis*, Final Report, February 2010. Zanzibar: VSO, SNV and ZAT.

Tjora, A.H. (2006) Writing small discoveries: An exploration of fresh observers' observation. *Qualitative Research* 6 (4), 429–451.

UNESCO (2012) World Heritage Centre. Stone Town of Zanzibar. http://whc.unesco.org/en/list/173 (accessed 1 December 2012).

World Bank (2010) Doing business in Zanzibar, The World Bank, Washington, DC. http://subnational.doingbusiness.org (accessed 26 May 2013).

Yin, R.K (2009) *Case Study Research: Design and Methods* (4th edn). Thousand Oaks: Sage Inc.

Zanzibar Commission for Tourism (ZTC) (2001a) *Commission for Tourism in Zanzibar: Working Reports 2001*. Zanzibar: Zanzibar Commission for Tourism.

Zanzibar Commission for Tourism (ZTC) (2001b) Tourism policy statement. http://www.zanzibartourism.net/docs/policystatement.pdf (accessed 14 June 2013).

Zanzibar Commission for Tourism (ZTC) (2011) Tanzania tourist board statistics. www.zanzibartourism.net/news.php (accessed 10 December 2012).

Zanzibar Organic Spice Growers (n.d.) History. http://envaya.org/zanzibarorganicspices/history (accessed 9 May 2013).

# 7 The Role of Spice and Herb Gardens in Sri Lanka Tourism

## M.S.M. Aslam

The natural and manmade geography of Sri Lanka raised it as a destination for travellers from various corners of the world since the prehistoric era. Arabs were the popular traders of spices between Sri Lanka and Europe in early days. When sailing and world exploration became popular in Europe, Arabs were bypassed by Portuguese who reached the island before them. Although entering the country for the purpose of trading, later they invaded Sri Lanka in 1505 owing to its richness in natural resources. Coastally established Portuguese trading encountered the market for spices and herbs from all over the island. Spices and herbs began to play a complementary role locating Sri Lanka in the global travel and tourism map since they were icons of the Portuguese trading. In addition, Sri Lanka was the traditional hub on the east–west sea route and silk route. Subsequently, the Dutch invaded in 1658 and continued trading spice while occupying the coastal cities of the island. The last invader or the English rulers of the country also widened the spice trading from Sri Lanka, while introducing large plantations such as tea, rubber and coconut from 1796 to 1948.

Spices and herbs remained as key influential factors in attracting short-haul and long-haul tourists even after independence in 1948. However, the country could recognize tourism as an industry only after the 1960s, when it encountered socio-economic developmental challenges. Meanwhile, tourism is the fastest growing industry and provides solutions for many developmental challenges. Sri Lanka is one of the nations that recognizes tourism as a main pillar of socio-economic development.

Sri Lanka is a teardrop-shaped small island situated about 80 km east of southern tip of India (Aslam, 2005; Tsung-Wei Lai, 2002). Although it is only 65,610 square miles (Bandara, 2003) and stretches 350 km from north to south and 180 km from east to west (SLTDA, 2011; Tsung-Wei Lai, 2002), situated between 6° and 10° North and 80° to 82° East, it is located in a strategic position on the historical travel map (Aslam, 2005) separated from India by the Palk Strait. Plentiful natural geographical resources such as mountains, plains, waterfalls, rivers, streams, springs, forests, wildlife, caves, marine resources and beaches, with a huge diversity acessible across a short duration of travelling leads to the traveller experiencing different atmosphere and weather. The total population of Sri Lanka was estimated at 20.563 million in 2010 (Central Bank of Sri Lanka (CBSL), 2010). The population distribution among the Urban, Rural and Estate sectors is 21.5%, 72.2% and 6.3% respectively (Department of Census Statistics, 2010). Agriculture, Industry and Services remain as the major components of the national economy. Foreign exchange earnings from Foreign Remittance Rs. 465.1 billion (27%), Textile and Garment Industry Rs. 395.4 billion (23%), Tea Rs. 155.4 billion (9%), Transportation Services 130.5 billion (7.6%) and Tourism Rs. 65,018 billion (3.8%) and holding first, second, third, fourth and fifth respectively (SLTDA, 2010). Spices as minor export crops contributed US $165 million in 2010 and increased by 27% in comparison to 2009 (The Spice Council (TSC), 2010).

The purpose of this chapter is to identify the relationship of spices to tourism in Sri Lanka, in particular contributing to sustainable rural tourism through the establishment of spice gardens that are key components of standardized tours for tourists. The chapter reviews spices and herbs in relation to both the economy and tourism and then reports on a study of Sri Lanka's traditional spice garden attractions, identifying issues and challenges in fully integrating these attractions as key components of sustainable rural tourism in Sri Lanka. The chapter concludes with some comments on the possibility of moving spice-related tourism away from typical mass tourism and into some of the niche tourism areas in order to improve visitor experience and satisfaction and to enhance the viability of the spice gardens as part of sustainable rural tourism in the country.

## Spices and Herbs in Sri Lanka

As spices and herbs have traditionally been a significant component of Sri Lankan economy, cultivation and further enhancements have been continued. During the post-independence decades from the 1960s to 1990s a number of legislative enactments, institutions, programmes and projects were introduced to preserve and expand the cultivation of spices and herbs. This included cultivating spices in uneconomic tea lands as alternate crops, introducing spices and herbs as inter-planting crops in tea, rubber and coconut lands and establishing the Department of Export Agriculture (DEA) by a Parliamentary Act (Act. No. 46 of 1992) are benchmark interventions

(DEA, 2012). Over 70% of spices and herbs on cultivated land are smallholdings and home gardens with minimum utilization of chemical fertilizers, pesticides or herbicides (De Silva, 2012). Sri Lanka possesses a number of world-renowned spices and herbs, such as cinnamon, pepper and clove, and their quality is also maintained to retain the demand globally.

Popular Sri Lakan spices include are cinnamon (*C. Zeylicum of Lauraceae*), cardamom (*Elettaria Cardamom of Zingiberaceae*), clove (*Eugenia Caryophyllus of Myrtaceae*), peper (*Piper Nigram L. of Piperaceae*), areca nut (*Areca Catechu L of Palmae*), Betel (*Piper Betel L of Piperaceae*), cocoa (*Theobroma Cacao of Sterculaceae*), ginger (*Zingiber Officinale of Zingiberaceae*), lemon grass (*Cymbopogon Citatus/Flexosus of Graminae*), nutmeg (*Myristica Fragrans of Myristaceae*), citronella (*Cymbopogon Nardus/C. Winterianus of Graminae*), turmeric (*Curcuma Domestica of Zingiberaceae*), coffee (*Coffee Arabica and C. Canephora of Rubiaceae*) and goraka (*Garcinia Quaecita Pierra of Clusiaceae*) (DEA, 2012). These spices are used as dried whole or ground form, powder form, flavourings, and provide aroma in food, pharmaceutical and perfumery industries, and Ayurvedic and Chinese medicine (DEA, 2012). Coffee and cacao are also included as spices by DEA and TSC, as they possess similar value in commerce and consumption. See Table 7.1 for the estimated productions of major spices and herbs.

As south Asian people possess a traditional habit of chewing the betel, areca nuts are in first and second positions in the export table (Table 7.2).

**Table 7.1** Estimated production of spices and herbs (2003–2009)

| Crop | Estimated production (Mt.) | | | | | | |
|------|------|------|------|------|------|------|------|
|      | 2003 | 2004 | 2005 | 2006 | 2007 | 2008 | 2009 |
| Cinnamon | 14,153 | 14,879 | 15,898 | 15,792 | 16,795 | 14,691 | 15,690 |
| Pepper | 13,778 | 11,016 | 14,303 | 14,801 | 16,377 | 12,897 | 12,306 |
| Clove | 2907 | 3988 | 6077 | 3505 | 2886 | 8553 | 3032 |
| Cardamom | 64 | 65 | 74 | 79 | 80 | 70 | 61 |
| Nutmeg & Mace | 1865 | 1605 | 2054 | 2092 | 2267 | 2265 | 2379 |
| Cocoa | 1084 | 527 | 902 | 1055 | 1336 | 1696 | 2453 |
| Coffee | 3139 | 3035 | 3086 | 3145 | 2979 | 3081 | 3125 |
| Areca nuts | 19,114 | 19,462 | 19,693 | 23,389 | 22,605 | 24,955 | 23,540 |
| Betel | 29,968 | 30,039 | 29,841 | 29,739 | 32,716 | 30,571 | 30,454 |
| Citronella | 21 | 23 | 23 | 29 | 19 | 22 | 7 |
| Total | 86,092 | 84,639 | 91,950 | 93,625 | 98,061 | 97,105 | 93,048 |

*Source*: Department of Export Agriculture – 2010

**Table 7.2** Value of exports of spice and herb products (2006–2009)

Value (Rs. Mn)

| Products | H. S. Code | 2006 | 2007 | 2008 | 2009 |
|---|---|---|---|---|---|
| Cinnamon | 09061001 | 6879 | 8380 | 9428 | 8467.8 |
| Pepper | 090411 | 1672 | 3165 | 3047 | 1873.6 |
| Cloves | 09070002 | 1245 | 985 | 3768 | 1333.6 |
| Clove Stems | 09070003 | 41 | 29 | 93 | 45.9 |
| Nutmeg | 090810 | 507 | 658 | 788 | 605.4 |
| Mace | 090820 | 148 | 184 | 183 | 212.3 |
| Cardamom | 090830 | 16 | 14 | 29 | 27.9 |
| Essential Oils | 330190 | 496.4 | 800 | 580 | 24966 |
| Cocoa Beans | 18010001 | 0 | 5 | 5 | 773.4 |
| Coffee | 09011101 | 4 | 15 | 0.2 | 15.3 |
| Areca nut | 08029001 | 205 | 92 | 344 | 151.6 |
| Garcinia | 08134009 | 128 | 101 | 172 | – |
| Tamarind | 08134001 | 91 | 28 | 31 | – |
| Cashew Nuts | 080132 | 119 | 111 | 152 | – |
| Vanilla | 090500 | 0.6 | 0.8 | 0.8 | – |

Source: Adapted from Statics of The Sri Lanka Spice Council – 2012

Sri Lanka produces the best quality cinnamon in the world, more than 14,000 tonnes annually, contributing 51% of total spice export earning, over 85% of global cinnamon export and 14.5% of world cinnamon market (TSC, 2010). Further, pepper is also produced, more than 11,000 tonnes annually, and is in high demand in the world market. However, still Sri Lanka finds seasonal and insufficient production of spices and herbs, while having the extensive demand and potential (DEA, 2012) for further expansion. Although unfavourable weather conditions led to decline in clove, pepper and coffee production in 2011, production of cinnamon and cocoa increased in 2011 (Central Bank of Sri Lanka – CBSL, 2011). Spices and herbs as a minor export contributed to gross domestic product (GDP) and gross national product (GNP) Rs. Million 11,028, 14,955 and 12,114, in 2009, 2010 and 2011 respectively (CBSL, 2011). Export earnings from different spices and herbs are given in Table 7.2. However, within the last few decades the spice and herb industry has encountered a greater impact from tourism globally (Spice Master, 2008). Also, demand in the hotel industry has increased the consumption of spices and herbs in Sri Lanka substantially (Jaysuriya, 2011). Tourism therefore plays a catalyst role in the expansion of the global market and production of spices and herbs.

# Method

This study adopted the qualitative case study methodology due to inadequate understanding and meaning provided by the quantitative approach researches or surveys (Havitz, 1994; Henderson & Bedini, 1995; Hollinshead, 1996; Riley, 1996; Walle, 1997). This approach facilitates the study to bring forth the multiple realities of a socially constructed world of people (Merriam, 2009; Nicholls, 2009), who are owners, operators, employees or visitors of spice gardens. In order to acquire the views of respondents in their own words, semi-structured in-depth interviews (Esterberg, 2002) were carried out with seven experienced operators or managers from seven spice gardens. Spice gardens such as New Paradise, Surathura, Happyland, Diana, International Spice Walk, were very helpful and supportive of participative observation, while others were reluctant. These observations enabled the researcher to gain first-hand data from the natural setting of the spice gardens (Esterberg, 2002; Merriam, 2009). The interest, response and reactions, facial and body language of tourists were observed during the demonstration tours and promotion of products and additional services magnified the authenticity of the data. In addition, tourists' feedback and comments on spice gardens were reviewed through travel websites such as Lonely Planet, TripAdvisor and VirtualTourist. Interviews, observation and review of feedback and comments' electronically posted allowed for data triangulation to identify prevailing conditions and challenges of spice gardens. Comparison with literature on concepts of sustainable tourism was carried out to envisage the integration of spices and herbs within diverse alternative tourism products to ensure rural sustainable development.

# Spices and Herbs in Modern Tourism of Sri Lanka

Although, spices were key elements bringing Sri Lanka into the ancient travel map under different names and attracting many pilgrims and other travellers, it was only during the British colonial period that a constant flow of tourists was created (deBruin & Nithiyanandam, 2000). Soon after Sri Lanka lost self-sufficiency of the economy in the 1960s while facing various problems and constraints in the local economy (Lackshman, 1997), neo-liberalization and modernization led to industrialization influencing the adoption of tourism as a strategic tool for development (Awang, 2006; Bandara, 2001; Scheyvens, 2002) in Sri Lanka. Meanwhile, the Ceylon

Tourist Board – CTB (Sri Lanka Tourism Development Authority) as a regulator body or National Tourism Organization under Parliament Act no: 10 of 1966 (Government of Ceylon, 1966a) and Ceylon Hotel Corporation alias Sri Lanka Institute of Tourism and Hospitality under Act no. 14 of 1966 (Government of Ceylon, 1966b) were established in 1966. Since then, development of the tourism industry has continued gradually (Jayawickrama, 2000) in order to take up the advantages of conventional mass tourism. This was further strengthened by the Tourism Development Act No. 14 of 1968 (Government of Ceylon, 1968). Yet the Ceylon Tourist Plan from 1967 to 1976 was carried out with the target of 307,000 total tourist arrivals in 1976 (Harris, Kerr, Foster and Company, 1967).

Although tourist arrivals had been over estimated and could not reach the target, arrivals increased within the stipulated timeframe. One of the objectives of the plan; 'to develop tourism industry plants that best utilise the attractions and opportunities of all of Ceylon with respect the requirements and potentials of international tourism' (Harris, Kerr, Foster and Company, 1967: 1) pushed tourism towards diverse natural and manmade attractions. Hence, tea, rubber and coconut plantations together with spice and herb plantations became popular in catering for the diverse needs of a large volume of tourists. Besides, increasing tourist arrivals tended to increase consumption and demand for spices and herbs for the purpose of cooking, medicine, souvenirs and fragrance (Jayasuriya, 2011). Rich spices and herbs were added to daily Sri Lankan dishes for pungent flavours and heady aromas and the custom to use herbal medicine to cure common illnesses (Renique, 2009) astonished tourists in Sri Lanka. Conventional tourists too have been delighted by the Sri Lankan spices and herbs. Experience of exotic gastronomy, rejuvenation with health and spa treatments and pleasure within nature are all provided by spices and herbs.

As spices and herbs are kinds of catalysts in developing conventional tourism, the local community is given an opportunity to present and demonstrate them for the tourists. However, before the 1970s tourists had to visit different spice gardens to witness spices and herbs. Although a small number of tourists were interested in visiting the spice gardens, after the introduction of mass tourism through charter flights, the number of visitors rapidly increased for spice gardens. Visiting different spice gardens to see different spices and herbs meant a lengthy visit, and tourists found it difficult to see a number of them during a single visit.

One of the interviewers from Suratharu (formerly Wadiwel), the oldest spice garden, explained that in late 1970 Mr Kulasekeram, an estate worker, started to carry leaves and nuts to show the tourists who visited rubber plantations in Matale. Subsequently, he was encouraged to present those spices and herbs at the origins of the home garden. Later, his presentation and demonstration of many spices and herbs at a single garden led many people to grow diverse spices and herbs in a garden and open to visitors beside Colombo–Kandy (A1) Road and Matale–Dambulla (A9) Road in addition to a few in other places as shown in Figure 7.1. These spice gardens have become established particularly for tourism and are required to register under the Specified Tourist Service Code – 1984/Tourism Development Act (No. 14 of 1968; SLTDA, 2011). There are 33 registered spice gardens (SLTDA, 2011)

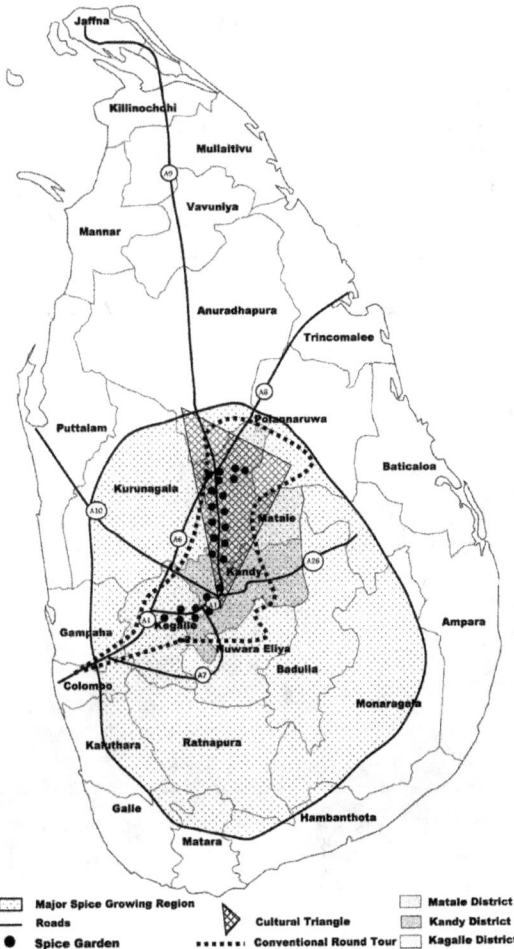

**Figure 7.1** Spice and herb growing regions and spice gardens in Sri Lanka tourism map
*Source*: Adapted from Survey Department of Sri Lanka, 2011 and Field Survey 2012

some of which function very well, others are not operated actively and a few of them no longer function.

Spice gardens, developed for tourism, offer a memorable visit. A short tour or a walk into these small lands enables the visitors to acquire a basic understanding of most spices and herbs in Sri Lanka. Tourists are guided by skilled and experienced people, even with different languages (Figure 7.2). Visitors are allowed to taste, touch, sense and smell most of the spices from original plants. The land areas of these spice gardens range from 2 acres to 12 acres. Even in the large gardens, small areas are marked out and spices grown for short demonstration tours, which take about half an hour to one hour. Most of the conventional round tours (Figures 7.1 and 7.3) covering a cultural triangle (Figure 7.1) and hill country within seven days or three days include a spice garden as a site to visit. In addition, day excursions to Kandy or the cultural triangle also include a spice garden visit. Visitors are welcomed by the operators with their own traditions and do not charge any entry fee. Upon arrival, visitors are offered a herbal drink or a spiced black tea to introduce the value of spices and herbs. Visitors are assigned a guide, who speaks their native or another common language. Most guides are very capable of explaining the various features and characteristics of spices and herbs such

**Figure 7.2** Demonstration by a guide at Surathura Spice Garden

**Figure 7.3** Arrival of a round tour group at New Paradise Spice Garden

as botanical names, origin, physical characteristics, gastronomic and medicinal values, method of consumption, forms of products, and so on (Figure 7.2). However, guides have not undergone any professional qualifications or training for this purpose. After a comprehensive demonstration tour in the garden, visitors are taken to a product presentation, which is called a spice and herb museum in some gardens. Here tourists are encouraged to buy different kinds of spice and herb products for consumption or as souvenirs. In addition, some spice gardens promote instant herbal therapies or Ayurvedic massages, and others hold cooking demonstrations.

Tourism as a service, encompasses inherent characteristics such as intangibility, perishability and variability (Kotler, 1997), and its satisfaction lies between expected and experienced service quality (Reichel et al., 2000). The traditional image and history of Sri Lankan spices and herbs induces tourists to visit spice gardens, but the quality of experience while there determines their satisfaction. Although a large number of clients are very satisfied with the services of spice gardens, a considerable percentage are disappointed with the ways the services are provided (Figure 7.4) and products are sold (Figure 7.5). In addition, the researcher observed that many tourists raise questions about the authenticity of the products. On one hand, garden operators are compelled to promote sales in order to maintain the garden and retain the

**Figure 7.4** Providing mini herbal therapy at Surathura Spice Garden

**Figure 7.5** Selling spices and herbs at Regent Spice Garden

business. On the other hand the commission-integrated business structure has led them to sell the products at inflated prices. Consequently spice gardens today face many challenges due to conventional mass tourism.

## Challenges Faced by Spice Gardens

Although mass tourism led to the invention of tourism-oriented spice gardens in Sri Lanka, today many challenges have been generated by traditional stereotypical tourism for spice gardens. Lack of regulatory mechanisms, missing certification or authorization for guiding, insufficient time for the tourists to spend, inappropriate commission structure, domination of guides and tour operators, depending on sales for survival, unfavourable weather conditions and verifying authenticity are challenges identified through interviews and observations.

The dilemma for further development of spice gardens could be attributable to the absence of proper visitor records and user feedback. Unavailability of past statistics together with interviews and observations revealed that none of the spice gardens maintain visitor records and user feedback for planning and decision making (see Table 7.3), although some hold records of sales. These facts and figures could be useful for owners or operators to plan the business for the long term.

Although spice gardens are approved by the Sri Lanka Tourism Development Authority (SLTDA) under The Specified Tourist Service Code (TSTC) – 1984 (SLTDA, 2011), the latter does not provide clear criteria for establishing and operating of spice gardens. Hence, huge variations were observed in size, number of spice and herb plants, landscaping, duration of tours, standard of services, presentation of spice and herb products, pricing

**Table 7.3** Unavailable information due to poor recordkeeping

| | *Unavailable information* |
|---|---|
| 1 | Number of visitors for a day or a weak or a month or year |
| 2 | Type and other characteristics of tourists |
| 3 | Tourists' interest and preference |
| 4 | The duration of time a tourist spend |
| 5 | Further services and facilities required by tourists |
| 6 | Willingness to revisit |
| 7 | Intention to recommend for friends and future visitors |

*Source*: Field Survey 2012

of the products, and so on. Although, at present SLTDA approved most of the spice gardens run by the experts and skilled teams, there is a possibility for anybody to enter this market. As Jenkins et al. (1998), Sharpley (2002), Pearce (2002), Page and Getz (1997), Roberts and Hall (2001) and Timothy (2005) note, policy guidelines and strategies play a crucial role in sustainable tourism development. Lack of policies, guidelines and strategies prevent the development of appropriate standards, reliability in spice gardens, even though spice garden visitors are one of the most popular tourist services in Sri Lanka.

Guides are the ambassadors or walking encyclopaedia of spices and herbs in Sri Lanka. Lack of certification and licensing of spice garden guides results in various issues and problems, such as anyone can become guide at anytime, inability to differentiate between really skilled and unskilled guides, possibility to duplicate or cheat at anytime, lack of commitment and ethical responsibility and the possibility for misinterpretation and misguiding. Hence, visitors cannot expect similar standards or quality of service from every guide in the spice gardens. Furthermore, guides also find it difficult to determine their wages or earnings due to lack of barriers and criteria for a new person to become a guide. Proprietors or operators are also unable to measure and trust the quality of the guiding services to retain and expand their business. Ultimately, misinterpretation and misguiding tends to affect the entire tourism system and destination services.

Too brief a visit, insufficient time allocation and mismatch with packaged round or circular tours (see Figure 7.1) are another challenge to continuing the spice gardens. As a spice garden visit is included in the packaged tours as an optional item, tourists are provided with limited time within the scheduled itinerary. Very often the short visit is not enough to understand and experience the spices and herbs. Besides, many tourists are not interested in visiting spice gardens since they have already decided on other items or programmes in the scheduled itinerary. As tours are packaged with several items, tour leaders are forced to rush the spice garden operators and spice garden guides to finish the tour within a short time. Incomplete tours and inadequate information on spices and herbs leads the tourists to interpret their experience unfavourably.

Another common issue is the prevailing commission structure. As stated above, the spice garden business is determined by distribution of commission, while taking care of its own cost of purchasing, wages, rent and overheads. The commission has to be distributed among the tour operators, travel agencies, tour leaders, guides, drivers and assistants. A few interviewees clearly stated that 'If we want to retain the business or receive tourists continuously, we should pay competitive and higher commission for the people who direct and bring tourists'. This causes unnecessary competition, resulting in many variations and irregularities in services and quality of operations.

The no entry fee policy is an added burden for the continuation of spice garden businesses. Although spice gardens incur various costs in acquiring land, developing, gardening, maintaining, hiring facilitators, paying commissions and taxes, visitors are charged no admission. Hence the entire costs and financial commitments need to be recovered from the sales revenue of spice and herb products and additional services. Depending on sales revenue causes many operational deficiencies, such as the fact that the few tourists who purchase the products and service are loaded with the entire cost of spice gardens. Eventually this has led the visitor to publish many negative criticisms such as: 'quite expensive could the same stuff be bought elsewhere cheaper' (Solovika, 2009); 'well over priced of course', 'head for the nearest local pharmacy, here you will find everything on sale at spice garden at a much lower cost' (Dave, 2009); 'we enjoyed the tour and also mini massage, and we decided to buy something from their shop, we only bought some sandlewood cream and cinnamon oil (not even sure it's even the right stuff as it doesn't even have smell and is certainly not worth much) the total cost was 5900 rupees' (Furby England, 2010). As an entry fee is not charged, tourists fall into embarrassing situations and buy something to compensate for the efforts of the spice gardens.

Unfavourable weather conditions also interrupt the stable business of spice gardens. During the drought seasons it is difficult to keep the spice and herb plants healthy and green. Controversially, when tourists arrive during periods or rain for a brief visit, they are reluctant to move around the plants and bushes. Missing these opportunities deprives the business expectations of employees and operators.

Thus, building a spice garden for tourism tends to give an impression of staged authenticity for some visitors. Seldom are visitors allowed to pluck or pick-up things from original plants and the extraction and production of spice and herbal products is not demonstrated. Most of the time tourists find it difficult to verify the authenticity and raise question on the genuineness of products. While an inherent characteristic of conventional tourism product is staged authenticity (Cohen, 1988; MaCanell, 1973), tourist products, facilities and services are provided according to the convenience of tourists. Similarly, the original form of Kandyan home gardens have been replicated as spice gardens along the waysides for the convenience of tourists' short visits. Those tourists who are interested in experiencing the authentic spices and herbs integrated into traditional livelihood, food culture and healing of common illnesses of rural community, are not provided with adequate opportunities.

# Emerging Trend of Sustainable Tourism and Spices and Herbs

At present the sustainability of spices and herbs tourism is the dominant issue, as they form significant components of the tourism industry of Sri Lanka. McCool and Moisey (2008) categorize sustainable tourism as (1) 'sustaining tourism; maintaining business of tourism industry over a long time', (2) 'sustainable tourism; small-scale and gentle form of tourism with minimum negative impacts' and (3) 'what to sustain; as tool for socio-economic development'. Spices and herbs should be transformed into forms of sustainable tourism in order to secure long-term business while ensuring local socio-economic development with minimum negative impacts. D'Hautserre (2005) argues that conventional tourism does not resolve the challenges on sustainability and 'alternative' or 'soft' tourism is a path to sustainability. The emergence of new forms of tourism, such as ecotourism, community-based tourism, alternative tourism, rural tourism and green tourism (whatever the name given all these forms of tourism) are integrated into sustainable tourism, which leads to overcoming deficiencies in conventional tourism development (Aslam, 2005; Mowforth & Munt, 1995). As traditional mass tourism denies incorporating spices and herbs comprehensively to provide holistic experience and enjoyment, alternative forms of tourism are required to ensure the sustainability in spice-related tourism.

Seeking authentic and unique experiences in consumption of local foods and beverages lets the tourists get close to the host culture (Plummer *et al.*, 2004). Food and beverages are playing a critical role in tourism (Cohen & Avieli, 2004; Henderson, 2009; Hjalager & Corigliano, 2000; Tourism Kwazulu-Natal – TKZN, 2011), while spices and herbs are widely used to maximize the value for food and beverages through natural flavourings and fragrances (Jayasuriya, 2011). Firmino's (2010) in-depth analysis of organic farmers and spice plantations in the Ponda region of Goa, India elucidates the importance of integration of spice and herbs into tourism in a wider perspectives, which includes historic, heritage, culture, organic, nature and health dimensions of tourism (also see Chapter 5). Tourist statistics in India recorded 80% of the tourists arriving in the district of Kerala state stay in spice plantations (Radhakrishnen, 2011). Further, Chase and Burch (1998) and Middleton (2000) presented an empirical study in Zanzibar, a spice island of Tanzania, which stated that spices are a vital component in the broad spectrum of tourism and recreation. Although gourmet or gastronomic tourism is not new or unusual (Muntean *et al.*, 2010), presently food and beverages diversity pertaining to geographical and cultural diversity is an influencing factor of tourism.

The alternative forms of tourism increased demand and recreation activities in rural areas, where the majority of spices and herbs originate. At present globally peripheral regions possess approximately 10–20% of tourism activities (Roberts & Hall, 2001), over 70% of all Americans participate in rural recreation (OECD, 1994) and 23% of European holidaymakers choose the countryside as their destination annually (EuroBarometer, 1998). Since the environment, socio-culture and livelihood of rural community are interwoven with alternative tourism and recreation, spices and herbs amalgamating culture, nature and history of rural Sri Lanka will be a complementary factor in exploiting potential. Although rural communities encountered a decline in traditional sources of trading and merchandizing their local produce, tourism could be identified as a non-traditional alternative to regenerate rural livelihoods, while preserving the culture and nature (Fleischer & Pizam, 1997; Sharpley, 2002, 2003; Tribe et al., 2000; Timothy, 2005). Spices and herbs can be incorporated as a supportive component of alternative tourism, which ensures sustainability.

Rather than setting up spice gardens for a short visit of mass tourists, they can be part of a complete tourism product for special interest tourists, who place a higher value on the experience (Roberts & Hall, 2001). Such tourists assume that the experience benefit outweighs the cost of the visit. Although, every tourist does not have an interest particularly in spices and herbs, gastronomy, herbal therapies and natural atmosphere and fragrances can maximize value and satisfaction of the product. Combining spices and herbs with historical, anthropological, ethnographical, ecological and geographical resources widens the tourists' experience and can multiply demand. Emerging alternative concepts of tourism can therefore be underpinned with spices and herbs, which have more meanings and values for different interest groups.

## Conclusion

Spices and herbs began to exist in travel and tourism during 16th and 17th centuries with Portuguese discoveries on plant exchange between continents (Ferrão, 1994). The East West Silk Route made the Asian region (Radhakrishnen, 2011) into the heart of tropical spices and herbs, and Sri Lanka received the most recognition. The rich diversity and unique geographical features here facilitate the production of varieties of high-quality spices and herbs, and position the island in the transnational trading and global travel and tourism map. However, the impossibilities and inconvenience of witnessing many spice and herb plants at one place within a short time led to building contemporary spice gardens along the waysides for short visits of conventional mass tourists. These spice gardens provide a remarkable experience and basic understanding of prominent spices and herbs of Sri Lanka; nevertheless, they seemed to demonstrate staged authenticity. In-depth interviews and participative observation enabled the researcher to report on many challenges and issues in sustaining the spice gardens according to socially constructed interpretations of people, who are the topic of interest. Envisaging the potential of sustainable tourism is essential in the regeneration of the declining traditional livelihood of the rural community, who are the custodians of spices' and herbs' authenticity. Combining spices and herbs with different sustainable tourism concepts would bring forth more meaning and value through a wide experience.

## References

Aslam, M.S.M. (2005) An empirical study on reasoning for and determinants of sustainable tourism development, A case study of Kandy, MSc Dissertation, Colombo: University of Sri Jayewardenepura.

Awang, K.W. (2006) Tourism development in peripheral area of Malaysia: A case study of Kelantan, PhD thesis, Aberstwyth: University of Wales.

Bandara, H.M. (2001) *Tourism Development Planning in Developing Countries: A Critique.* Colombo: Stamford Lake.

Bandara, H.M. (2003) *Tourism Planning in Sri Lanka.* Colombo: Stamford Lake.

CBSL (2010) *Annual Report.* Colombo: Central Bank of Sri Lanka.

CBSL (2011) *Annual Report.* Colombo: Central Bank of Sri Lanka.

Chase, H. and Burch, B. (1998) Zanzibar: The Spice Island in The Sun. *Crisis: Travel and Leisure* 105 (3), 68–69.

Cohen, E. (1988) Authenticity and commoditization in tourism: *Annals of Tourism Research* 15, 371–386.

Cohen, E. and Avieli, N. (2004) Food in tourism: Attraction and impediment. *Annals of Tourism Research* 31 (4), 755–778.

Dave (2009) Sri Lanka forum: Spice gardens: Real or fake, TripAdvisor. http://www.tripadvisor.ie/ShowTopic-g293961-i8983-k3118480-Spice_gardens_real_or_fake-Sri_Lanka.html (accessed 30 August 2012).

de Bruin, A and Nithiyanandam, V. (2000) Tourism in Sri Lanka: 'Paradise on Earth'? In C.M. Hall and S. Page (eds) *Tourism in South and South East Asia* (pp. 235–247). Oxford: Butterworth Heinemann.

De Silva, S. (2012) *Supply Chain Challenges for Spice Producers.* Worl Spice Congress, 9–11 February 2012, Pune, India. http://www.worldspicecongress.com/; http://112.133.204.82/wsc_pune/ (accessed 20 May 2012).

Department of Census and Statistics (2010) *Population and Housing Statistics – Mid Year Report.* Colombo: Department of Census Statistics of Sri Lanka.

Department of Export Agriculture (DEA) (2012) Overview, department of export agriculture. http://www.exportagridept.gov.lk/web/index.php?option=com_content&view=article&id=51&Itemid=57&lang=en (accessed 20 February 2012).

D'Hauteserre A.-M. (2005) Tourism, development and sustainability in monaco: Comparing discourses and practices. *Tourism Geographies* 7 (3), 290–312.

Esterberg, K.G. (2002) *Qualitative Methods in Social Research*. Boston, MA: McGraw-Hill.

EuroBarometer (1998) *Facts and Figures on the Europeans' Holiday, EuroBarometer DG XXIII*. Brussels: European Commission.

Ferrão, J.E.M. (1994) *The Adventure of Plants and the Portuguese Discoveries*. The Institute of Tropical Scientific Research, The National Commission for Commemoration of the Portuguese Discoveries. Rio Tinto: José Berardo Foundation.

Firmino, A. (2010) New challenges for organic farmers in India: Tourism, spices and herbs. *Journal of Geography* 5 (1), 101–113.

Fleischer, A. and Pizam, A. (1997) Rural tourism in Israel. *Tourism Management* 18 (6), 367–372.

Furby England (2010) Sri Lanka forum: Spice gardens: Real or fake, TripAdvisor. http://www.tripadvisor.ie/ShowTopic-g293961-i8983-k3118480-Spice_gardens_real_or_fake-Sri_Lanka.html (accessed 30 August 2012).

Government of Ceylon (1966a) *Ceylon Tourist Board Act No. 10 of 1966*. Colombo: Government Press.

Government of Ceylon (1966b) *Ceylon Hotel Corporation Act No. 14 of 1966*. Colombo: Government Press.

Government of Ceylon (1968) *Tourist Development Act No. 14 of 1968*. Colombo: Government Press.

Harris, Kerr, Foster and Company (1967) *The Ceylon Tourist Plan*. Hawaii, Honolulu: Harris, Kerr, Foster & Company.

Havitz, M.E. (1994) *A Personal and Collective Critique of Methodological and Ethical Concerns in Consumer Behavior Research*. Keynote presentation at the National Recreation and Park Association Leisure Research Symposium, Minneapolis, MN.

Henderson, J.C. (2009) Food tourism reviewed. *British Food Journal* 111 (4), 317–326.

Henderson, K.A. and Bedini, L.A. (1995) Notes on linking qualitative and quantitative data. *Journal of Therapeutic Recreation* 29, 124–130.

Hjalager, A.M. and Corigliano, M.A. (2000) Food for tourists – Determinants of image. *International Journal of Tourism Research* 2 (4), 281–293.

Hollinshead, K. (1996) The tourism researcher as Bricoleur: The new wealth and diversity in qualitative inquiry. *Tourism Analysis* 1, 67–74.

Jayasuriya, S. (2011) Spice industry benefit from tourism. *Daily News*, 3 January 2011.

Jayawickrama, A.J.M. (2000) Tourism in Sri Lanka recent trends. *Economic Review* 26 (2), 5–7.

Jenkins, J.M., Hall, C.M. and Troughton, M. (1998) The restructuring of rural economies: Rural tourism and recreation as a government response. In R. Butler, C.M. Hall and J.M. Jenkins (eds) *Tourism and Recreation in Rural Areas* (pp. 19–42). Chichester: Wiley.

Kotler, P. (1997) *Marketing Management: Analysis, Planning, Implementation and Control* (6th edn). Englewood Cliffs, NJ: Prentice Hall.

MacCannel, D. (1973) Staged authenticity: Arrangement of social space to tourist setting. *American Journal of Sociology* 79 (3), 589–603.

McCool, S.F. and Moisey, R.N. (2008) Introduction: Pathways and pitfalls in the search for sustainable tourism. In S.F. McCool and R.N. Moisey (eds) *Tourism, Recreation and Sustainability* (pp. 1–15). Wallingford: CAB International.

Merriam, S.B. (2009) *Qualitative Research: A Guide to Design and Implementation*. San Francisco: Jossey-Bass.

Middleton, N. (2000) Totally tropical. *Geographical* 72 (2), 46–53.

Mowforth, M. and Munt, I. (1998) *Tourism and Sustainability: New Tourism in the Third World*. London: Routledge.

Muntean, M.-C., Nistor, C., Nistor, R. and Sarpe, D. (2010) Oeno-Gourmet tourism – A new way of Romanian Tourism Boost. Accessed at http://www.wseas.us/e-library/conferences/2010/Corfu/CUHT/CUHT-37.pdf (accessed 13 May 2014).

Nicholls, D. (2009) The qualitative research: Part three-method. *International Journal of Therapy and Rehabilitation* 16 (12), 638–647.

OECD (1994) *Tourism Strategies and Rural Development*. Paris: OECD.

Page, S.J. and Getz, D. (1997) *The Business of Rural Tourism: International Perspectives* (pp. 6–7). London: International Thomson Business Press.

Pearce, D.G. (2002) Tourism and peripherality: Perspectives from Asia and the South Pacific. *Tourism and Hospitality Research* 3 (4), 295–309.

Plummer, R., Telfer, D., Hashimoto, A. and Summers, R. (2004) Beer tourism in Canada along the Waterloo-Wellington Ale Trail. *Tourism Management* 26 (2005), 447–458.

Radhakrishnen, S.A. (2011) Adding spice to Tourism. *The Hindu*, India's National News Paper, 7 March 2011. http://www.hindu.com/2011/03/07/stories/2011030751300200.htm (accessed 21 June 2012).

Reichel, A., Lowengart, O. and Milman A. (2000) Rural tourism in Israel: Service quality and orientation. *Tourism Management* 21, 451–459.

Renique, A. (2009) Healing powers of herbs and spices in Sri Lanka: Quick cure for common ailments can be found in kitchens and gardens, natural medicine, Suit – 101. http://suite101.com/article/healing-powers-of-herbs-and-spices-in-sri-lanka-a169109 (accessed 20 April 2011).

Riley, R.W. (1996) Using grounded theory analysis to reveal the underlying dimensions of prestige in leisure travel. *Journal of Travel and Tourism Marketing* 5 (1/2), 21–40.

Roberts, L. and Hall, D. (eds) (2001) *Rural Tourism and Recreation: Principles to Practice*. Wallingford: CAB International.

Scheyvens, R. (2002) *Tourism for Development: Empowering Communities*. Harlow: Pearson Education Limited.

Sharpley, R. (2002) Rural tourism and the challenge of tourism diversification: The case of Cyprus. *Tourism Management* 23, 233–244.

Sharpley, R. (2003) Tourism, modernization and development on the island of cyprus: Challenges and policy responses. *Journal of Sustainable Tourism* 11 (2 & 3), 246–265.

SLTDA (2010) *Annual Statistical Report*. Colombo: Sri Lanka Tourism Development Authority.

SLTDA (2011) *List of Spice Gardens Registered Spice Gardens Under. The Specified Tourist Services Code – 1984*. Colombo: Sri Lanka Tourism Development Authority.

Solovika (2009) Sri Lanka forum: Spice gardens: Real or fake, TripAdvisor. http://www.tripadvisor.ie/ShowTopic-g293961-i8983-k3118480-Spice_gardens_real_or_fake-Sri_Lanka.html (accessed 30 August 2012).

Spice Master (2008) *Would Madame Like Some Ground Pepper with Her Barramundi?* Paper presented at World Spice Congress, 25 January 2008. http://www.spicemasters.com.au/news/newsitemview.asp?id=1 (accessed 13 May 2011).

Timothy D.J. (2005) Rural tourism business: A North American overview. In D. Hall, I. Kirkpatrick and M. Mitchess (eds) *Rural Tourism in Sustainable Business* (pp. 41–62). Clevedon: Channel View Publications.

TKZN (2011) *Food and Beverage Tourism*. Occasional Paper – 86, Zulu Kingdom.

Tribe, J., Font, X., Griffiths, N., Vickery, R. and Yale, K. (2000) *Environmental Management for Rural Tourism and Recreation*. London: Cassell.

TSC (2010) TSC Statistics: Value of export agricultural products, The Spice Council. http://www.srilankanspices.com/statistics.html (accessed 2 August 2012).

Tsung-Wei Lai (2002) Promoting sustainable tourism in Sri Lanka. In T. Hundloe (ed.) *Linking Green Productivity to Ecotourism Experiences in the Asia–Pacific Region* (pp. 208–214). Tokyo: Asian Productivity Organization.

Walle, A.H. (1997) Quantitative versus qualitative tourism research. *Annals of Tourism Research* 24 (3), 524–536.

# 8 The Tropical Spice Garden in Penang, Malaysia

## Azilah Kasim

Penang, Malaysia has a rich historic connection to spice owing to its strategic location and its colonization history, which began in 1786. The success of Captain Francis Light's negotiation to have the island in exchange for security protection of Kedah's Sultan – the original ruler of Penang (Mohammed *et al.*, 2006) is the pinnacle of Penang and its spice journey. Light took over Penang on behalf of the East Indian Company and turned the island from a sleepy, sparsely habituated place to a buzzing trade port for tea, textiles from India and spices such as locally produced star anise and nutmeg, and black pepper from China. These, boosted by the booming regional tin and rubber trading that followed, transformed the tax-free trade zone of Penang into a significant civilization and buzzing meeting point of traders from Europe, China, India, Thailand, Myanmar and the Malay archipelago (Mohammed *et al.*, 2006).

Subsequently, the island became home to many races – the English, the Malay from the Peninsula and Sumatra, the Chinese and the Indian labourers who left their countries in search of a better place to live. In 1957, Penang became independent from the English and became part of Malaysia in 1963 (Penang Municipal Council public relation officer; personal communication). It was the English occupation that has led Penang to become an important trading port for spices. The resulting multicultural society of Penang naturally became significant contributors to spice related tourism in Penang today. Specifically, the use of spices in the multicultural society of Penang has led to the creation of unique and diverse variety of cuisines that lifted Penang's image as a gastronomic destination. The significant role of spices in the local cuisines has inspired a Penang entrepreneur to develop a spice garden from a land which was formerly a rubber plantation. The Tropical Spice Garden (TSG), which will be described in detail later in the chapter, has won several awards (Table 8.1) and is increasingly popular among

**Table 8.1** Awards received by the Tropical Spice Garden

| Year | Award |
| --- | --- |
| 2004 | Malaysian International Landscape and Garden Festival Award |
| 2004 | Laman Floral Garden Award |
| 2005/6 | Merit Award |
| 2010 | Best Man Made Attraction Award |
| 2012 | Most Outstanding Tourism Attraction Award |

*Source*: TSG

international travellers. It is also a primary attraction in Penang promoted by the state government intended in selling Penang as a spice tourism destination (Jalleh, 2012).

# Methodology

This chapter adopts a case study approach to uncover the theoretical link between food and tourism, the historic and culinary foundations of spices in Penang; and the workings of the TSG in Penang tourism. The approach enables the researcher to critically assess and investigate something and to do an in-depth analysis of the relevant research problem. Young (1982) has proposed that a fairly comprehensive study of a person or group is called a *life* or *case history*. In this sense, a comprehensive study of a social unit – a person, a group, a social institution, a place, or a community is then called a case study. A case study approach usually analyzes a contemporary phenomenon within its real-life context, when the boundaries between phenomenon and context are not clearly evident (Yin, 2003). Therefore, case study approach is highly suitable for examining all aspects, processes and complexity of factors of a social unit, as well as understanding their complex relationships as a whole.

The research procedure began with a literature search. It was then followed by the rigorous qualitative methods of observation, and an in-depth interview with the TSG General Manager (GM) and triangulated with a phone interview with a Penang Municipal Council officer. The observation method was helpful to provide personal insights into the physical outlay of the garden, the products (i.e. the herbs and spices) and any observable management and marketing issues facing TSG. The author acted as a paying customer to perform the evaluation so that an objective perspective can be generated about what was observed. A semi-structured interview was conducted for gathering the primary data. According to Hancock (1998) semi-structured interviews require a series of open ended questions based on the topic areas that the researcher wants to cover. He further asserts that, 'the open-ended nature of the question defines the topic under investigation but provides opportunities for both interviewer and interviewee to discuss some topics in more detail'. Hence, this approach was effective, as it illuminated unexpected and insightful information.

The interview respondent was a long time employee of TSG who has worked her way up to the managerial position. The interview session was recorded and transcribed afterwards. As English was used throughout the entire conversation, there was no need for back translation as is often the case when interviewing a Malaysian (owing to the tendency to either use Malay or a mixed language in conversations). Upon completion of initial analysis, the interviewee was contacted for confirmation of facts and conclusions. A phone interview was also conducted with an officer of the Penang Municipal Council. However, this interview is only to help the study verify some information about Penang found on the council's website.

# Findings

## The theoretical link between food and tourism

Desk research showed that food and tourism have strong relation. Food is often a major consideration for potential tourists when choosing a destination. Middle East tourists for example, have specific food requirement for meat when they travel. This is one of the reasons that draw them to Malaysia during their summer holiday destination (Alfandi & Kasim, 2011). The availability of a wide range of 'Halal' food (prepared according to the Islamic specifications, without pork and following particular procedure for the slaughtering of animals) in Malaysia make travel easier and more pleasurable for them.

Boyne et al. (2003) observed that there is a continuum of food tourists. This can range from 'the highly committed', i.e. taking food is an important driver for holiday travelling (for example, the case of Middle East tourists mentioned above), to 'the searcher', i.e. actively scavenging information on the local availability and heritage of gastronomy to 'the disinterested', i.e. those who have little or no food interest. Therefore, with appropriate promotion that highlights unique tangible and intangible products and services, local cuisines can offer a destination the potential point of differentiation (Boyne et al., 2003). There were also perspectives on the psychological side of food in tourism. Frochot (2003) for example, insists that food related tourism can provide tourists the avenue to achieve relaxation, excitement, escapism, status, education and lifestyle. Meanwhile, Quan and Wang (2004) contend that food acts as primary or secondary motivator for travel. Food also enhances the image of a destination (Boniface, 2003; Long, 2004). These authors are correct in the sense that strong relationship between certain localities and certain types of food is often the reason many popular destinations such as Thailand, Italy and Belgium are preferred. Those countries are commonly perceived to offer delicious tasting food along with other equally important tourism attributes such as monuments, traditions and nature. As Hughes (1995) emphasized, there is a perceived natural relationship between a region's land, its climatic conditions and its food. A geographical characteristic's influence on the distinctiveness of regional culinary traditions has been used in tourism promotions. According to Munsters (1994) regional gastronomic routes may be attributed to specific cultural tourism product such as an asparagus route, a mussel route and others (cited in Zainal et al., 2010). These seasonal routes reflect the connection between agricultural cycles and local food production.

Munster's and Hughes's linking of geography and food also applies in the context of Malaysia. According to Zainal et al. (2010), Malaysian cuisine has traditionally been strongly influenced by traders from countries that are geographically in close proximity with Malaysia – such as Indonesia, India, the Middle East, China and others. Thus, there was a fusion of local and foreign flavours that are unique but varied, reflecting a strong relationship between food and identity. Food in Malaysia also plays the role of a place marker, creating an invisible 'food trail' that lets tourists experience an authentic cultural experience by sampling the different varieties of local cuisines.

The government was quick to realize the role of food as a significant place marker in tourism promotion. Food is used to represent a state's, a region's and a community's specific specialties (the Ninth Malaysia Plan, 2006–2010). The plan highlighted the 'Malaysia Kitchen' concept which reflects the multi-culturally influenced cuisines of Malaysia. The concept was introduced to bring Malaysian cuisines to the world. The resulting programme encourages entrepreneurs to set up of Malaysian restaurants in every major city. More recently, Penang has been selected as the 'Food Spice Trail' destination which shows increasing recognition on the importance of spice in tourism (Jalleh, 2012). However, while all these programmes and events are plausible, it seems that the existing policy of Malaysia Tourism has overlooked a very important avenue for showcasing food and local spices – the home-stay tourism programme. Home stay is a popular tourism product showcasing the traditional *kampong* (village) lifestyle that

**Table 8.2** Various medicinal and gastronomic uses of spices in Malaysia

| Spices | Medicinal benefits | How it is used in Malaysian cooking |
|---|---|---|
| Star anise | • Anti colic <br> • Aids digestion. | A family of liquorice, star anise gives a hint of sweetness and aroma to soupy and curry dishes. It is normally fried whole at the initial stage of soup/curry making to release the aroma and sweetness. |
| Ceylon cinnamon [true cinnamon] | • Anti fungal <br> • Reduces diabetes <br> • When combined with honey, cinnamon can reduce a number of ailments ranging from heart disease to weight issues. | Commonly used to accompany cloves, cardamom and star anise in korma dishes. It is also used in marinating chicken for chicken rice dishes. |
| Black pepper | • Reduces bloating <br> • Aids digestion <br> • Anti oxidant <br> • Reduces anaemia. | As many Malaysian dishes use chillies to give additional spiciness, not many local dishes use black pepper as flavour enhancer. However, for dishes specially made for post-partum malay women, black pepper is used as not only a flavour enhancer but also 'body warmer' to those women. |
| White pepper | • Reduces bloating <br> • Aids digestion <br> • Anti-oxidant <br> • Reduces anaemia <br> • Anti-fungal. | White pepper is often used as flavour enhancer for fried or soupy noodles as well as fried rice. It is as spicy as black pepper, but without the dark colour. It is used more in Malaysian Chinese cooking and is used in much the same way as black pepper is the western culture, |
| Ginger | • Reduces bloating <br> • Reduces nausea. | Dried ginger is often used as flavouring for drinks. On the other hand, regular ginger is usually minced together with shallots and garlic to form a base for many of Malaysian curries and sauces. |

*(Continued)*

**Table 8.2** (*Continued*)

| Spices | Medicinal benefits | How it is used in Malaysian cooking |
|---|---|---|
| Turmeric | • Anti-aging<br>• Antioxidant<br>• Anti-fungal. | Turmeric is often used in powder form. Although rich in antioxidants, it is primarily used for the vibrant yellow colour to curry and sauces. |
| Lemongrass | • Anti-cancer<br>• Calming to the skin<br>• Aids digestion. | This herb is very common in Thai and Malay cuisines. It gives lemony, fragrant effect on dishes and can be used in sauces, curry as well as rice dishes. |
| Curry leaves | • Aids digestion<br>• Reduces diabetes. | Curry leaves have very strong aroma that significantly enhances curries smell and flavours. It is often fried in a little oil along with cloves, coriander and other curry spices to release the aroma before the remaining ingredients are added in. |
| Nutmeg [from Penang] | • Brain tonic<br>• Relieve pain<br>• Aids digestion<br>• Treats bad breath<br>• Detox liver and kidney<br>• Skin care Aids sleeping (Fitday, 2000–2001). | In local dishes nutmeg is not often used in regular cooking despite its abundance in Penang. However, some cakes do use nutmeg as flavour enhancer. Most common use of nutmeg is as preserve. |
| Cloves (from Penang) | • Pain killer for toothache | This herb is often used together with star anise and cardamom in local curries. |
| Galangal | • Anti-cancer<br>• Anti-inflammation<br>• Aids digestion<br>• Reduces diarrhoea. | Malaysia's favourite dish called Rendang relies heavily on galangal to give it its distinctive flavour. |

*Source*: Developed by author

attracts young visitors from all over the word. In home stays, visitors are exposed to the traditional Malay lifestyle, culture, ceremonies and food. However, reading through the country's Economic Plan and based on recent events as well as the author's personal observation, there is evidently no emphasis about utilizing home-stay villages to showcase the production (planting and harvesting) and usage of herbs and spices in the Malay food. This seems like a 'missed opportunity' and should have been considered further in the country's quest to promote Malaysia's identity to the world.

On the other hand, choosing Penang as a Food Spice Trail destination can be deemed as a wise move. Penang is a popular island tourism destination in Malaysia. It is located in the northeast of Malaysian Peninsula and is connected to the mainland via Penang Bridge and a ferry system first developed during the English occupation of the island. The island is known internationally as rich in history and culture. However, to regional and local tourists, it is more renowned as a gastronomic heaven. Penang food relies heavily on spices. As the population is very multicultural – Chinese, Indian, Malay, Indian Moslem, Nyonya and Baba (combination of Chinese and Malay) etc., food preparation in Penang has been greatly influenced by the cooking style of all these cultures. While varied in taste and appearance, all these cultures use spices heavily in their cooking. Commonly used spices in their respective cooking include ginger, curry leaves and tamarind. Such dependency is not only attributable to the role of spices as flavour enhancer, but also the medicinal value spices have to human health (see Table 8.2).

This list is by no means exhaustive as there are plenty of other spices that are used in the cooking and healing processes in Penang. The TSG Manager (personal communication) stressed that going to a *Seng Seh* (or the traditional Chinese medicine stores – found everywhere in Penang) would introduce one to a lot more exotic looking and tasting combinations of spices and herbs intended for medicinal purposes.

As mentioned earlier, Penang has a rich historic connection to spice owing to its strategic location and its history of being colonized by the English. In line with Munsters (1994) contention about food and product route, the food culture of Penang can also be attributed to specific product (spice) route. Since it is a tiny island located in the midst of the Malay Archipelago, the historical importance of spices in Penang is very much embedded in the history of spice trade routes of Southeast Asia (Chomchalow, 1996). Whereas the ancient history of the routes (documented in medieval Chinese and Muslim texts) are complicated and is beyond the scope of this chapter, a more modern account of the history showed Southeast Asia to be the origin of spice trade route that ultimately ended in the Mediterranean market as well as to China and India (Manansala, 2001). These are known as the 'Cinnamon Route' and the 'Clove Route'. The so-called Cinnamon Route began somewhere in the Malay Archipelago before reaching the Indian Ocean to Madagascar, and eventually to the East African trading ports in Rhapta. The spices were then hauled by merchants towards the North via Adulis in Ethiopia, then to Muza in Yemen and finally to Berenike in Egypt.

Egypt was the hub for spices that later made their way to the markets of Europe and West Asia (Miller, 1969, cited in Manansala, 2001). Miller further suggested that as there were prehistoric settlements of Madagascar by Austronesian seafarers, then Austronesian traders must have been the first to have brought spices to African markets via the southern maritime route. As for the Clove Route, the author suggested that it originated from the southern of Philippine, particularly Maluku. Then the spice travelled first to the South China and Indochina before moving south to the Strait of Malacca to India and further west (Chomchalow, 1996).

During the age of exploration that sees competing quest for spices and precious metals, early explorers such as Magellan and Sebastian Cabot were said to be on the quest to find spices and precious metal on islands called Tarshish and Ophir. This led to the circumnavigation of Africa and the world, and the coming of the Europeans to colonize Asia. It was reported that the Portuguese explorers often use Penang (at the time known as Pulo Pinao) as a stopping point in their quest searching for the Spice Islands. This effectively put Penang on the spice trade route map. In 1786, during the British colonization, Penang was designated as a pepper port which gave the British great power to control the spice trade route (Manansala, 2001; Penang Municipal Council officer, personal communication).

While Penang is a big spice consumer (to be used in its culinary), it is not a big spice producer. In fact, Penang, and Malaysia in general import spices from India – mainly coriander (5072.4 metric tonnes per year), small cardamom (331 metric tonnes per year), turmeric (2895.4 metric tonnes per year) and cumin (1214 metric tonnes per year) (see Press Trust of India, 12 June 2009). This can be seen as an unsustainable practice because as with any products, dependence on imports is often subjected to price changes, safety and security issues. Thus, reducing dependency on imported spices and focusing on locally produced spices would be a more sustainable option.

However, Penang produces nutmeg – an important spice often used in sweet dishes, juices and cakes. Nutmeg is commonly found in Balik Pulau and Teluk Bahang. Although technically a fruit, its spicy and sweet flavour effectively rendered it as a spice. Nutmeg can be produced and processed into powder, pickled and dried form to be used in cooking. It can also be turned into balm, medical oils or face cream owing to its antiseptic and soothing nature (Fitday, 2000–2001). The oils and balm are often used externally to treat headaches, nausea, colds, stomach aches, minor burns, dry cough and stomach gas.

Penang also produces cloves. Prior to the millennium, cloves used to be grown commercially in Penang. However, this gradually disappeared as time goes by, leaving few remaining farms used for research by the Ministry of

Agriculture. Vanilla is also planted on a small scale, whereas other herbs such as Kafir lime leaves, lemongrass and tamarind are normally planted in people's yards or back garden. The main reason for low commercial production of spice in Penang is the emphasis on other economic activities such as manufacturing and property industries. It is more economically viable to source spices from the Mainland Peninsular, which can easily be accessed using the Penang Bridge (Chomchalow, 1996).

## The Tropical Spice Garden

The significance of spice in Penang has given an expatriate named David Wilkinson the inspiration to turn his land into a privately managed spice garden. His idea is not far-fetched. Gardens have long been an important tourism attraction for many destinations. In almost every city destination in the world, gardens and parks provide either the main or secondary tourism pull factor. The most common garden found in many tourism destinations is the botanical garden. Other typical gardens and parks include butterfly gardens/farms and bird parks/sanctuaries. These tourism products are built mainly for two fundamental objectives – conservation and education. The products encourage conservation because the main element – be it flowers, insects or bird – are cared for and protected. It encourages education because these parks are often equipped with passive and/or active interpretive tools. In fact, garden projects that possess outstanding quality can attract international tourists thereby earning valuable foreign exchange earnings for a destination. As Quintal (2011) pointed out, gardens occupy one of the top ten attractions for tourists from England, Germany, USA, Japan and Australia. For this reason, many destinations strive to develop unique garden landscape to attract tourists. Some successful and internationally renowned gardens include The Eden Project and the modern Alnwick Garden in England; the Botanical Garden of Curitiba in Brazil; the Buchart Gardens in Vancouver Island as well as Van Dusen Botanical Garden in Vancouver, Canada; and the Kirstenbosh National Botanical Garden in Cape Town (listed in 2004 as a World Heritage by UNESCO) (Quintal, 2011).

However, the above-mentioned gardens mostly concentrate on commonly known flowers such as tulips, roses etc. Spice garden on the other hand, is a relatively a new concept. Unlike the obvious beauty of flower blooms, spice plants generally lack the visual aesthetics since they are normally planted for medicinal and gastronomic reasons. However, TSG has successfully developed a visually pleasing spice garden, by integrating spice plants with other features such as flowers, trees and water features rendering it to be one of the most popular tourism attractions in Penang. 'Fresh', 'shady' and 'relaxing' are some of the adjectives that come to mind when entering this garden (personal observation). The land, which is essentially a slope that faces the open sea along Penang's North western shores, makes it perfect for panoramic sceneries. According to the GM, Wilkinson formed a team comprising landscape architect Lim In Chong and project manager Frederick Walker to set the place up. Along with his wife Rebecca, and funded by Bertam Consolidated Rubber Co. Ltd, David started to landscape the garden using an environmentally friendly approach. He ensured the original species on site were protected and worked around the contour of the hilly terrain as is with all the boulders etc. and building our landscape around the existing plants/terrain. Later, Katharine Chua (GM) and husband Kenneth Khoo took over and continued the effort, thereby transforming the once overgrown plot into a uniquely designed garden that strives to represent the ecotourism and gastronomic tourism of Malaysia.

With the mission of developing the garden into 'an internationally recognized garden and botanic institution focussed on enhancing knowledge and understanding for the responsible management of our natural resources' (GM; personal communication), the 8-acre garden's landscape was designed to give visitors the feeling of mystery. There are three trails weaving through the valley and the hill – the Ornamental trail, the Spice trail and the Jungle trail. Herb planting was designed according to the topography of each trail and planted to give visitors an 'Alice-in-Wonderland' feeling. In other words, the plants are positioned such that passing each bend would give visitors an opening to a new vista (Figure 8.1).

An older bungalow house, thought to have been built in the 1940s was redeveloped as the garden's gift-shop. The shop now sells a variety of dried spices, ground spices and curry spices. In addition to those spices, there are also a range of handicrafts, household scented items, aromatherapy products, body oils, stationary, Penang/botanical related books/local and contemporary craft being sold to visitors. In deciding the products to be sold in the garden shop, the management seeks to select items that are fairly traded to protect the local farmer/artisan over imported goods (GM, personal communication). They strive to select items that carry an interesting story and are unique while staying away from common, run on the mill and 'touristy' items. Thus, tourists can find unique things such as dried Stevia leaves (a natural, purportedly healthier replacement of sugar), soap bars made from selected herbs, and home-made spice blends (Table 8.3).

In terms of services, the garden provides daily guided tours in English, Arabic and Mandarin and specifically designed packages for corporate team-building, boutique garden weddings and daily hands-on cooking classes.

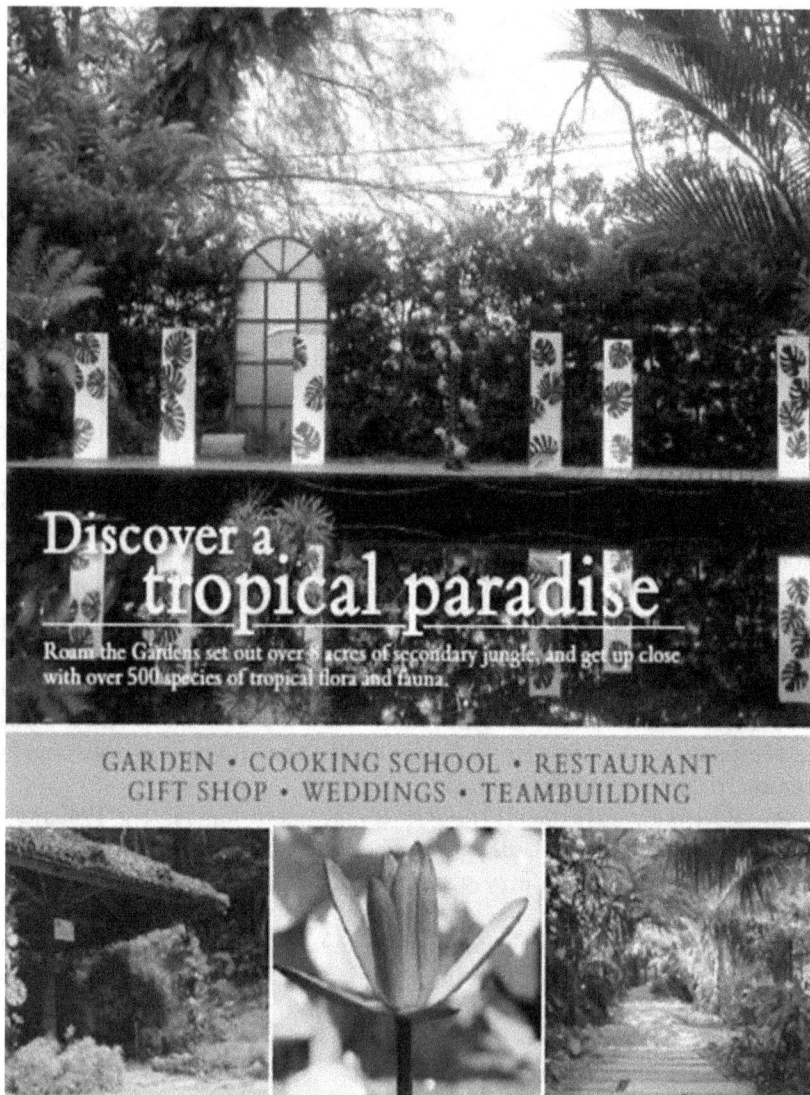

**Figure 8.1** Range of products and services offered at the Spice Garden

The cooking classes have been a top selection for many foreign visitors because of the values they offer – a hands-on familiarity to Asian cooking as well as understanding on the types and uses of tropical herbs and spices (see *Tripologist: Travelling the World on a Backpacker's Budget*, 26 March 2012 for an

**Table 8.3** Blended spices and curries

| Blended spices | Herbs and spices used |
| --- | --- |
| Cajun spices | Cumin, coriander and fennel seeds |
| Tandoori spices | Cumin, coriander, cayenne |
| Garam masala spices | Cardamom, peppercorn, cumin, cloves, nutmeg, cinnamon |
| Biryani spices | Turmeric, ginger, cumin, garlic, shallot |
| Korma spices | Coriander seeds, garlic, cardamon pods, chilli, cayenne pepper, tumeric, ginger and cumin |
| Chinese 5 spices | Fennel, anise, ginger, cinnamon, cloves |
| Green curry | Galangal, ginger, lemongrass, bird's eye chillies |
| Red curry | Cardamom, peppercorn, cumin, cloves, nutmeg, cinnamon, dried chillies |
| Yellow curry | Turmeric, cardamom, peppercorn, cumin, cloves, nutmeg, cinnamon, dried chillies |
| Rendang | Galangal, ginger, lemongrass, kafir lime leaves, chillies |
| Nasilemak | Pandanus leaves |
| Lamb gosh | Ginger, garlic, white pepper |
| Tom yam | Galangal, ginger, lemongrass, kafir lime leaves, chillies |

Source: Developed by author

independent review of the cooking class offered at TSG). The cooking class is well equipped with work tables and modern stoves and can accommodate up to 10 participants at any given time (*The Star*, 11 May 2011). Depending on the chosen menus or package, participants will be guided by one or three resident chefs of TSG using herbs and spices that are harvested from the garden itself (Figure 8.2).

On a section of its slope, TSG erected a restaurant that offers both contemporary and traditional (sitting cross-legged the floor, facing a low dining table) seating styles overlooking the ocean. Here tourists can choose a variety of local dishes while enjoying the view and the traditional decor of the restaurant. One of the main foods showcased in TSG's restaurant is '*Nasi Kandar*'. This dish consists of rice accompanied by several curried based dishes, boiled lady fingers and eggs as well as fried '*Papadom*' (crispy fried crackers). This dish is much sought after by locals and tourists alike due to the distinctive flavours it offers. The curried dishes use carefully selected, well-proportioned variety of spices such as cumin, coriander, fennel seeds,

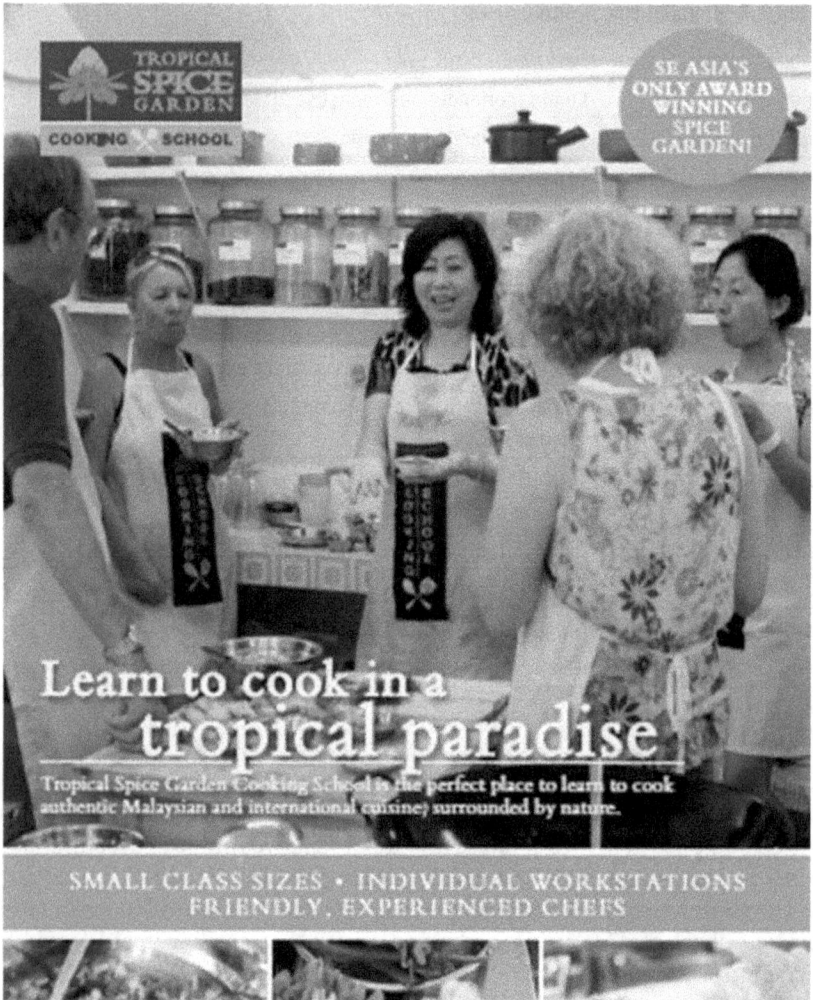

**Figure 8.2** Cooking lessons using local spices
*Source:* Courtesy of TSG

cloves, turmeric and ginger. Even the *papadom* is often laced with cumin seeds to give them added tastiness. In the past, *Nasi Kandar* was often carried on two baskets that hang on both ends of a pole, which the seller would carry on his shoulder from place to place in search of customers. In modern times however, the dish is sold in simple yet comfortable eateries and restaurants.

**TSG COOKING SCHOOL**
Learn to cook authentic Malaysian and international cuisine in our purpose built cooking school. Our friendly team of expert chefs will teach you about the fabulous diversity of spices and herbs and make your cooking class a fun and unforgettable experience.

**UNFORGETTABLE EVENTS**
Weddings, parties, book launches, music fests, corporate teambuilding events, you name it, TSG has hosted it. Speak to us about tailor-making your own special event.

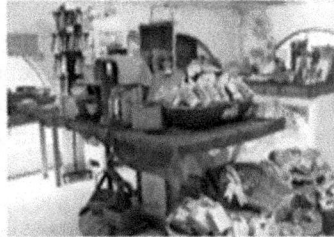

**SLIDES & LADDERS**
Snakes & ladders comes to life! Slides & Ladders is our latest kids attraction with slide tubes, candy coloured platforms and a spinning disc set in the rainforest. Children's parties can be booked in advance.

**UNIQUE SPICE GIFTS**
Our well-stocked gift shop offers a wide range of spices, spa products, original local crafts, art and books all under one roof. If you're looking for something different, you've come to the right place!

**Figure 8.3** Range of activities for visitors to the Spice Garden

Beside *Nasi Kandar,* there are plenty of other local delicacies offered such as *Laksa Penang,* (noodle in hot sour sauce), Penang Red Curry and *Pasembur* (Penang salad) that depend on spices for flavouring. Table 8.3 presents some other combination of spices that are used in TSG restaurant or sold in its souvenir shop, depicting the use of spices in Malaysia generally, and in Penang specifically:

The traditional *Teh Tarik* (a local favourite that uses strong tea and condensed milk) is often offered with ginger (ginger tea) to give drinkers the added benefit of reducing bloated or gassy feelings. Mint also have the same effect, and is often used in local another favourite dish called *Asam Laksa* or noodle in sour soup.

The landscaping of the garden took one and half years to complete. One of the primary challenges faced by TSG management in this process was to harmonise over 500 species of tropical flora with the natural landscape of the garden. Keeping indigenous flora and fauna as well as working with the natural topography of the site were perceived as crucial because they wanted to give the garden a timeless natural feel (Figure 8.3). Thus the existing terraces in the disused rubber plantation were put to good use in deciding planting positions. This helped the management to avoid dependency on heavy machinery to cut hills or change the natural topography. In addition, the already mature rubber trees worked as shade and shelter to wildlife found in the garden and to visitors. Man-made attractions in the garden were constructed in part using building materials salvaged from local antique stores and torn down pre-war shop houses. Those antiques now add to the attractiveness and uniqueness of the garden.

A prominent part of the landscape is a water feature that comprises a cascading small waterfall and a serene pond filled with African lilies (Figure 8.4). The water body was skilfully designed by re-routing water from the nearby waterfall using a system of man-made canals. The water collects into the pond. An advantage of the man-made canal system is that visitors can hear the gentle, relaxing gurgle of water meandering through the grounds in many parts of the garden. This adds to the tranquil feeling of being in the green and shady garden (Figure 8.5).

According to the GM, the landscaping strategies of TSG follow an environmentally friendly pathway. This entails commitment to use organic fertilizer to grow and maintain their plants, to adopt poison-free pest control methods, to focus on recycling and to collect dead leaves and garden waste for composting. These environmentally friendly practices are part of TSG's commitment to environmental protection. Their successful implementation is accredited to the support of a 'tight knit bunch of workers' (GM, personal communication) that are hired from the local community. The GM believes

**Figure 8.4** The cascading small waterfall

**Figure 8.5** Tranquil pond scenery at the Spice Garden

that hiring locally can help create a family environment that would ensure better cooperation and team spirit between management and workers. At the time this chapter's field data were collected, TSG has 18 full-time staff; three part time staff; 10–12 freelance guides. TSG emphasizes good communication with its employees to ensure good teamwork that will bring good for the organization. As mentioned by the GM (personal communication):

> Our philosophy is one of open, honest and clear communication that workers of all ranks are to be valued for what they can contribute in terms of ideas, suggestions etc. I believe in taking a personal interest in the staff and building them up as people and not just as workers – as we are a small team I was and still to some degree able to do that. I do wonder how I can still be personally as involved as we grow and expand. It's ultimately about believing in my team and liking and loving them as people and all they bring to the table and workplace.

Suppliers of TSG are primarily small local vendors and traders with the purpose of creating a mutually supporting business environment in the community as well as 'giving back' to the community and projecting an image of a responsible and caring organization.

As with managing any tourism product, TSG counters a range of challenges. But two main challenges it is facing are (1) marketing; and (2) government red tape on expansion or renovation. In marketing, the TSG management found that visually classy, colourful and bold marketing strategies are no longer suitable. While those have worked quite well in previous years giving TSG a strong brand presence and image as spice-based aromatherapy consultant, rising competition from similar class of tourism products in Penang (such as the Butterfly Farm and Tropical Fruit Orchard) has affected tourists flow to the garden. This forces the management to rethink its marketing strategy. Since TSG is essentially a small company with limited capacity to reach the market, they decided to develop a good website (www.tropicalspicegarden.com) and started to network effectively with food bloggers, chefs and spice shop owners from all over the world. They also turned to social media tools such as Facebook and Twitter to reach their market. Another strategy was to shift from targeting high end tourists to mass and domestic markets to ensure continuous visitation during low season (see the dip in arrival in 2009 and 2010 in Table 8.4).

Another management challenge relates to the existing provincial law on renovation or expansion, which is perceived by businesses like TSG to be prohibitive in nature (GM, personal communication). This law makes it difficult or extremely time-consuming for a tourist attraction in Penang to get the permission to expand or renovate their product. Business owners perceive such red tape as unproductive and unsupportive of their businesses.

However, TSG management is generally optimistic about its future and feel that they are heading towards the right direction (GM, personal

**Table 8.4** Annual visitor arrival to TSG, 2004–2011

| Year | Visitor arrival (per annum) |
| --- | --- |
| 2004 | 22,392 |
| 2005 | 32,916 |
| 2006 | 46,696 |
| 2007 | 53,631 |
| 2008 | 52,849 |
| 2009 | 50,415 |
| 2010 | 56,824 |
| 2011 | Est. 62,000 |

*Source*: TSG

communication). Their networking and internet marketing initiatives are showing positive impacts (see tourist arrival for 2011). In addition, the more recent development of Penang being chosen as the country's 'Spice Tourism Trail' (Jalleh, 2012) is a significant indicator about the importance of spice in Penang tourism. Apart from issues such as the constant need to re-strategize their marketing approach to remain attractive, and the red tape facing businesses like TSG, the future seems set for this spice garden to grow and be successful as one of the key players of Penang tourism.

The TSG case provides us with few important lessons on using spice as tourism garden attraction. First there is a need to integrate spice planting requirements with the natural topography of an area to minimize environmental damage. In the case of TSG, the spices have been carefully selected to suit the natural topography and soil conditions of the area. Second, because spices are themselves not particularly attractive plants, their presence must be enhanced by different more attractive garden features such as water fountains, shady trees and the like. Third, other amenities and activities such as training kitchen (for cooking lessons), restaurant that offers thematic menu and souvenir shop would add to the attractiveness of a spice garden. TSG will be a passive and unattractive garden if it does not offer amenities and activities to elevate visitor experience. The fourth lesson is that 'going green' in managing a spice garden is a practical and beneficial option, and can readily be accomplished with managerial commitment and strong employee support. In the case of TSG, treating employees as family enhanced their sense of belonging and motivation to help the organization achieve its sustainable management philosophy. The fifth and final lesson to be learnt is that just like any other tourism products, social media has proven to be a significant and effective way to create and maintain a spice garden's brand presence. Therefore future marketing effort should not be wasted on traditional marketing, but focus more on new media channel instead.

## Discussion

Spices have had a historic significance in Penang. This significance now continues to be manifested in two forms related to tourism – food and garden attraction. In food, spices continue to add to the unique flavours of Penang food which represent the cultural diversity that the island has to offer tourists. This demonstrates Boyne et al.'s (2003) contention that unique tasting food can distinctly differentiate one destination from another. It also supports the theory that food can enhance the image of a destination (Boniface, 2003; Long, 2004).

As garden attraction, spices grown in TSG have now provided tourists with visual aesthetics to what used to be just a rubber plantation. This adds another important dimension of spices' role in Penang – as a means to educate future generations. People can see, smell, touch and taste raw spices that they might otherwise take for granted. With better knowledge about spices, people will better understand what they are using/consuming and perhaps be able to make informed choices about food and medicines that they consume. The garden also offers other benefit such as relaxation, escape, learning (through the cooking lessons). This is in line with Frochot (2003) contention that food related tourism can provide tourists the avenue to achieve relaxation, excitement, escapism, status, education and lifestyle. Perhaps another dimension that can be added to Frochot's benefit list is 'exploration'. As demonstrated in the context of TSG, food related tourism also provides tourists the opportunity for exploration of new touristic products and experiences. For example, foreigners can explore the different tastes of local cuisines at the restaurant. In addition, youngsters may be more interested to explore about spices (which they may otherwise ignore or take for granted) during a visit to a spice garden. The hands-on, interactive style of imparting knowledge as is offered through guided tours of the garden, would be more 'attention-grabbing' and encourage youngsters to explore more about the varieties, physical characteristics, medicinal and gastronomy values of locally grown spices.

Furthermore, to better support the importance of spices in Penang tourism, it is imperative that linkage between spices and the daily living of Penangnites is showcased to tourists in a more fashionable and systematic way. As mentioned earlier in the chapter, there is currently no policy promoting the use of home stay to showcase local spice production and usage. A home-stay village has tremendous potential to develop the home-stay experience into a 'living museum' on the planting, harvesting and usage of spices in traditional cuisines and medicines. Depending on the creativity that one has, such exhibition could be manifested in many ways and approaches that would educate and entertained visitors and tourists. While TSG showcase spices in the context of a garden landscape, the home-stay village can showcase spices in day-to-day living, behind people's houses etc. Home-stay tourists can be entertained beyond the normally offered activities such as rubber tapping, wedding ceremony and handicrafts (see Tourism Malaysia, 2011), by teaching and involving them in the planting, harvesting and usage of local spices such as lemongrass, ginger and birds-eye chillies and galangal. This would expand the tourists' opportunity to learn about spice beyond the context of a spice garden.

It is equally important to continue supporting TSG's development as the pioneer of the official spice tourism attraction in Penang. Tax breaks, incentives, and joint promotion are alternatives the local tourism authority can help TSG to develop further, and be more successful. Another possible type of support is for the government to ease licensing requirement and renovation project approvals. Less red tape and speedier processing of applications could motivate further physical improvement of local tourism products. The ultimate benefit of this is the sustainability of the tourism industry in general.

Perhaps a more holistic approach to improving spice tourism in Penang specifically and in Malaysia generally is to take initiatives that can result in the reduction on spice import. Focusing more on production and usage of locally grown spices using available arable land is an alternative that can be pursued by various stakeholders in the country. In this way, it will be easier to sustain the presence (and therefore role) of spices for local uses.

# Conclusion

This study shows that spices do have strong presence and role in Penang tourism. Over the years, the dependence of Penang cuisines on spices and the increasing popularity of spice related attraction such as the TSG are strong indicators of the role of spices in Penang tourism. Local culinary adventure will not have achieved its current popularity had it not been for the unique taste developed using selected spices offer. Similarly, the current location of TSG would remain as nothing more than an old rubber plantation, had it not been developed into an attractive tourism attraction that it is today. In essence, spices have played a role as a place marker (see Zainal et al., 2010) for Penang. However, the significance of spice in Penang tourism can be enhanced by showcasing spice using 'living museums' such as a home-stay village. This objective can also be achieved by assisting the growth and development of existing attraction such as TSG and reducing dependency on imported spices. These improvements would not only improve the overall travel and learning experience of tourists, but also ensure sustainability of supply of spices for local use.

## References

Alfandi, A.A. and Kasim, A. (2011) Long-term communication effects of Tourism Malaysia marketing communications on the awareness and perceived destination image dimensions among potential tourists from the Gulf Countries (GC). In M. Alvarez and D. Gursoy (eds) Proceedings of Advances in Tourism and Hospitality Marketing and Management *(ATHMM2011)* (pp. 230–236). June 2011, Istanbul, Turkey.

Boniface, P. (2003) *Tasting Tourism: Travelling for Food and Drink New Directions in Tourism Analysis.* Ashgate: London.

Boyne, S., Williams, F. and Hall, D. (2003) Policy, support and promotion for food related tourism initiatives: A marketing approach to regional development. *Journal of Travel and Tourism Marketing* 3 (4), 131–154.

Chomchalow, N. (1996) Spice production in Asia – An overview. An unpublished paper presented at the IBC'c Asia Spice Markets 96' Conference, Singapore. http://www.journal.au.edu/au_techno/2001/oct2001/article6.pdf (accessed 20 April 2012).

Fitday (2000–2001) 7 benefits nutmeg provides. http://www.fitday.com/fitness-articles/nutrition/healthy-eating/7-health-benefits-nutmeg-provides.html (accessed 2 April 2012).

Frochot, I. (2003) An analysis of regional positioning and its associated food images in French tourism regional brochures. *Journal of Travel and Tourism Marketing* 14 (3/4), 77–96.

Hancock, B. (1998) Trent focus for research and development in primary health care: An introduction to qualitative research. UK: Trent Focus. Accessed: http://faculty.uccb.ns.ca/pmacintyre/course pages/MBA603/MBA603_files/IntroQualitativeResearch.pdf (accessed 20 May 2012).

Hughes, G. (1995) Food, tourism and Scottish heritage. In D. Leslie (ed.) *Tourism and Leisure* (pp. 109–128). Brighton, LSA: Cultural, Heritage and Participation.

Jalleh, J. (21 May 2012) Hot and Spicy Penang Launched as part of Penang Rebranding. http://thestar.com.my/news/story.asp?file=/2012/5/21/nation/11329176&sec=nationon (accessed 1 June 2012).

Long, L.M. (2004) *Culinary Tourism (Material Worlds).* Lexington: KY University Press of Kentucky.

Manansala, P.K. (2001) The spice routes. http://asiapacificuniverse.com/pkm/spiceroutes.htm (accessed 2 April 2012).

Mohammed, N., Salleh, M., Musa, M. Halimi, A.J., Othman, M.I. and Abd Aziz, S. (2006) Sejarah Awal Pulau Pinang. Unpublished Research Report. http://eprints.usm.my/4843/1/Sejarah_Awal_Pulau_Pinang.pdf (accessed 12 June 2012).

Ninth Malaysia Plan, 2006–2010 (31 March 2006) Speech by the Prime Minister at the Dewan Rakyat. http://www.parlimen.gov.my/news/eng-ucapan_rmk9.pdf (accessed 21 May 2012).

Press Trust of India (12 June 2009) Malaysia 2nd largest importer of Indian spices. http://www.business-standard.com/india/news/malaysia-2nd-largest-importerin dian-spices/15/24/64525/on (accessed 6 May 2012).

Quan, S. and Wang, N. (2004) Towards a structural model of the tourist experience: An illustration from food experience in tourism. *Tourism Management* 25 (3), 297–305.

Quintal, R. (2011) The Importance of Garden Tourism in Madeira Island. http://www.scribd.com/doc/54522834/The-Importance-of-Garden-Tourism-in-Madeira-Island (accessed 29 May 2012).

Tourism Malaysia (2011) Activities and sports: Home stay. http://www.tourism.gov.my/activities/?xtvt_id=11 (accessed 30 May 2012).

*Tripologist: Travelling the World on a Backpacker's Budget* (26 March 2012). http://tripolo gist.com/south-east-asia/learning-to-cook-malay-at-penangs-tropical-spice-garden (accessed 12 April 2012).

*The Star* (11 May 2011) TSG cooking school launched. http://thestar.com.my/metro/story. asp?file=/2011/5/11/north/8636432&sec=north (accessed 12 April 2012).

Yin, R.K. (2003) *Case Study Research Design and Methods* (3rd edn). California: Sage Publications, Inc.

Young, C. (1982) The everyday accountant and researching his reality. *Accounting Organisation and Society* 8 (4), 686–705.

Zainal, A., Zali, A.N. and Kassim, M.N. (2010) Malaysian gastronomy routes as a tourist destination. *Journal of Tourism, Hospitality and Culinary Arts*, 15–24. http://www.jthca.org/Download/pdf/V2%20IS1/chap%202.pdf (accessed 5 April 2012).

# Part 3
# Spice Product Studies

# 9  Australian Native Spices: Building the 'Bush Tucker' Brand

## Leanne White

This chapter examines Australia's native spices and related tourism products. Australian native spices are often referred to colloquially as 'bush tucker'. For more than 40,000 years, bush food has been consumed by Australia's indigenous communities. Despite that history, knowledge about Australian native cuisine is not particularly widespread. Although the chapter focuses on Australian native spices, bush foods or native foods include animals, fruits and berries, and herbs, spices and seeds. Some examples of bush foods are: kangaroo, crocodile, wallaby, emu, witchetty grubs, Davidson plum, Kakadu plum, quandong, finger lime, bush tomato, warrigal greens, macadamia nut and riberry.

With their intense flavours, native herbs and spices are the backbone of Australia's true native cuisine. Some of the more popular are: lemon myrtle, wattle seed, native pepper (both the pepper berry and leaf are used), native thyme and native mint. The chapter discusses some popular native Australian herbs and spices and their heritage; examines the development of the bush tucker brand; explores some of the bush tucker tourism product options in the market; explore various discourses of nationalism; and finally, looks at both the culinary experience and future of Australian native foods.

## The Australian Native Food Industry

As chef Jean-Paul Bruneteau explains, Australian cuisine has existed since the Aborigines hunted game, collected fruit, harvested nuts and berries, and fished the rivers and seas. Indigenous Australians hunted out 'berries, seeds, leaves, bulbs, roots and fruits' for their mainly vegetarian diet (Symons,

1982: 6). Although now generally consumed for culinary purposes, some bush foods have considered beneficial for their medicinal qualities.

Although indigenous food had been well-known to Australia's original inhabitants, Symons reported in 1982, that the only indigenous plant to be commercially harvested was the macadamia nut (Symons, 1982: 255). More than 30 years later, this situation has changed dramatically with many bush food options available to a global market.

The Rural Industries Research and Development Corporation (RIRDC) provides a definition and expands upon the European origins of native food:

> while 'bushfood' has been the staple of Australia's Aboriginal people for millennia, the impetus for the establishment of 'a bushfood industry' has been attributed to pioneers such as Vic Cherikoff and to the restaurateurs Jean-Paul Bruneteau and Jennifer Dowling who introduced native foods into their menus during the early and mid-1980s. In addition to being uniquely Australian, such food was perceived to be clean, healthy, organic and environmentally friendly. The term native food was adopted in the late 1990s to reflect the new cuisine and uses being made of Australian plants that built on and complemented traditional uses. (RIRDC, 2008: 5)

The RIRDC explains that the native food industry in Australia is extremely diverse. It incorporates both native harvest and cultivation from the production of Kakadu plums in the Australia's north and wattle seed in the dry interior, to mountain pepper in Australia's southern island state – Tasmania. Although some products are now being cultivated, Australian native herbs and spices are generally found in the wild – in rainforest areas, in deserts and in woodlands.

The beginnings of a slow appreciation for Australian native food began (at least for non-indigenous people) in the 1980s. As pioneer Vic Cherikoff argues, 'From the time of the European invasion of Aboriginal Australia up to the mid 1980s, there have been no national culinary landmarks in Australian gastronomy; not a single dish which is proudly and identifiably Australian; nor any attempt to create a discernable food culture' (Cherikoff, 1992: 14). Indeed, Australia's early colonists looked in horror at the eating habits of the Aborigines and concluded that bush foods were generally 'not tolerable' although could occasionally be 'flavourless but sustaining' (Isaacs, 1987: 14).

## Popular Australian Native Herbs, Spices and Seeds

Although there are numerous Australian native herbs, spices and seeds, three of the more popular ones – wattle seed, lemon myrtle and mountain pepper – will be briefly examined.

## Wattle seed

A popular Australian native seed can be found in the dried pods of a wattle tree. The flavorsome seed is said to taste something like raisin and chocolate. Wattle seeds also constitute a complete food source as they contain fibre, carbohydrates, protein and fat. They are also meant to be good for you as they have a 'very low glycaemic index' (Kirton, 2009: 226). The Gang Gang cockatoo is just one of Australia's native parrots that enjoys feasting on the dried seeds (see Figure 9.1).

Aboriginal people have known about the positive health benefits of the seed for thousands of years. Although there are around 1000 different species of Australian wattle, only a small number are suited to culinary uses (McKean, 1999: 248). Bruneteau's rolled wattle seed pavlova has become world famous, whereas Kirton claims that wattle seeds are 'delicious in baked goods, custards and creams' (Kirton, 2009: 226). Both Australians and New Zealanders lay claim to being the inventors of the popular dessert – pavlova.

When processing wattle seeds for consumption, the seeds are roasted and ground. Seeds are then boiled to soften and can also be made into a liquid

**Figure 9.1** The Gang Gang Cockatoo enjoys a feast of wattle seed

extract. The wattle seed can be incorporated into marinades, or combined with other ingredients to make a crumb for meat or fish. The extract is used to produce wattle ice cream, pancakes and even wattle-flavoured coffee. Bruneteau proudly predicts that this particular seed will eventually become as popular as chocolate and vanilla (Bruneteau, 1996: 200).

## Lemon myrtle

Another popular Australian native plant is the aromatic lemon myrtle (*Backhousia citriodora*). Lemon myrtle has a more intense flavour than lemon grass and can be used 'in marinades or as a skewer for seafood' (Kirton, 2009: 223). When crushed, the lemon myrtle leaf releases a taste similar to a combination of lemon grass and lemon leaves. Lemon myrtle can be used to make herb butter or custard, and can be added to breads and biscuits. The product is widely available in various forms – as dry leaf, ground herb or oil. The herb was used by Australian soft drink manufacturer Tarax to flavour their lemonade during World War II when there was a shortage of lemon essence (Bruneteau, 1996: 126). Commercial farming of lemon myrtle began in 1991 and there are now a number of large producers of the plant.

Some of the recipes that can be made with lemon myrtle include: lemon myrtle, barley and potato risotto; lemon myrtle crusted ocean trout with riberry, mango and coriander salsa; lemon myrtle fishcakes with wild lime chilli ginger sauce; lemon myrtle prawn laksa; and lemon myrtle shortbreads (Outback Spirit, 2013). The lemon myrtle has been described as 'undoubtedly the best Australian Rainforest Spice' (Kurrajong Australian Native Foods, 2008).

## Mountain pepper

Australia's native peppers can be found in a number of mountainous regions in the country. One of the tastier peppers – the Tasmanian mountain pepper (*Tasmania lanceolata*) – is made from berries found in the rainforests of Tasmania. Inside the pepper berry are numerous small hot seeds.

The Tasmanian native pepper can be purchased from a number of suppliers including Diemen Pepper. The name of this company came about as a result of the former title for the Australia's island colony – Van Diemen's Land. Diemen Pepper is run by former academic Chris Read, who completed a doctoral thesis on the Tasmanian mountain pepper. As early as 1811, it was noted that this 'spice tree' possesses a strong aroma and exudes 'a more pungent quality than pepper' (Low, 1989: 183).

Peppers have traditionally held a special place in the spice world. Australian chef Christine Manfield explains that they were once the most highly prized spice to be found on the trade routes, 'holding equal value to gold' (Manfield,

2005: 25). Black pepper has a stronger taste than green pepper along with a slightly sweetened flavour. Tim Low also points out that Australia is located not too far from the Spice Islands of Indonesia so it is not surprising that our spices are closely aligned to some of those in Asia (Low, 1989: 182–83).

Interest in the Tasmanian native pepper largely came about from the work of botanist Stephen Harris (Bruneteau, 1996: 54). In 1990, Harris presented a conference paper about the bountiful supply and significant potential of the native pepper. However, within 20 years of the presentation by Harris, the RIRDC reported that the supply of the mountain pepper berry had become unreliable owing to heavy logging and the establishment of plantation trees in some parts of Tasmania. They also reported that not all operators were using best practice methods in processing the berry, and some operators were indeed unlicensed (RIRDC, 2008: 9).

# Building the Bush Tucker Brand

When it comes to building awareness of the bush tucker brand, the role played by Vietnam veteran Major Les Hiddins – Australia's first 'Bush Tucker Man' – must be acknowledged. His *Bush Tucker Man* television series displayed his bush survival skills just after the time when Paul Hogan's on-screen character Mick (Crocodile) Dundee became internationally known. Graeme Turner describes the *Crocodile Dundee* films as exhibiting the 'familiar "bush myth" nationalism' (Turner, 1993: 151). As Nancy Rivenburgh and colleagues have argued, Australia's 'two most influential cultural ambassadors' as far as the United States is concerned 'are, without question, *Crocodile Dundee* (Paul Hogan) and the kangaroo' (Rivenburgh *et al.*, 2004: 22). In more recent times and until his death in 2006, Steve Irwin – possibly better known as 'The Crocodile Hunter' – became an exceptionally popular symbol of Australia on a global scale. A selection of organizations that have developed the bush tucker name generally in Australia and around the world terms of product, tours and the dining experience will now be examined.

# Bush Tucker Produce

## Outback Spirit

Outback Spirit is a bush tucker brand produced by Robins Foods. The company was established by Ian and Juleigh Robins in 1986, and now sells to a number of markets around the world. The Outback Spirit food range includes: preserves, chutneys, sauces, dressings and herbs. The website

explains that the company 'is committed to making a contribution to breaking the ongoing cycle of poor education, poor health, high unemployment,
passive welfare dependence and poverty that typifies the majority of
Indigenous Australians' (Outback Spirit, 2013). The organisation set up a
foundation in order to 'give Indigenous Australians the opportunity to help
themselves to achieve a higher level of economic independence'. Their strategy involves assisting with 'sustainable agricultural programs for remote
communities that encompass the Indigenous culture and sense of country',
and 'providing Indigenous youth opportunities to pro-actively contribute to
their own future' (Outback Spirit, 2013).

Outback Spirit employed the services of the well-known Aboriginal
former athlete Cathy Freeman to promote their products and services.
Freeman has enjoyed sponsorship dealings with a wide range of companies
including: Nike, Qantas, Australia Post, Mitre 10, Channel Seven, Milo,
News Corporation, Balarinji Design Studio, Kellogg's, Ford, Telstra, Optus,
Oakley sunglasses, AstraZeneca pharmaceuticals, First Nations Australian
Credit Union, PowerBar, Athletics Australia and Outback Spirit. In lighting
the cauldron at the Sydney Olympic Games before a global television audience of around 3.7 billion, along with winning her historic 400 m run at
Stadium Australia, Cathy Freeman became one of Australia's most admired
and respected athletes. It was Australia's 100th gold medal at an Olympics
event and the first individual gold medal for an Indigenous Australian. The
company may well be hoping that some of Freeman's popularity might
transfer to their bush tucker brand.

## Vic Cherikoff Food Services

Vic Cherikoff is widely regarded as probably the key authority on Australian
bush foods. Cherikoff has a background in clinical pharmacology and nutri-
tional science. In 1987 he started a company called 'Bush Tucker Supply' which
later became part of the current company that bears his name. The company
sells indigenous food products and is involved in book publishing and producing
television programs. Cherikoff is the author of a number of books on Australian
native food including: *The Bushfood Handbook, Uniquely Australian,* and *Dining
Downunder Cookbook* which he co-authored with Benjamin Christie.

The company is based in Sydney and distributes to 18 countries around
the world. The website explains that their suppliers include 'remote community Aborigines' and other 'foragers, growers and farmers'. He explains that
as the industry is growing, the ingredients are only 'just being introduced to
global markets'. As a result, his customers are experiencing 'the future of
Australian food' (Cherikoff, 2005).

Cherikoff claims to have invented wattle seed as a bush spice in 1984 by over-roasting seeds once only eaten by Australian Aborigines. His website explains that wattle seed 'is roasted in a similar way to coffee', then ground to produce a 'highly versatile and nutritious flavouring' (Cherikoff, 2005). His company also sells a wattle seed extract that can be used as a key ingredient in making sauce, creme brulee, ice cream and pavlova. Cherikoff explains that 'wattleccino' is made by diluting a tablespoonful of the extract with a quarter of a cup of hot water, then topped with hot milk.

### Kurrajong Australian Native Foods

A more recent player in the bush food market is Kurrajong Australian Native Foods who sell a range of bush food products in retail outlets and via their online store known as the 'Bush Tucker Shop'. The company was founded by Lee Etherington who describes himself as 'a passionate naturalist and foodie' (Kurrajong Australian Native Foods, 2008). The business developed from the making of a lilli pilli conserve which Lee gave to the tourists of his adventure tours company in the Blue Mountains, west of Sydney.

The flagship product of the company is a wild hibiscus flower in syrup. The flowers are packaged in jars or 11 but can also be purchased in larger jars of 50 and 100. The product is most often used as a decorative addition to a glass of champagne – or sparkling wine (as it is known in countries other than France). Product information on the website explains that the flower sits at the base of the glass while 'all the bubbles stream off and subtly open the flower' (Kurrajong Australian Native Foods, 2008). The edible flower, which is sold in a number of countries around the world, has a raspberry and rhubarb flavour that balances with the sweet syrup.

# Australian Native Food and Tourism

## Sounds of Silence and Tali Wiru

The culinary tourism option known as 'Sounds of Silence' is described on the Voyages website as an 'award-winning dining experience under the stars' (Voyages Travel Centre, 2013). It is explained that diners will feast on 'authentic Australian delicacies' such as 'barramundi, kangaroo and crocodile, bush salads and classic desserts, complemented by Australian wines' (Voyages Travel Centre, 2013).

While the menu items that guests select from are subject to change, some of the options have been known to include: paprika-rubbed kangaroo with native chutney mousse; lemon myrtle marinated crocodile Caesar salad;

barramundi rubbed in wild lime; chicken skewers rubbed in lemon myrtle; kangaroo fillet in wild pepper berry; beef fillet with native mint; and peach and wild lime topped with wattle seed crumble.

Although Sounds of Silence has been considered the ultimate dining experience for tourists in the Uluru (Ayers Rock) region for many years, an even more exclusive option has now entered the market. 'Tali Wiru' which means 'beautiful dune' in the local Aboriginal language offers a four-course dinner matched with Australian wines. A local storyteller also provides information about the Aboriginal history, language and culture. The dinner is promoted as 'a unique dining experience for no more than 20 guests' (Voyages Travel Centre, 2013). One of the items featured on the menu is native wattle seed with hot chocolate.

A more focused bush tucker option offered by the Voyages group, which effectively have a monopoly on much of the accommodation and dining options in the area, is the 'Aboriginal Guided Bush Tucker Tour' which presents the traditional bush food of the area. Those who take the tour can 'taste a selection of the bush foods, grind native seeds and have the opportunity to talk with your Aboriginal host about desert life' (Voyages Travel Centre, 2013). Some of the luxury bush tucker menu items include: wattle seed rubbed roo carpaccio; native thyme and garlic grilled wagyu; and macadamia and lemon myrtle flavoured barramundi (Lobley, 2013).

## Diverse Travel Bush Tucker Tours

A less mainstream, and possibly more 'authentic' tourist experience is offered by a group known as Diverse Travel. The company website explains that they offer a wide range of tours that 'explore Aboriginal culture and history through the eyes of Aboriginal guides'. They also claim they are dedicated to 'capturing the unusual experiences that reflect the unique essence of Australia' offering the best 'nature-based, eco and cross-cultural tourism Australia has to offer' (Diverse Travel Australia, 2013).

One of their popular tours is known as 'Bush Tucker Tour Uluru'. It consists of a two hour tour with a local Aboriginal (Anangu) guide where tourists can taste a selection of native foods and learn how the original inhabitants of the land survived in the desert.

## RT Tours Australia

A smaller player on the market is Bob (Penuka) Taylor's company, RT Tours Australia. For more than 25 years Bob worked as a chef in Australia and Europe. He is the 'host, guide and private chef' for his clients and offers a range of tours from short lunches and dinners through to nine day packages and tailor-made private charter tours (RT Tours Australia, 2013). Bob informs his potential clients, 'Get your Aboriginal culture from Aboriginal people. We've lived it and live it. The tours will give you an understanding of what it is to be an aboriginal in modern Australia' (RT Tours Australia, 2013).

When journalist Andrew Bain accompanied Taylor on a 'Mbantua Dinner Tour' at the foot of the West MacDonnell Ranges, he was treated to macadamia nuts roasted with wattle seed, native pepper, lemon myrtle and bush tomatoes; emu salami; beef hotpot with native thyme; yam fritters with saltbush; and white chocolate and wattle seed steamed pudding. His verdict was simply, 'No bush tucker restaurant could ever hope to compete' (Bain, 2012).

# Dining Australian Native Style

## Roadkill Cafe

Possibly taking bush food to extremes is a small operation in the Northern Territory known as Roadkill Café. Their blatant and potentially offensive slogan is 'You kill it, we grill it'! The food stall operates from Darwin's popular Mindil Beach Market twice a week (see Figure 9.2). Although it might seem that the men who run the food stall drive around collecting freshly killed Australian fauna from the side of the road... they don't. At Roadkill Café, the

**Figure 9.2** The Roadkill Café where the slogan is 'you kill it, we grill it!'

satays are made from crocodile, kangaroo, camel, emu, possum, wallaby and buffalo. All meat products are legal, hygienic and cooked by a qualified chef.

## From Rowntrees to Woolloomooloo

Jean-Paul Bruneteau was the first to open a restaurant dedicated to serving Australian cuisine. He and his partner, Jennifer Dowling, opened 'Rowntrees – The Australian Restaurant Restaurant' in the Sydney suburb of Hornsby in 1984. Bruneteau has played a pioneering role in native cuisine and his was the first 'Australian' restaurant to be listed in the telephone book. He explains that it took until 1988 (Australia's Bicentennial year) for the cuisine to be recognised as 'legitimate'. In that year he was awarded a gold medal at the International Cooking Festival for 'Most Original Cuisine' (Bruneteau, 1996: 12). He later opened a second restaurant, 'Riberries – Taste Australia' in 1991.

Bruneteau published *Tukka: Real Australian Food,* and proudly boasts that the book is used as a core training manual for chefs, and sits on the shelves of Australian embassies around the world including London, Paris, Hong Kong and Beijing (Bruneteau, 1996: 8). After his successes in Australia, he returned to Paris to become the food director for the successful Australian restaurant chain Woolloomooloo. The popular Woolloomooloo Group has 'Steakhouse' style restaurants in Hong Kong and Singapore (see Figure 9.3).

**Figure 9.3** Woolloomooloo: A bush tucker option in Hong Kong and Singapore

## Outback Steakhouse

A more mass-market version of 'bush tucker' cuisine can be found with the international chain Outback Steakhouse (see Figure 9.4). The company currently has stores in the following 19 countries: Australia, Brazil, Canada, Costa Rica, Dominican Republic, Guam, Hong Kong, Indonesia, Japan, Korea, Malaysia, Mexico, Philippines, Puerto Rico, Singapore, Taiwan, Thailand, United States and Venezuela.

The company describes itself as 'an Australian themed steakhouse restaurant' with a marketing strategy of differentiating its restaurants from others by: 'emphasizing consistently high-quality food and service, generous portions at moderate prices and a casual atmosphere suggestive of the Australian Outback' (Outback Steakhouse, 2013). The headquarters of Outback Steakhouse are in Florida where the parent company Bloomin'

**Figure 9.4** Outback Steakhouse markets a unique outback experience around the world

Brands also operates a range of other successful restaurant chains across the United States including: Bonefish Grill, Carrabba's Italian Grill, Fleming's Prime Steakhouse and Wine Bar, and Roy's Restaurant.

Instead of appetizers, the menu presents 'Aussie-Tizers' designed to be shared such as: Aussie cheese fries and grilled shrimp on the barbie. Outback Steakhouse offer a range of menu items with Australian names including: walkabout soup of the day, Alice Springs chicken, outback burger, chocolate thunder from down under, and Sydney's sinful sundae. However, it would appear from examining the menu that they do not use any specific Australian native herbs or spices.

# The Bush Tucker Brand and Nationalism

This chapter undertook an empirical analysis of bush tucker and its evolution since the 1980s. A number of significant developments for Australian native food along with the transition to an internationally recognised brand are evident. Since their beginnings, bush tucker companies (in their various forms such as produce, tourist attraction and dining) have been in the business of selling nationalism and patriotism (adopting commercial nationalism). Indeed, sometimes bush tucker product forms overlap. For instance, the international tourist might purchase a bush tucker product for family or friends, and later attempt to re-live and share a similar experience in an Australian-themed restaurant.

From a theoretical perspective, similarities and differences exist between 'official nationalism' (principally generated from the federal government or government departments via significant public events and advertising campaigns) and commercial nationalism – the brand of nationalism generated by private companies. It is useful to understand the complex relationships and interconnections between these discourses of nationalism and how they might work in the context of the bush tucker brand.

Commercial nationalism describes the style of nationalism promoted by and advertisers as it encompasses the suggestion that commerce and the nation are deliberately constructed entities. The term refers to the patriotic aspects in commercials but also alludes to the notion that the once clearer boundaries of the domains of official and commercial nationalism have been eliminated and that the broader concept of nationalism, which deals with ideas and beliefs, has combined with the economic forces in the world of commerce which compete for the consumer dollar. Thus, commercial nationalism is essentially a paradox – two potentially conflicting sectors combining their influences and occupying the same space. Commercial nationalism is a continuation and extension of the overall theme, style and symbols of official nationalism as generated by the nation-state.

The dual discourses of commercial and official nationalism are directly related. Both contribute to the total discourse on nationalism in a community – be it 'imagined' (Anderson, 1991) or real. The official and commercial strands of nationalism are not binary oppositions – there is a significant degree of overlap between the areas. Commercial nationalism operates like a paradigm – it continues the pattern that has been firmly established by the official body. It is not in the interests of the private company to create conflict between these two types of nationalism; they are merely used for different purposes (White, 2004: 28).

Commercial nationalism (often a more vociferous manifestation of official nationalism) manifests itself in consumer-related uses of national symbols, images and icons. National signifiers such as the country's flag or landmass are adopted by the world of commerce for consumption in the market. Although 'popular nationalism' and commercial nationalism generally perform a different function to official nationalism, these nationalisms often overlap. Images of the nation and types of nationalism intersect and change (depending on the use to which they are put).

A diagram and explanation of the relationship between official nationalism, popular nationalism and commercial nationalism is outlined below (see Figure 9.5). Official nationalism is the civic, formal and ceremonial nationalism such as the Australian Federal Government's planning of the Bicentennial celebrations in 1988 or the Centenary of Federation celebrations in 2001. National anthem, flag and official symbols are part of official nationalism. The concept of popular nationalism was introduced by Russel Ward and can include nationalist messages and images as depicted in popular culture texts such as Australian film, television drama, popular songs and sport. Ward's archetypal text *The Australian Legend* attempted to 'trace the historical origins and development of the Australian legend or national mystique' (Ward, 1966: v).

Commercial nationalism refers to consumer-related uses of these national symbols, images and icons. It is the material, everyday nationalism represented by companies and brands such as Foster's Lager, Qantas, Vegemite, Outback Spirit and Outback Steakhouse. For many years, the phenomenon of commercial nationalism has been evidenced in advertising slogans that occasionally develop into popular jingles such as 'Aussie Kids are Weet-Bix Kids', 'I'm as Australian as Ampol' and 'Football, Meat Pies, Kangaroos and Holden Cars'.

Although popular and commercial nationalism generally play a subservient role to official nationalism, these forms of nationalism occasionally overlap. An example of all three forms of nationalism intersecting in

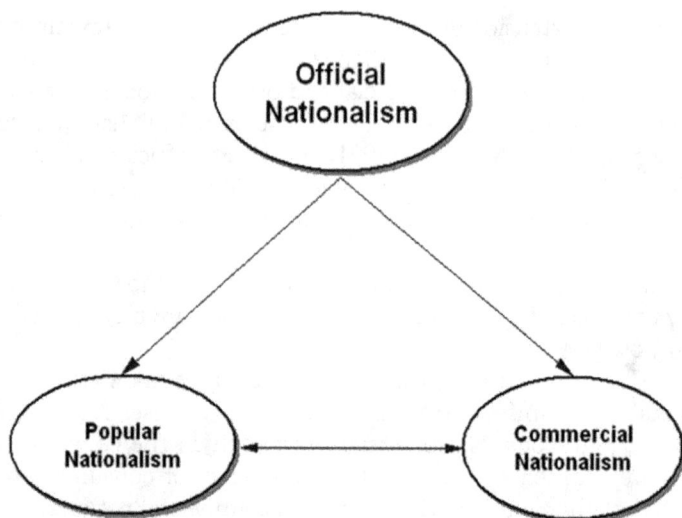

**Figure 9.5** Official nationalism is the dominant pool of nationalism that primarily emerges from the nation-state. Both popular and commercial nationalism fall under the larger umbrella of official nationalism. Some popular and commercial images swim to the top, whereas others sink to the bottom and do not develop currency

Australian culture would be former Prime Minister John Howard's admitting to being a 'cricket-tragic', the widespread popularity of the Australian cricket team, and the selling of green and gold merchandise to cricket fans so that they can overtly show their support for Australia and the team.

## Conclusion

In 1987, bush food expert Jennifer Isaacs wrote, 'most Australians have never even tasted bush foods' (Isaacs, 1987: 11). Two years later, Low argued that Australian native herbs and spices are the least known of Australian native foods and are yet to be fully explored (Low, 1989: 177). The trend towards using wild ingredients in mainstream cooking began in the late twentieth century (Kirton, 2009: 223). A large number of restaurants boasting their bush food options can now be found in Australia and throughout the world. And while Australia's first settlers showed very little interest in Australian native foods, we are now starting to appreciate our indigenous foods thanks in part due to waves of migration from Europe, Asia and the Middle East (McKean, 1999: 248).

Bruneteau claims that it is 'illogical to deny the existence of an Australian cuisine', and it is furthermore 'discourteous and embarrassing' for all Australians to suggest that there is no such cuisine (Bruneteau, 1996: 8). He argues that understanding native food is essential for the development of an Australian cuisine, and 'the native ingredient is the catalyst' (Bruneteau, 1996: 12).

A wide range of Australian native food suppliers now exist to supply the market with bush tucker products. Some of the names of the companies include: Outback Chef, Outback Pride, Australian Bush Spices, Bushfood Australia, Brushtail Bushfoods, Barbushco, Oz Tukka, and A Taste of the Bush. Even well-known Australian entrepreneur and Australian-made and owned advocate Dick Smith offers a 'Bush Foods Breakfast' available at the local supermarket which includes ingredients such as strawberry eucalyptus leaves, lemon myrtle, rosella flower, and wattle seeds.

It seems that 225 years after European settlement, one of the oldest cuisines in the world is finally starting to come of age through the use of native ingredients such as herbs and spices.

# References

Anderson, B. (1991) *Imagined Communities: Reflections on the Origins and Spread of Nationalism* (2nd edn). London: Verso.

Bain, A. (2012) Dinner with a desert chef. *The Sydney Morning Herald (Traveller)*, 28 July. http://www.smh.com.au/travel/activity/food-and-wine/dinner-with-a-desert-chef-20120726-22u2 k.html (accessed 6 January 2013).

Bruneteau, J. (1996) *Tukka: Real Australian Food*. Frenchs Forest, NSW: New Holland Publishers.

Cherikoff, V. (1992) *Uniquely Australian: A Wild Food Cookbook*. Gladesville, NSW: Bush Tucker Supply Australia.

Cherikoff, V. (2005) *Vic Cherikoff: The essence of Australia*. http://www.dining-downunder. com/shop/index.php?main_page=about_us (accessed 12 December 2012).

Diverse Travel Australia (2013) We are the creators of journeys. http://www.diversetravel. com.au/site/welcome.htm (accessed 5 January 2013).

Isaacs, J. (1987) *Bush Food: Aboriginal Food and Herbal Medicine*. Willoughby, NSW: Weldon Publishers.

Kirton, M. (2009) *Harvest: A Complete Australian Guide to the Edible Garden*. Millers Point, NSW: Murdoch Books.

Kurrajong Australian Native Foods (2008) *The Bush Tucker Shop*. http://www. bushtuckershop.com/index.htm (accessed 2 November 2012).

Lobley, K. (2013) Spirit of the ancestors. *The Age (Traveller)*, 12 January, p. 13.

Low, T. (1989) *Bush Tucker: Australia's Wild Food Harvest*. North Ryde, NSW: Angus and Robertson.

Manfield, C. (2005) *Spice*. Camberwell, Vic: Lantern (Penguin Group).

McKean, C. (1999) *Australian Food: The Complete Reference to the Australian Food Industry*. East Melbourne: Agrifood Media.

Outback Spirit (2013) Outback spirit. http://outbackspirit.com.au (accessed 7 December 2011).

Outback Steakhouse (2013) Outback steakhouse. http://www.outback.com (accessed 8 January 2013).

Rivenburgh, N., Louw, E., Loo, E. and Mersham, G. (2004) *The Sydney Olympics and Foreign Attitudes Towards Australia*. Gold Coast: Cooperative Research Centre for Sustainable Tourism.

RT Tours Australia (2013) Aboriginal Chef's tours. http://rttoursaustralia.com.au (accessed 5 January 2013).

Rural Industries Research and Development Corporation (RIRDC) (2008) *Native Foods: R&D Priorities and Strategies, 2007–2012*. Barton, ACT: RIRDC.

Symons, M. (1982) *One Continuous Picnic: A History of Easting in Australia*. Ringwood, Vic: Penguin.

Turner, G. (1993) *National Fictions: Literature, Film and the Construction of Australian Narrative* (2nd edn). St Leonards, NSW: Allen and Unwin.

Vogages Travel Centre (2013) Voyages Indigenous Tourism Australia. http://www.voyages.com.au (accessed 4 January 2013).

Ward, R. (1966) *The Australian Legend*. Melbourne: Oxford University Press.

White, L. (2004) The bicentenary of Australia: Celebration of a nation. In L.K. Fuller (ed.) *National Days/National Ways: Historical, Political and Religious Celebrations around the World* (pp. 25–39). Westport, Connecticut: Praeger.

# 10 Pure, Fresh and Simple: 'Spicing Up' the New Nordic Cuisine

Laufey Haraldsdóttir and Guðrún Þóra Gunnarsdóttir

Being an Arctic tourism destination, Iceland is not easily placed on the world map of food trails and tourism, and nor are the other Nordic countries. In recent years the image of the Nordic countries as worthwhile food tourism destinations has systematically been developed and promoted through the joint Nordic project *New Nordic Cuisine* (Larsen, 2010; Musgrave, 2011). The simplicity and pureness of the Nordic cuisine has been highlighted and closely related to nature imagery and spectacular scenery. The short light summers and long dark winters are an important background for the Nordic cuisine imagery and discourse, not the least in relation to herbs used as spices.

This chapter focuses on the role of herbs and wild plants in the context of food tourism in Iceland. It looks at the ways in which herbs and plants used as spices connect spice-related tourism to a new destination such as Iceland, as well as contributing to global culinary trends. The chapter, furthermore, demonstrates how the herbs and plants work as active agents connecting the culinary culture to the Nordic nature and in that way contribute to the experience of tourists seeking uniqueness and authenticity. Based on a qualitative methodology, the chapter includes a case study (Berg, 2009) at the Restaurant Dill (Yourgrau, 2010) in the capital city Reykjavik. Data were collected through a variety of methods, including interviews with the owner and chef, participant observation, reviewing of audio-visual material and media coverage related to the subject. In addition, field work was conducted at several tourist shops in the region of Reykjavik in order to explore the selection of herb products.

The chapter starts with an overview of how Iceland has been represented as a tourism destination. We then introduce the project *New Nordic Cuisine* and give a short historical overview of the use of herbs in Iceland and the other Nordic countries. Thereafter, we explore the case study of Restaurant Dill and conclude the chapter with a discussion of the role of herbs and plants as souvenirs.

## Iceland – Capitalizing on Nature

Iceland has been promoted as a tourism destination since the mid-20th century, and in recent years the Icelandic tourism authorities have placed increasing emphasis on image making through various marketing exercises (Johannesson et al., 2010). Throughout, Iceland has been marketed as a nature tourist destination with an emphasis on the clean and pure wilderness (Alessio & Johannesdottir, 2011; Gunnarsdóttir, 2011). Surveys that have been carried out among foreign tourists have clearly confirmed that nature is the main reason for visiting Iceland (Icelandic Tourist Board, 2012). Since 1999, Iceland has, for example, been promoted in the United States by a marketing consortium labelled 'Iceland Naturally' (Icelandic Tourist Board, 2010), in which Icelandic products, tourism as well as water, lamb, fish and designer clothes, are framed and branded in the context of a pure and unspoiled northern nature. As the slogan indicates, nature has been emphasized as the main attraction for Iceland as a tourism destination, with the different actors (Ren, 2011) taking part in enacting the image. In recent years, food has become an important destination actor and food production in Iceland has been highlighted in relation to tourism (Haraldsdóttir, 2009; Pálsdóttir, 2008), resulting in changes in food production sites and services into spaces of touristic experience (Everett, 2012; Haraldsdóttir, 2012).

Various food tourism projects have been launched around the country, many of them as a result of certain rural development initiative that emphasize a cluster approach on a regional basis (Haraldsdóttir, 2009; Gunnarsdóttir & Haraldsdóttir, 2009; Murray & Haraldsdóttir, 2004). Those food tourism clusters all emphasize local products and knowledge, where the traditional is entwined with innovational initiatives aiming to sharpen the image of the destination as a worthy touristic place.

Regional imagery has recently become more and more important on the global tourism market, and this has been especially noticeable with the promotion of quality food products (Boniface, 2003; Everett, 2008). In this context, initiatives regarding food localization have been emphasized (MacEntee, 2010; Sims, 2010) and a mixture of innovation and traditions used to make place narratives, where creation and sharing of stories regarding local food are part of the tourists consumption and experience (Lichrou *et al.*, 2008; Messeni & Savino, 2012).

During the last few years the marriage of food and nature has been an increasing focus in Iceland, visible, among other things through the 'Iceland Naturally' campaign and at the annual, weeklong 'Food and Fun' festival in Reykjavík (Brandau, 2006; Parseghian, 2005) launched in 2002, where culinary events are framed by images of fresh ingredients and closeness to nature. According to Gyimóthy and Mykletun (2009: 260) regional products and cuisines are important features in destination branding. By underlining regional identities through its food and food culture, it becomes possible to 'turn rural destinations into fashionable places to visit'. The promotion of the *New Nordic Cuisine* project is a good case in point.

# The New Nordic Cuisine

In 2004 twelve leading chefs in the Nordic countries wrote the *New Nordic Cuisine Manifesto*. Building on landscape and climate, products and culture based values, the chefs listed 10 new commandments for the Nordic Kitchen (Messeni & Savino, 2012). The aim of the manifesto was to give a new image to the Nordic cuisine, suffering at the time from a rather negative perception. This negative perception manifested, for example, in comments made by some public figures claiming the Scandinavian food to be one of the worst in the world (Friedman, 2008; Küchler, 2006). In 2005 the Nordic governments supported this initiative by launching a joint programme: *New Nordic Food*, fostered by the Nordic Council of Ministers. With the aim of conducting a gastronomic revolution in the Nordic countries, the programme is now in its second phase lasting until 2014.

Several restaurants in all of the Nordic Countries market themselves under the label of *New Nordic Cuisine*. Restaurant *noma* in Copenhagen, recently declared the best restaurant in the world is the flagship of the project. Noma was launched in 2004 and has been awarded two Michelin stars (Larsen, 2010). A quote on the restaurants homepage underlines the ethos of the joint project, referring to tradition and innovation in relation to landscape; 'In an effort to shape our way of cooking, we look to our landscape and delve into our ingredients and culture, hoping to rediscover our history and shape our future' (noma, ed).

The restaurant firmly grounds itself in a specific locale and culture, thereby emphasising its unique identity. In a global world where verticalization and agricultural productivism dominate the scene, often at the expense of traceability and health, highlighting a place of origin is an effort to firmly ground the food production and reconnect consumers and producers (Sims, 2010; Wilson & Whitehead, 2012). The local, as well as small-scale food production, is often considered to be authentic, symbolising place and culture (Sims, 2009), which appears to be attractive to the modern consumer. This has been seen as a countermove to globalization but at the same time a marketing tool for food producing destinations seeking unique selling points in an ever more competitive environment. This is clearly reflected in the five areas highlighted in the New Nordic Food project, listed below:

- branding the New Nordic Food;
- enjoyment and identity;
- healthiness;
- experience economy/tourism and creative industries;
- small-scale production.

The Nordic *terroir* and authenticity are key concepts in this context. (Larsen, 2010; Messeni & Savino, 2012). *Terroir* is a concept originating in the wine production but it is also used in food production, among other in the *New Nordic Cuisine* project. *Terroir* refers to local climate and soil composition and defines the character and taste of its products (Trubek, 2009). This emphasis on the geographical identity of food is closely intertwined with the concept of authenticity which in the ideology of the *New Nordic Cuisine* embraces at the same time the local and the traditional (Messeni & Savino, 2012). The above-sited quote on the *nomas* homepage shows how the Nordic narratives refer to a past rooted in a landscape from which the food as well as the culture is rediscovered; authentic and exotic at the same time. The method of telling stories of one's origin is a common strategy in strengthening local consumption cultures in a globalizing world (Jackson, 2004). This is evident in the branding exercises of the *New Nordic Cuisine*, not the least when it comes to herbs used as spices that in recent years have become more and more prominent players in the Nordic cuisine, along with the narrative of the Nordic *terroir*. The cool climate and the interplay between dark and light in the Nordic countries is said to cause a slow growth and leave its characteristics in the product (Hermansen, 2012; Risvik, 2007), hence reflecting Nordic landscape and culture.

## Herbs Used as Spices – The Nordic Context

The culinary history of the Nordic countries is better characterized with scarcity and matters of survival than gourmet cuisines (Bringéus, 2001;

Gísladóttir, 1999). Nevertheless, different berries and wild plants were already used in Nordic cookery in the Viking Age (Notaker, 2009). Many herbs were also used, even though their main uses were connected to dietetic or medical purposes, not as flavour to the food. Survival recipes from the Middle Ages include imported spices such as cloves, nutmeg, cardamom, pepper and cinnamon. These recipes are found in small manuscript leaflets, for example in Iceland. Notaker (2009) argues that prevalent peasant dishes that are documented under the early modern period, originate from the Middle Ages. The medieval dishes including actual spices were primarily meant for the elite, while most people used domestic roots and herbs such as angelica, marjoram, anise and onion as seasonings in their food.

There were, of course, regional and social variations of cooking traditions and methods in the Nordic countries. Iceland, being a faraway island in the North Atlantic Ocean, had and still has its specialities. Harsher climate condition than in the other Nordic countries and a profound isolation from the rest of the world periodically, resulted in a limited use of vegetables, herbs and plants in the local diet.

## Herbs in Iceland – tradition and innovation

Written documents about the use of herbs and wild plants in Iceland through the centuries are rather sparse. References in the Sagas, different proverbs, quatrains and tales indicate that herbs and plants have been used for medicinal purposes and likewise as nourishment in the forms of extracts, soups and porridges. Examples of those are the Iceland moss (*Cetraria islandica*), Angelica (*Angelica archangelica*), Dulse (*Palmaria palmata*) and Scurvywort (*Cochlearia officinalis*). With few exceptions, documents say little about common people using wild herbs or plants to spice up their food (Gísladóttir, 1999; Notaker, 2009). Angelica was used to spice up soups, porridges and jams, and Caraway is mentioned in references from the 17th and 18th century as a spice in bread, liquor and coffee. After 1800, herbs such as chervil and thyme are more often mentioned along with actual spices such as salt, pepper, clove, nutmeg, cinnamon and ginger (Gísladóttir, 1999). A lack of the tradition of using wild and/or cultivated plants as spices in food is therefore apparent, at least up until the 18th century. The use of herbs and wild plants as spices in meat and fish dishes didn't become common in Iceland until the late 20th century, reflecting the fact that Iceland entered the stage of global consumerism relatively late compared to other Western nations. In the following section we will take a closer look at Restaurant Dill in Reykjavík that actively operates in the spirit of the *New Nordic Cuisine* ideology.

# Restaurant Dill

Located in the Nordic House in Reykjavik, a building designed in the late 1960s by the Finish architect and designer Alvar Aalto (1898–1976), the Dill Restaurant seems to be the perfect place to bring about the ideology of the *New Nordic Cuisine*. The Nordic House, operated by the Nordic Council of Ministers, organizes a variety of cultural events and educational initiatives, which aim to foster and strengthen the cultural bonds between the Nordic Countries. The food culture is no exception. The restaurant opened in 2009, and the name refers to the herb dill (Anethum graveolens). The herb is not perennial in Iceland and cannot be said to be traditional in the country, but the use of the herb is very common in the Nordic countries. One can hardly image pickled salmon or potato salad in Norway or Sweden without the green feathery herb on the top. This makes the name of the restaurant presumably Nordic in the eyes of the world.

The house itself is a building surrounded by a green area in the middle of the city. Outside the restaurant, the guests can enjoy a walk in nature immersed with waters, birds and a great variety of plants. Chervil (Anthriscus sylvestris) and Angelica (Angelica archangelica) plants that are very much used by the chef in the Dill Restaurant literally cover the area. A garden attached to the restaurant contains different plants and herbs, both immigrant plants and plants indigenous to the Icelandic nature. There is also a greenhouse in the garden where the chef cultivates different types of the herb dill. Inside the interior, furniture and tableware have been designed by classic and contemporary Nordic designers and artists.

Values and ideas are often clearly reflected in the dishes chefs serve and the way they cook (Võsu & Kannike, 2012). This is the case at Dill where the chef likes to keep things simple and fresh. Brought up in a small town in northern Iceland by a father who passionately grew plants and herbs, he says he looks for herbs and plants for his cooking wherever he goes, emphasizing his desire to use natural ingredients. The chef claims that vegetables, herbs and plants are always the base of his dishes while fish and meat come second – if they feature at all. Asked if he considers herbs as spices, he replies 'isn't everything that gives flavour in food spices?' (Gunnar Karl Gíslason, interview 22 June 2012). At the time of a visit to the restaurant in the summer of 2012, seven out of nine dishes in the constantly changing menu included some kind of herb, whereas only four included seafood or meat. This is somewhat unusual for Icelandic restaurants that are not vegetarian.

To make the herbs and plants available in the wintertime, the Dill Restaurant uses preservation methods such as pickling and drying. Herbs and plants are used in creams, oils, soups and sauces – and as aesthetic decoration on desserts such as sorbet – giving a prominent colour and flavour to the dishes. In that way they are not only used as spices and flavour enhancers, but also as significant performance medium (Gunnell, 2010; Larsen, 2010) in the setting of the plate. Their green, simple and fresh appearance gives an overall performance of the *New* – back to earth – *Nordic* (Figure 10.1).

The restaurant setting and the professional and creative direction of the meal experience are an analogy to theatrical performances (Võsu & Kannike, 2012), where both human and non-human agents play multiple roles. All in all, the Nordic House, its surrounding and Restaurant Dill give a performance of the Nordic in past and present, a mixture of tradition and innovation, in a creative production which enhances the tourist experience.

In general, the ideology of the *New Nordic cuisine* and its interpretation in Restaurant Dill, can be said to be in line with the philosophy of many gourmet restaurants today (Larsen, 2010). Rhetoric of locality, freshness and simplicity, the idea of reconnecting producers and consumers, along with authenticity and tradition are fairly usual encounters in promotional material from a trendy modern restaurant. Although this rhetoric might seem to support a rather romantic discourse (Pratt, 2007), it also connects to complex modern consumption patterns, reflecting different attitudes and values that contribute to people's self-identities and lifestyles. Food has an interdisciplinary recognition as an important medium in human communication

**Figure 10.1** Herbs are central ingredients in all the dishes at Dill
*Source*: Laufey Haraldsdóttir

(Barthes, 1979; Belasco, 2008). It communicates personal, social and cultural identities, and characterizes sites and places. Through consumption behaviour people express their visions and values. Such things as attitude towards health, concerns about the agro-industrial food system, environmental issues and sustainability and animal welfare (Mak *et al.*, 2011; Zukin, 2008) are among the values that influence consumers decision making and affect people's experiences, for example while travelling. Hence, the making of a place with image rooted in simplicity and tradition, as well as in clean and unspoiled nature, is an important marketing tool in the making of the North as a worthwhile tourist destination and in the making of the *New Nordic Cuisine*. In this imagery the herbs and plants used as spices play an important part as tourist products.

## Herbs as Tourist Products in Iceland

When it comes to food, Iceland is better known for its fish and seafood, than vegetables and herbs. The use of wild and cultivated herbs as spices in Iceland seems to be a modern phenomenon which recently has gained an increased popularity among chefs and the public (Haraldsdóttir, 2012; West Tours, 2009; Zimmer, 2012). The chef at Restaurant Dill emphasizes herbs and plants as spices in his cooking largely to highlight the *New Nordic Cuisine* ideology. However, other restaurants, and hotel restaurants in Iceland also celebrate herbs and plants without being part of the *New Nordic* or being vegetarian. Furthermore, the growing micro-brewery industry in Iceland is also embracing Icelandic herbs in an attempt to produce beers with a distinct flavour, and in a cookbook recently published in Iceland, the gastronomic potential of plants better known for their medical purposes, is explored (Eiríksson, 2012).

While the appearance of herbs on restaurant menus has increased gradually over time, perhaps the most prominent newcomer on the market are herbs in travel-friendly packaging that are found in various tourist locations in Iceland (Figure 10.2). Our field research in tourist shops and farmers market-like store in the capital city Reykjavik, as well as at the international airport in Keflavik, revealed a selection of herb products presented as tourist souvenirs. Whereas herbal tea products have been common for some time, herbs prepared as spices are now appearing on the shops shelves. Those include products such as 'Artic Herb Salt', 'Birch-flavoured sea salt', 'Icelandic wild herbs', 'Arctic Thyme' and 'Rhubarb Angelica Salt'. Most come from small producers around Iceland and the sales outlets are often described on their homepages if they have one. A survey of those webpages reveals that the products are typically offered in speciality stores, tourists' shops, handi-craft shops and markets such as Christmas markets. Cafes and restaurants are also common on the list of sales outlets, but only in one case, is a super-market mentioned.

An examination of the packaging of herbal products from three different producers showed that the packages are generally small and neat, in modern design and easy to transport. The overall colour schemes of the packaging are in earthy tones, with dominance of green and brown – varying in shades and nuances. The languages used on the labels are a mixture of Icelandic and English, usually with emphasis on the latter. The Icelandic flag appears on packages from one of the three producers, and the labelling 'Made in Iceland'

**Figure 10.2** Herb products presented as tourist souvenirs
*Source*: Laufey Haraldsdóttir

or 'Icelandic' indicates the origin of the product from two of them. One of the producers, located in rural East Iceland, indicates the specific production place in Iceland on the packaging. Notably, one of the producers puts the products in a historical context by using drawings from Old Icelandic manuscripts and carvings, as well as texts from the Old Norse poems Havamal, as themes on the labels. The producers, not surprisingly, all try to evoke connection with nature through the naming of their companies: urta.islandica, Hills and Heaths, The Thyme Field. The names of the products further evoke the image of the northern nature by using the word 'wild' or 'Arctic', sometimes both.

Souvenirs, including food souvenirs such as the herb packages described above, are an important part of the tourist product at a destination and souvenir purchases are, therefore, an important part of the overall tourist behaviour and experience. Although those herb products are highly functional, fusing tourism and everyday life (Morgan & Pritchard, 2005) with the tourists bringing them back to their homes and kitchen, they are also highly symbolic, carrying messages from places and people. Furthermore they materialize the travel with the tourists' consumption of souvenirs. In their symbolic role, souvenirs can represent geographical, cultural, as well as social aspects (Morgan & Pritchard, 2005; Sims, 2009) and with their earthy tone and reference to Icelandic history, the herb souvenirs are a symbol of Icelandic nature and culture. Souvenirs as material objects are also a way of extending and continuing the tourist experience (Pietikäinen & Kelly-Holmes, 2011) as they are brought back home along with memories of a place. The herbs on the shelves in the tourists shops in Iceland are an example of a creative commodification (Võsu & Kannike, 2012), integrating herbs used as spices into the tourism products in Iceland. It is an innovation meant to meet contemporary consumer trends (Everett, 2008; Gyimothy & Mykletun, 2008) as well as being a symbol for a culture and a place. Just like the herbs and plants on the plates in Restaurant Dill, those products give an image of a landscape and culture with its natural appearance and historic connection.

## Conclusion

Through increasing emphasis on its food as an important aspect of destination attachment, Iceland is perhaps making its place on the world map of food tourism. One of the agents used increasingly for that purpose are the wild and cultivated plants used among other things as spices in food. Although many of the culinary herbs and plants that are used in contemporary Icelandic cuisines are imported, immigrant plants or cultivated in protected surroundings, a variety of wild Icelandic plants can be used as spices in food. Plants are readily related to nature and Iceland's focus on nature in its branding exercises, for example in the 'Iceland Naturally' campaign, puts it in perfect line with the ideology of the joint Nordic project *New Nordic Cuisine*. In recombining existing resources such as nature, food production and culture, the Nordic countries use innovative processes and history to underline the image of a pure and fresh culinary destination.

The herbs and the plants, so prominent on the menu at Restaurant Dill, serve as destination actors in that setting, where the destination is Iceland and *the Nordic*. The herbs as souvenirs are analogous destination actors, representing Icelandic landscape and culture at tourists' sites. In the restaurant setting, herbs used as spices play with other non-human actors the 'trendy' part alongside the more traditional part of smoked meat and salted fish. Together with the human actors and their narrative presentation of the dishes served, they enact the image of the destination. They are symbolic of the Nordic nature and landscape, performing the green and fresh – back to earth *New Nordic Cuisine imagery* on the plate. On the shelves of the tourist shops the herbs represent the interplay between terroir, its products, Icelandic culture and creative innovation, and act as destination actors contributing to a trendy culinary image. Overall, the herbs used as spices – at the restaurant and in the shelves – are performative, that is to say they serve as an expression of something that implies authenticity and a sense of place. Performing an artistic innovation, where reinvented tradition and natural conditions are 'spiced-up' to meet global culinary consumption trends, a new culinary tradition is created and a new image is constructed – the image of the New Nordic Cuisine.

## References

Alessio, D. and Johannesdottir, A.L. (2011) Geysers and 'girl', Gender, power and colonialism in Icelandic tourist imagery. *European Journal of Women's Studies* 18 (1), 35–50.

Barthes, R. (1979) Towards a psychosociology of contemporary consumption. In R. Foster and O. Ranum (eds) *Food and Drink in History* (pp. 166–173). Baltimore: Johns Hopkins University Press.

Belasco, W. (2008) *Food: The Key Concepts*. Oxford: Berg.

Berg, B.L. (2009) *Qualitative Research Methods for the Social Sciences* (7th edn). Boston: Pearson International Edition.

Boniface, P. (2003). *Tasting Tourism: Travelling for Food and Drink*. Burlington: Ashgate.

Brandau, M. (2006) Food and Fun Festival showcases Icelandic Ingredients. *Article in Nation's Restaurants News*, 27 March. http://web.ebscohost.com/ehost/pdfviewer/pdfviewer?sid=dd5ed751-4227-431c-9258-261684e0dd97%40sessionmgr114&vid=2&hid=105 (accessed 19 December 2012).

Bringéus, N.A. (2001) *Man, Food and Milieu: A Swedish Approach to Food Ethnology*. East Lothian: Tuckwell Press.

180    Part 3: Spice Product Studies

Eiríksson, A. (2012) *Ljúfmeti úr lækningajurtum [Delicacy out of medical plants]*, blog. http://www.alberteldar.com/2012/10/06/ljufmeti-ur-laekningajurtum-2/ (accessed 7 January 2013).
Everett, S. (2008) Beyond the visual gaze? The pursuit of an embodied experience through food tourism. *Tourist Studies* 8 (3), 337–358.
Everett, S. (2012) Production Places or Consumption Spaces? The Place-making Agency of Food Tourism in Ireland and Scotland. *Tourism Geographies: An International Journal of Tourism Space, Place and Environment* 14 (4), 535–554.
Friedman, J. (2008) Appreciating Anthony Bourdain (with almost no reservations). *Seattlest article*, 9 June. http://seattlest.com/2008/06/09/appreciating_an.php (accessed 25 September 2012).
Gísladottir, H. (1999) *Íslensk matarhefð [Icelandic Food Culture]*. Reykjavík: Mál og menning.
Gunnarsdóttir, G.Þ. (2011) Reflecting images: The front page of Icelandic tourism brochures. In S. Ísleifsson and D. Chartier (eds) *Iceland and Images of the North* (pp. 531–551). Québec: Presses de l'Université du Québec and The Reykjavík Academy.
Gunnarsdóttir, G.Þ. and Haraldsdóttir, L. (2009) Culinary tourism project in northern Iceland. In C.M. Hall, D.K. Müller and J. Saarinen (eds) *Nordic Tourism: Issues and Cases* (pp. 117–121). Bristol: Channel View Publications.
Gunnell, T. (2010) Introduction. Performative stages of the Nordic world. *Ethnologia Europaea* 40 (2), 5–13.
Gyimóthy, S. and Mykletun, R.J. (2009) Scary food: Commodifying culinary heritage as meal adventures in tourism. *Journal of Vacation Marketing* 15 (3), 259–273.
Haraldsdóttir, L. (2009) Að borða mat en bragða svæðið. Þarfir og væntingar ferðamanna til veitinga á ferðalögum [To eat the food but taste the place. Demands and expectations of tourists while travelling]. In I. Hannibalsson (ed.) *Rannsóknir í Félagsvísindum X [Research in Social Sciences X]* (pp. 399–412). Reykjavík: Háskólaútgáfan (University of Iceland Press).
Haraldsdóttir, L. (2012) Hreint, ferskt og einfalt. Ný norræn matvæli og sviðslistin [Pure, fresh and simple. The performance in New Nordic Cuisine]. In S. Eggertsson and Á.G. Ásgeirsdóttir (eds) *Rannsóknir í Félagsvísindum XIII [Research in Social Sciences X]* (pp. 1–8). Reykjavík: Háskólaútgáfan (University of Iceland Press). Electronic version. http://skemman.is/stream/get/1946/13380/32087/1/LaufeyHaraldsdottir_Hreint_ferskt_og_einfalt.pdf (accessed 15 December 2012).
Hermansen, M.E. (2012) Creating terroir: An anthropological perspective on new Nordic cuisine as an expression of Nordic identity, research blog on *nordicfoodlab*, 7 August 2012. http://nordicfoodlab.org/blog/2012/8/creating-terroir-an-anthropological-perspective-on-new-nordic-cuisine-as-an-expression-of-nordic-identity (accessed 27 October 2012).
Icelandic Tourist Board (2010) Fjölbreytt verkefni Iceland Naturally 2010, *news*, 19 January. http://ferdamalastofa.is/Category.mvc/DisplayElement?moduleid=220&catid=676&sid=5360 (accessed 12 December 2012).
Icelandic Tourist Board (2012) Tourism in Iceland in figures. Online document: http://www.ferdamalastofa.is/upload/files/Tourism_in_Iceland_in_figures_May_%202012.pdf_ferdatjonusta_i_tolum_mars2011.pdf (accessed 12 December 2012).
Jackson, P. (2004) Local consumption cultures in a globalizing world. *Transactions of the Institute of British Geographers* 29 (2), 165–178.
Johannesson, G.T., Huijbens, E. and Sharpley, R. (2010) Icelandic tourism: Past directions – future challenges. *Tourism Geographies* 12 (2), 278–301.

Küchler, T. (2006) Finland prepares culinary wonders for presidency, *euobserver's news*, 17 May. http://euobserver.com/political/21624 (accessed 25 September 2012).

Larsen, H.P. (2010) Performing Tasty Heritage. Danish Cusine and Playful Nostalgia at restaurant noma. *Ethnologia Europaea* 40 (2), 90–102.

Lichrou, M., O'Malley, L. and Patterson, M. (2008) Place-product or place narrative(s)? Perspectives in the marketing of tourism destinations. *Journal of Strategic Marketing* 16 (1), 27–39.

MacEntee, J. (2010) Contemporary and traditional localism: A conceptualisation of rural local food. *Local Environment* 15, 785–803.

Mak, A.H.N., Lumbers, M., Eves, A. and Chang, R.C.Y. (2011) Factors influencing tourist food consumption. *International Journal of Hospitality Management* 31 (3), 928–936.

Messeni, P.A. and Savino, T. (2012) Search, recombination, and innovation: Lessons for haute cuisine, long range planing. http://www.sciencedirect.com/science/article/pii/ (accessed 6 December 2012).

Morgan, N. and Pritchard, A. (2005) On Souvenirs and metonymy: Narratives of memory, metaphor and materiality. *Tourist Studies* 5 (1), 29–53.

Murray, I. and Haraldsdóttir, L. (2004) *Developing a Rural Culinary Tourism Product: Considerations and Resources for Success*. Quebec: Administrative Sciences Association of Canada (ASAC). Online at http://luxor.acadiau.ca/library/ASAC/v25/articles/ Murray-haraldsdottir.pdf (accessed 6 December 2012).

Musgrave, S. (2011) Cool modern food trending north; Nordic cuisine's renaissance at home draws attention abroad, *article in Edmonton Journal*, 21 May 2011. http://www.canada. com/edmontonjournal/news/story.html?id=23b6fbb8-5d12-427f-bb14-ee33985ea7fe (accessed 6 December 2012).

Noma (n.d.) (ed.) Welcome. http://noma.dk (accessed 4 December 2012).

Notaker, H. (2009) *Food Culture in Scandinavia*. Westport: Greenwood press.

Pálsdóttir, I.H. (2008) Country Case Inside – Iceland. The case of Iceland Naturally – Establishing an umbrella brand to increase country image impact and coherence. In K. Dinnie (ed.) *Nation Branding: Concepts, Issues, Practice* (pp. 181–187). Oxford: Elsevier.

Parseghian, P. (2005) Chefs of Iceland showcase cuisine at annual Food & Fun festival. *Article in Nation's Restaurants News*, 11 April. http://web. ebscohost.com/ehost/ pdfviewer/pdfviewer?sid=5a9f9d5f-003b-4f58-b5f4-3f79cbe7e952%40sessionmgr (accessed 19 December 2012).

Pietikäinen, S. and Kelly-Holmes, H. (2011) The local political economy of languages in a Sámi tourism destination: Authenticity and mobility in the labelling of souvenirs. *Journal of Sociolinguistics* 15 (3), 323–346.

Pratt, J. (2007). Food values: The local and the authentic. *Critique of Anthropology* 27, 285–300.

Ren, C. (2011) Non-human agency, radical ontology and tourism realities. *Annals of Tourism Research* 38 (3), 858–881.

Risvik, E. (2007) Trendy nordisk mat. *Nofirma news,* 8 May. http://www.nofima.no/ nyhet/2009/02/8684281094891412457 (accessed 15 October 2012).

Sims, R. (2009) Food, place and authenticity: Local food and the sustainable experience. *Journal of Sustainable Tourism* 17 (3), 321–336.

Sims, R. (2010) Putting place on the menu: The negotiation of locality in UK food tourism, from production to consumption. *Journal of Rural Studies* 26, 105–115.

Trubek, A.B. (2009) *The Taste of Place: A Cultural Journey into Terroir*. Berkley: University of California Press.

Võsu, E. and Kannike, A. (2012) My home is my stage: Restaurant experiences in two Estonian lifestyle enterprises. *Journal of Ethnology and Folkloristics* 5 (2), 19–47.

West Tours (2009) Learn how to cook delicious food from wild plants. *West Tours news*, 27 July. http://www.vesturferdir.is/index.php?p=426&lang=en& (accessed 15 October 2012).

Wilson, G.A. and Whitehead, I. (2012) Local rural product as a relic spatial strategy in globalised rural spaces: Evidence from County Clare (Ireland). *Journal of Rural Studies* 28, 199–207.

Yourgrau, B. (2010) Table Hopping. Dill in Reykjavik. *Article* in *The New Your Times Style Magazine*, 28 April. http://tmagazine.blogs.nytimes.com/2010/04/28/table-hopping-dill-in-reykjavik/ (accessed 6 December 2012).

Zimmer, E. (2012) Snapshots from Iceland: Eldhús, the Smallest Icelandic Restaurant on Wheels. *Serious eats*, article, 2 April. http://www.seriouseats.com/2012/04/snapshots-from-iceland-eldhus-little-house-on-wheels-dinners-smallest-icelandic-restaurant.html (accessed 15 October 2012).

Zukin, S. (2008) Consuming authenticity. From outposts of difference to means of exclusion. *Cultural Studies* 22 (5), 724–748.

# 11 Recognition of Spices and Cuisine as Intangible Heritage

Lee Jolliffe

> *What is clear is that intangible heritage, and, within its field, gastronomic and food heritage, is in a moment of expansion, of recognition and awareness of its protection.*
> Montanari, 1994: 197

The customs of food and cuisine have not traditionally been considered worthy of recognition and protection. However, recognition of the links between food and culture and changes in attitudes towards the tangible and intangible nature of heritage (Schmitt, 2008) are contributing to seeing food-related traditions as heritage. Cuisine is now recognized for its value as part of culinary tourism and the sustainable tourism experience (Sims, 2009). Traditional foods and ancient foodways are an important part of the food-related tourism appeal and image of many countries (Wang & Tang, 2011). These food images are often a symbol of authenticity for the prospective visitor.

Spices are part of the history of food and cuisine. The story of spices is intertwined with medieval trade as traders searched for spices desired for both their medicinal and culinary uses (Dalby, 2000). Exploration, and trade as well as wars were related to this search for spices contributing to the establishment of spice trading routes. Through colonization spice cultivation was spread around the world. Migration furthermore led to the spread of the use of spices through the cuisine of the migrants (Civitello, 2008). Many destinations and their cuisines around the world are therefore associated with spices.

Globally spices are integral to cooking food, reflecting various foodways, gastronomic and multi-cultural customs. Spices are tangible, but the traditions and conventions regarding their use are an intangible part of both local and global culinary traditions. The appeal of spicy food depends on culinary traditions. In tourism, local foods are adapted for tourist tastes, a process that creates an authentic food in the view of the tourist (Cohen & Avieli, 2004).

This chapter examines how the immaterial heritage of spices is recognized and interpreted through cuisine, discussing how this might affect the tourism experience. A case study approach is utilized, identifying the recognition through international (UNESCO) designations of cuisines in which spices are an element. First, the chapter draws from the literature related to the recognition and interpretation of culinary traditions and knowledge. Second, examples of the interpretation of spices through cuisine are drawn from both culinary tourism literature and the field experience of the researcher. Third, case studies are identified through the examination of UNESCO cuisine related recognitions. Fourth, a comparative approach is taken, discussing the case studies of the recognition of cuisine.

The examples of the listings and designations draw upon secondary sources including UNESCO nomination documents and reports, related web sites, as well as literature from both the academic and the popular press on the subject. Literature on culinary history, foodways, migration, globalization, culinary and gastronomic tourism provides a framework for identifying how the intangible aspects of spices are adapted and conveyed through both cuisine and culinary-related tourism.

## Culinary Studies and Foodways

Literature in this area contributes to understanding how cuisine has developed. Spices are both a tangible and intangible part of culinary traditions and foodways (Civitello, 2008). Studying foodways of a people, location, or region provides perspective for examining the intangible cultural heritage of cuisine. Foodways are more than just food, as food is physical and tangible whereas foodways incorporates intangible traditions regarding food ingredients, practices and customs (Timothy & Ron, 2013). There is a trend towards the appreciation of local food (Feagan, 2007) in particular as countering conventional globalizing food systems.

## Migration and Globalization

The literatures on both migration and globalization provide a lens through which to examine the intangible heritages of cuisine and spices. The geographical spread of the use of spices through cuisine is due in part to migration and studies in this area are relevant to examining the intangible aspects of cuisine and spices. Globalization has likewise had an impact on spreading culinary traditions, as is the case with Mexican cuisine (Pilcher, 2008). DeSoucey (2010) puts forth a theory of gastronationalism that counters that of globalization, postulating that food production and consumption sustains nationalist sentiments that can in turn influence the production and marketing of food.

## Culinary and Gastronomic Tourism

Research on both culinary and gastronomic tourism is useful for the examination of cuisine and spices in relationship to tourism. Through culinary tourism visitors experience the intangible aspects of cuisine including the use of spices. A higher end of culinary tourism, gastronomic tourism (Scarpato, 2002) also has a relationship to spices. Culinary tourists specifically seek to experience local cuisines, with food acting as both attraction and destination (Long, 2003).

## Spices and Cuisine

Cuisine as a regional and national identity marker is a lure for food related tourism (Ab Karim & Chi, 2010). Some locales, such as Hong Kong, employ local and international cuisine in tourism marketing efforts (Okumus et al., 2007). Some destinations are enhancing their association with spices, such as the rebranding of Penang, Malaysia as 'Hot and Spicy Penang' reflecting both their tangible (spice production and sale) and intangible (history as a spice trading route, reputation for a spicy cuisine) spice heritages (Jalleh, 2012). This rebranding included the introduction of a Spice Trail Tour, incorporating a visit to the Tropical Spice Garden, profiled earlier in Chapter 8. Other destinations branding themselves as spice island(s) include for example: the Maluku Islands (Indonesia), Grenada (West Indies) and Zanzibar (Tanzania).

At destinations a number of types of venues interpret the tangible and intangible aspects of both spices and cuisine (Table 11.1). Attractions not built for tourism have an inherent authenticity and vibrancy related to communicating aspects of the spice industry, such as local spice markets and bazaars, restaurants, spice farms and gardens. Other attractions designed for tourism compliment these naturally occurring attractions while utilizing spices, such as spas, cooking schools, culinary lodgings and souvenir shops. Attractions related to spices with educational objectives include museums and exhibits specifically designed for tourism.

**Table 11.1** Venues for interpreting spices and cuisine

| Venue | Tangible | Intangible |
|---|---|---|
| Markets | Spices displayed for sale. | Spice knowledge of vendors. |
| Restaurants | Spices experienced through cuisine. | Spice traditions conveyed through culinary traditions. |
| Farms and Gardens | Spices growing and being harvested. | Interpreting indigenous knowledge of spices and uses. |
| Spas | Spices are part of treatments and teas served. | Knowledge inherent in spice related treatments. |
| Cooking Schools | Spices as tangible ingredients for recipes. | Recipes, instructor knowledge of spices and local foodways. |
| Lodging | At working spice garden homestays visitors see spices at their source. | Hosts interpret spice cultivation conveying intangible heritages. |
| Souvenir Shops | Spices and spice related souvenirs. | Souvenirs cookbooks convey intangible spice heritages. |
| Museums | In exhibits spices can be seen, and perhaps smelled. | Intangible spice heritage conveyed through exhibits. |
| Visitor Attractions | At spice garden attractions visitors can see, smell, touch, and taste spices. | Local guides convey traditional knowledge regarding spice use. |

There is a growing awareness of foodways being valued for the intangible knowledge embodied by both the production and preparation systems, as in the case of Chinese cuisine (Cheung, 2013). At a broad range of venues noted above where they may be experienced, spices through cuisine are part of the tourism experience, forming a valuable part of the heritages of both their producing and consuming communities. However, there is little recognition of this local and global heritage, which is largely intangible. This situation may be changing with UNESCO's efforts to protect global intangible cultural heritage, as profiled through the case studies below.

# Case Study: UNESCO's ICHC Culinary Listings

The 2003 UNESCO Convention for the Safeguarding of the Intangible Cultural Heritage known as the Intangible Cultural Heritage Convention (ICHC) recognized the value of intangible heritages (UNESCO, 2003). In part the ICHC is considered to be an antidote to the more Western-oriented 1972 UNESCO Convention Concerning the Protection of the World Cultural, Natural Heritage known as the World Heritage Convention (WHC) (Smith & Akagawa, 2009). The authors note that the ICHC reinforces relevance of world heritage to Asian, African, South American and indigenous communities. Implementation of the ICHC has challenged traditional heritage views of material culture, requiring a more free-flowing interpretation of culture and heritage as constantly changing (Brown, 2005). For example spaces in which intangible cultural heritage is conveyed are now able to achieve recognition (Schmitt, 2008).

Only a few cuisines have been identified on the ICHC, namely the transnational case of the Mediterranean diet (2010), the national cases of Traditional Mexican Cuisine (2010) and the Gastronomic Meal of the French (2010) and these inscriptions and designations are profiled below. Although cuisine and gastronomy is not officially a category on the UNESCO list of ICHC, a recent best practice study of intangible heritage and tourism has included this category (UNWTO, 2012).

## Mediterranean diet

The Mediterranean diet application received in 2008 was inscribed on the ICHC in 2010. This transnational nomination was on behalf of the state parties of four countries in the region (Spain, Greece, Italy and Morocco) (UNESCO, 2010b). The listing recognizes the Mediterranean diet as being made up of a set of skills, knowledge, practices and traditions that range from the landscape to the table. This is considered to include crops, harvesting, fishing, conservation, processing, preparation and in particular consumption of food. The nomination documents describe the choice of four representative communities:

The four identified communities, in a symbolic way, are: Soria (Spain), Koroni (Greece), Cilento (Italy) and Chefchaouen (Morocco). In these communities, traditions and symbolisms based on food practices, from landscape to cuisine, as elements of social sharing and celebrations, are developed and transmitted from generation to generation. (UNESCO, 2010b: 2)

The Mediterranean diet recognizes the intangible food related traditions that are still alive within the four communities. The transnational nomination was made possible by the identification of these communities where elements of the Mediterranean diet are found in oral traditions and expressions, social practices, rituals and festivities. The nomination notes the essential role of spices in this cuisine:

> The Mediterranean Diet offers a nutritional model enriched by diverse cultures which, over centuries, has essentially maintained the same food structure and the same proportions: olive oil, grains and derivatives, fresh fruits and vegetables, nuts, and to a lesser extent, fish, dairy products and meat, with an essential presence of condiments and spices. (UNESCO 2010b: 4).

Research and promotion of the Mediterranean diet is encouraged through a network of organizations dedicated to the research, inventory, promotion and dissemination of traditions related to the cultural, social and health aspects of the diet. A connection between the Mediterranean diet and regional sustainable development is recognized (International Centre for Advanced Mediterranean Agronomic Studies, 2012). There are on-going discussions about ways to promote the Mediterranean diet.

## Traditional Mexican Cuisine

In 2010 Traditional Mexican Cuisine was inscribed on the ICHC. According to the nomination documents the listing is about much more than cuisine:

> Traditional Mexican cuisine – and in this case, the Michoacán paradigm– is an integral part of the ancient cultural system based on corn, beans and chili. This trilogy, along with numerous other associated original crops, has been a communal diet and at the core of ritual and ceremonial life. (UNESCO, 2010c: 3)

In this case a spice (chili) is part of the food system of corn, beans and chili that forms an integral part of the listing. The promotion and recognition of Mexican cuisine, through this listing contributes to both the local preservation and globalization of related culinary traditions (Pilcher, 2008). Reporting to UNESCO (UNESCO, 2012b) indicate that the nomination unleashed numerous activities promoting Mexican traditional cuisine.

## Gastronomic Meal of the French

The Gastronomic Meal of the French application received in 2008 was inscribed on the ICHC in 2010, with the following description:

> A customary social practice for celebrating important moments in the lives of individuals and groups, such as births, weddings, birthdays,

anniversaries, achievements and reunions. It is a festive meal bringing people together for an occasion to enjoy the art of good eating and drinking. This very popular practice, with which all French people are familiar, has flourished in France for centuries. It is constantly changing and being transmitted. (UNESCO, 2010a: 2)

The nomination does not refer to individual dishes or recipes but to an attitude towards eating, and is a constantly changing custom. Gastronomy relates to reflective cooking and eating and also can have a role in tourism planning and development (Scarpato, 2002). The intangible heritage of gastronomy is considered to be an essential part of tourism production and consumption.

The French gastronomic meal appears on the Inventory of Intangible Cultural Heritage of France, Mission of Ethnology of the Ministry of Culture. In addition elements of the meal appear on two other inventories. First, the Inventory of French Culinary Heritage lists traditional food and agricultural knowledge, along with related local products, that include herbs, spices and condiments etc. Second, is an inventory of the objects (for cooking and the table) that is included in the national inventory of artistic wealth.

Cuisine is one of the recognizable characteristics of French culture, and this listing of the French gastronomic meal serves to reinforce what DeSoucey (2010) refers to as gastronationalism.

# Case Study UNESCO Cities of Gastronomy

Intangible heritage of cuisine is also recognized is through UNESCO's Creative Cities Network (UNESCO, n.d.) which aims to celebrate and maintain the diversity of the member cities, as well as to promote local heritage by enriching cultural identity. It does this by focusing on the main products of excellence for example in the categories of Literature, Film, Music, Craft and Folk Art and Gastronomy. While member cities can thus apply for special recognition as a City of Gastronomy, the awarding of the designation is due to certain criteria and characteristics (Table 11.2).

The following profiles of the City of Gastronomy designations to date identify the nomination rationale and respective culinary and gastronomic activities.

## Popayan, Colombia

The city of Popayan, Colombia was the first to receive the UNESCO City of Gastronomy designation in 2005. The municipal government and the

**Table 11.2** Criteria for UNESCO City of Gastronomy

| |
|---|
| Well-developed gastronomy that is characteristic of the urban centre and/or region. |
| Vibrant gastronomy community with numerous traditional restaurants and/or chefs. |
| Endogenous ingredients used in traditional cooking. |
| Local know-how, traditional culinary practices and methods of cooking that have survived industrial/technological advancement. |
| Traditional food markets and traditional food industry. |
| Tradition of hosting gastronomic festivals, awards, contests and other broadly targeted means of recognition. |
| Respect for the environment and promotion of sustainable local products. |
| Nurturing of public appreciation, promotion of nutrition in educational institutions and inclusion of biodiversity conservation programmes in cooking schools curricula. |

*Source*: UNESCO (n.d.)

Popayan Gastronomy Corporation worked towards the recognition (City of Popayan, n.d.). The city was noted for its variety in gastronomic offerings, traditional ingredients and dishes, and in particular the attraction of international gastronomic events. Part of what happened here was the legalization by the Popayan city council of an informal gastronomy industry, introducing standards and publishing restaurant reviews led to the revival of the creative economy, and the increase of employment (Levickaitė, 2011). This new interest in gastronomy gave the locals opportunities to meet to exchange recipes, discuss ingredients and manufacturing processes and participate in international forums.

## Chengdu, People's Republic of China

The city of Chengdu was designated a UNESCO City of Gastronomy in 2010. Chengdu is well known for its spicy cuisine and the designation recognizes the city as a historical site of gastronomy and the birthplace of many culinary traditions, attributes reflected in its recognition as a culinary city (Liu, 2011). The culinary culture of the city is manifest in the tremendous number of local food outlets. An outstanding feature of Chengdu cuisine is the variety of flavours based on the five elements of: sweet, sour, bitter, spicy and salty (Quian, 2006). The nomination acknowledges the relationship of the gastronomy industry of the city, noted to drive the development of other creative industries and pursuits (Chendgu Municipal Government PRC, 2007). In 2010 representatives of both Popayan and Chengdu called for cooperation among such cities (Popayan Gastronomic Corporation & Chengdu

Restaurant's Union, 2010). As reported in a review the city seems to using its status as a City of Gastronomy to promote and develop it's culinary industry (UNESCO, 2012b).

## Östersund, Sweden

The city of Östersund was designated as a UNESCO City of Gastronomy in 2010. The rural and sparsely populated region here is known for a gastronomic culture, founded on a culinary tradition of locally produced and sustainable food (Östersund City, n.d.). The city is home to the Swedish National Centre for Small Scale Artisan Food Processing (Eldrimmer) that supports farmers and small entrepreneurs. With a culinary tradition strongly linked to nature and sustainability the nomination allows for the recognition of the city as a gastronomic centre and a contributor to the network of cities of gastronomy.

### Jeonju, Republic of Korea

The city of Jeonju was the fourth city to be designated as a UNESCO City of Gatronomy in 2012. The nomination acknowledged the policies of the city in terms of both safeguarding its culinary heritage and promoting food and culture in an integrated manner (Jeonju Municipal Government, n.d.). The city has a culinary infrastructure with many unique gastronomic assets and resources. These are promoted though local traditional markets and food festivals. The city is famous for its native dish of Jeonju Bibimbab (a typical Korean dish with regional variations mainly consisting of rice, vegtables, chili pepper paste and topped by an egg). According to the nomination document 'Jeonju cuisine has been developing at the center of the traditional food network that is based on rice civilization, beans, vegetarianism and fermented food' (Jeonju Municipal Government, n.d.: 5). In order to develop and preserve the native foods the city has since 1998 been designating Jeonju Native Traditional Food, traditional food that is unique to the region and has been cooked with agricultural, marine and forest products from the city and surrounding area (Jeonju Municipal Government, n.d.: 9)

# Discussion

This section compares the case studies of the recognition of cuisine as intangible cultural both through the ICHN and the City of Gastronomy designations by UNESCO.

The ICHN listings were all inscribed in 2010, although they had been nominated earlier. The City of Gastronomic listings date from 2005, 2010 and 2012. In all three ICHN cases cuisine local food traditions are central to the listings, as an integral part of food traditions in relation to society (Table 11.3). However, one listing is for a 'diet', another is for a 'cuisine' and a third is for a 'gastronomic meal'. The Mediterranean diet and Mexican Cuisine cases are more related to a cultural system of food whereas the French case is more about the customs surrounding the gastronomic meal, rather that the food recipes and preparation per se. Jurisdictions for the cases differ with two cases being national (Mexico and France) while one is transnational (Mediterranean) representing a cooperation of four countries

**Table 11.3** Culinary listings to UNESCO's ICHC

| Listing | Mediterranean diet | Traditional mexican cuisine | Gastronomic meal of the french |
|---|---|---|---|
| Year | 2010 | 2010 | 2010 |
| Rationale | Set of traditional knowledge, practice, skills, provides sense of continuity, generation to generation. | Central to community cultural identities, transmission generation to generation. | Active social role within its community, communicated as part of identity (generation to generation). |
| Jurisdiction | Transnational – Spain, Greece, Italy, Morocco | National | National |
| Participants | Representative organizations, relevant communities. | Practitioners, National Council for the Arts, Mexico | Communities, institutions, associations. |
| Safeguarding Measures | Transnational promotion to younger generation, research. | Promotion, research projects, practical training. | Promotion, research, educational system activities. |
| Examples of Related Listings | Intangible cultural heritage inventories (Spain, Greece, Italy, Morocco). | Inventory of the Intangible Cultural Heritage of Mexico. | Inventory of Intangible Cultural Heritage of France. |

*Source*: UNESCO (2010a)

in the same region, a nomination made possible by the identification of a representative or 'emblematic' community in each country. The City of Gastronomy designations brings the recognition of cuisine down to the local level.

All of the ICHC listings represent cultural systems for food production, preparation and consumption. The listings are closely tied to both production of local foods, preparation using local knowledge and consumption as part of society.

Safeguarding measures for the protection of the designated intangible heritage include practical training, research, and involvement with educational systems. Various elements of the ICHN and City of Gastronomy listings are also on registers of intangible cultural heritage, and dissemination activities continue to result from broad based interaction with stakeholders in some cases including communities. This is evidenced by activities implemented across Mexico since 2010 in conjunction with the listing of Traditional Mexican Cuisine and by the systematic recognition of local traditional foods to date by the nominated Cities of Gastronomy.

The listing of intangible heritage on national inventories begins the process of recognizing the significance of such heritage. Museums, including national and city level museums can through programming be involved in recognizing and communicating intangible heritage. Winfree Papuga (2005) suggests museums can portray intangible heritage of food through: food processes in the museum, museum presentations of food processes and museum collaboration to present food in traditional settings.

As outlined in Table 11.4, the listings for the UNESCO City of Gastronomy recognize both historic culinary traditions and systems of local cuisine.

The Cities of Gastronomy designations both predate and coincide with the ICHN culinary related listings. The programme appears to be gradually developing, with potential for network development signified by the Popayan Convention (Popayan Gastronomic Corporation & Chengdu Restaurant's Union, 2010) signed in 2010. The rationales for designation share the factors of culinary heritage and systems of foodways. In several cases (Popayan and Chengdu) the listings are related to historic gastronomy. Systems of local food heritage, including the involvement of small-scale producers are important to these designations (Östersund). The safeguarding measures appear to be more to do with creating standards for cuisine versus the more educational objectives of the ICHC culinary listings.

On an overall basis the listing as a City of Gastronomy highlights the recognition of local foodways and traditions that in several cases is characteristic of local cuisines (Chengdu and Jeonju) that are dependent on spices.

**Table 11.4** UNESCO City of Gastronomy designations

| Listing | Popayan, Colombia | Chengdu, PRC | Östersund, Sweden | Jeonju, Republic of Korea |
|---|---|---|---|---|
| Year | 2005 August | 2010 February | 2010 July | 2012 May |
| Rationale | Gastronomic offerings, traditional dishes/ foods, international gastronomic events. | Historical site of gastronomy, birthplace of many culinary traditions. | Gastronomic culture founded on culinary traditions of locally produced sustainable food. | Safeguarding culinary heritage and promoting food and cuisine in an integrated manner. |
| Participants | Municipality of Popayan, Popayan Gastronomy Corporation. | Chengdu City, Chengdu Restaurant's Union. | Östersund City, Eldrimmer (Swedish National Centre for Small Scale Artisan Food Processing). | City of Jeonju, Department of Traditional Culture Promotion, Jeonju Bibimbap Research Institute. |
| Safe-guarding Measures | Standards for gastronomy establishments. | Established Chengdu City of Gastronomy Promotion Association. | Search the old, create the new - neighbouring province traditional methods collaboration. | Recognition of native foods, see below. |
| Related Listings and Agreements | Gastronomic Declaration with Chengdu, PRC. | Gastronomic Declaration with Popayan, Colombia, 31 Sichuan cuisine items on Sichuan Intangible Heritage List. | Academy of Food recognitions and designations. | Native Traditional Food Recognition by City of Jeonju. |

*Source:* Creative Cities Network UNESCO (n.d.)

These recognitions of cuisine also contribute to enhancing the culinary and gastronomic images of destinations, potentially attracting more tourists to experience the designated cuisines and culinary destinations. Where the recognitions include the culinary use of spices, there both potential for tourists to have new culinary experiences but on the other hand the popularity of the recognitions may lead to the commoditization of the use of spices, and an altered form of the authentic in traditionally spicy foods.

## Conclusion

The use of spices in cuisine is gaining recognition as part of our global intangible heritage, as illustrated by UNESCO recognition of intangible cultural heritage of cuisines through both the ICHC and the Cities of Gastronomy listings.

The cases of the Mediterranean diet, the Mexican Traditional Cuisine and the Gastronomic meal of the French listed as ICHC provide a framework for the recognition and safeguarding of these intangible cultural heritages. Safeguarding and dissemination activities keep these intangible cultural traditions related to spices and cuisine alive. The City of Gastronomy designation likewise provides a framework for recognizing the intangible aspects of cuisine and for encouraging programmes and activities that will keep this knowledge for the future.

It is possible that these pioneering listings discussed in this paper will be influential in the recognition of other cuisines important to global heritage. For example (Cheung, 2013) outlines Chinese foodways and culinary resources as a system of knowledge inherited from the past, and (Wang & Tang, 2011) call for protecting the intangible cultural heritage of Shangdong cuisine. Many systems of cuisine, such as the regional variations in Chinese cuisine will be worthy of recognition and protection in order to counter the influences of globalization on local cuisines and the use of spices. However, since the nominations will need to be put forward by governments (national for the ICHC and municipal for the City of Gastronomy) there will always be politics involved in these initiatives.

With the growing global interest in culinary forms of culture the recognition of cuisine as intangible heritage on a universal and global basis should contribute to an awareness of the value of traditional local and regional cuisines to tourism. This is evidenced by a recent (UNWTO, 2012) report encouraging inclusion of intangible cultural heritage components that include gastronomy in the planning, development and management of tourism destinations. For the interpretation of spices in cuisine, examined in this chapter, the listings serve to educate regarding the importance of and role of spices in traditional systems of cuisine. Future research could examine on a more in-depth and longitudinal basis the impacts of the UNESCO culinary related designations on both the interpretation and safeguarding of the intangible heritages related to spices and cuisine.

## References

Ab Karim, S. and Chi, C.G.Q. (2010) Culinary tourism as a destination attraction: An empirical examination of destinations' food image. *Journal of Hospitality Marketing & Management* 19 (6), 531–555.

Brown, M.F. (2005) Heritage trouble: Recent work on the protection of intangible cultural property. *International Journal of Cultural Property* 12 (1), 40–61.

Chendgu Municipal Government (2007) Chengdu's application to join the UNESCO Creative Cities Network as a City of Gastronomy. http://www.unesco.org/new/fileadmin/MULTIMEDIA/HQ/CLT/pdf/CNN_Chengdu_Application_Gastronomy (accessed 5 June 2013).

Cheung, S.C. (2013) From foodways to intangible heritage: A case study of Chinese culinary resource, retail and recipe in Hong Kong. *International Journal of Heritage Studies* 19 (4), 353–364.

Cohen, E. and Alievi, N. (2004) Food in tourism: Attraction and impediment. *Annals of Tourism Research* 31 (4), 755–778.

City of Popayan (n.d.) Popayan Appliction for a City of Gastronomy (in Spanish). http://www.unesco.org/new/fileadmin/MULTIMEDIA/HQ/CLT/pdf/CNN_Popayan_Application_Gastronomy_EN.pdf (accessed 5 June 2013).

Civitello, L. (2008) *Cuisine and Culture: A History of Food and People* (2nd edn). Hoboken, NJ: John Wiley and Sons, Inc.

Dalby, A. (2000) *Dangerous Tastes: The Story of Spices*. London: British Museum Press.

DeSoucey, M. (2010) Gastronationalism: Food traditions and authenticity politics in the European Union. *American Sociological Review* 75 (3), 432–455.

Feagan, P. (2007) The place of food: Mapping out the 'local' in local food systems. *Progress in Human Geography* 31, 23–42.

International Centre for Advanced Mediterranean Agronomic Studies (2012) *The Mediterranean Diet for Sustainable Regional Development*. Paris: Presses de Sciences, International Centre for Advanced Medittterean Agronomic Studies.

Jalleh, J. (21 May 2012) 'Hot and Spicy Penang' launched as part of island rebranding. *The Star*. Selangor Darul Ehsan, Malaysis. http://thestar.com.my/news (accessed 1 April 2013).

Jeonju Municipal Government (n.d.) Jeonju's application to join the UNESCO creative cities network. City of Jeonju. http://www.unesco.org/culture/pdf/CCN-jeonju-application-EN.pdf (accessed 2 June 2013).

Levickaitė, R. (2011) Four approaches to the creative economy: General overview. *Business, Management and Education* 1, 81–92.

Liu, Y. (2011) Evaluation of Sichuan food culture and construction of the Gourmet City for Chengdu. *Journal of Sichuan College of Education* 4, 42–45.

Long, L.M. (2003) *Culinary Tourism*. Lexington, Kentucky: University Press of Kentucky.

Montanari, M. (1994) *The Culture of Food*. Oxford: Blackwell.

Okumus, B., Okumus, F and McKercher, B. (2007) Incorporating local and international cuisines in the marketing of tourism destinations: The cases of Hong Kong and Turkey. *Tourism Management* 28 (1), 253–261.

Ostersund City (n.d.) Application for Östersund City in the region of Jämtland, Sweden to the UNESCO 'Creative Cities Network.' http://www.unesco.org/new/fileadmin/MULTIMEDIA/HQ/CLT/pdf/CNN_Ostersund_Application_Gastronomy_EN.pdf (accessed 30 May 2013).

Parry, J.W. (1955) The Story of Spices. *Economic Botany* 9 (2), 190–207.

Pilcher, J. (2008) The globalization of Mexican cuisine. *History Compass* 6 (2), 529–551.

Popayan Gastronomic Corporation, and Chengdu Restaurant's Union (2010) *The Popayan Gastronomic Declaration 'Toward A World Union Of Gastronomic Cities'*. Popyan, Colombia: UNESCO Gasrtonomic Cities Program.

Quian, J. (2006) *Chengdu: A City of Paradise*. Chengdu: Author House.

Scarpato, R. (2002). Gastronomy as a tourist product: The perspective of gastronomy studies. In A-M. Hjalager and G. Richards (eds) *Tourism and Gastronomy* (pp. 51–70). London: Routledge.

Schmitt, T.M. (2008) The UNESCO concept of safeguarding intangible cultural heritage: Its background and marrakchi roots. *International Journal of Heritage Studies* 14 (2), 95–111.

Sims, R. (2009) Food, place and authenticity: Local food and the sustainable tourism experience. *Journal of Sustainable Tourism* 17(3), 321–336.

Smith, L. and Akagawa, N. (2009) Introduction. In L. Smith and N. Akagawa (eds) *Intangible Heritage* (pp. 1–9). London: Routledge.

Timothy, D.J. and Ron, A.S. (2013) Understanding heritage cuisines and tourism: Identity, image, authenticity and change. *Journal of Heritage Tourism* 8 (2–3), 99–104.

UNESCO (2003) *Convention for the Safeguarding of the Intangible Cultural heritage*. Paris: UNESCO.

UNESCO (2010a) *Nomination File No. 07491(French Gastronomic Meal) for Inscription on the Representative List of the Intangible Cultural Heritage in 2010*. Paris: UNESCO.

UNESCO (2010b) *Nomination File No. 007539 (Mediterranean Diet) for Inscription on the Representative List of the Intangible Cultural Heritage in 2010*. Paris: UNESCO.

UNESCO (2010c) *Nomination File No. 07530 (Mexican Cuisine) for Inscription on the Representative List of the Intangible Cultural Heritage in 2010*. Paris: UNESCO.

UNESCO (2012a) *UNESCO Periodic Report No. 00798/Mexico*. Paris: UNESCO.

UNESCO (2012b) *Reviewing Report on City of Gastronomy Chengdu China*. http://www.unesco.org/new/fileadmin/MULTIMEDIA/HQ/CLT/images/EvaluationReport_Chengdu.pdf (accessed 2 June 2013).

UNESCO (n.d.) Creative Cities Network, Gastronomy. http://www.unesco.org/new/en/culture/themes/creativity/creative-industries/creative-cities-network/gastronomy/ (accessed 1 June 2013).

UNWTO (2012) *Tourism and Intangible Cultural Heritage*. Madrid: United Nations World Tourism Organization.

Wang, R. and Tang, W. (2011) On Protection of Intangible Cultural Heritage of Shandong Cuisine. *Culinary Science Journal of Yangzhou University* 1, 6–9.

Winfree Papuga, D. (2005) A taste of intangible heritage: Food traditions inside and outside of the Museum. *Ethnological Researches* 1 (10), 57–62.

# Conclusion

# 12 Lessons for Spice-related Tourism Destinations, Attractions and Cuisines

## Lee Jolliffe

> *The Kochi Corporation will consider leasing warehouses of the Cochin Port Trust (CPT) for the proposed spice museum at Mattancherry*
> The Times of India, 2013

> *In order to add more spice to the tourism campaign, the Department of Tourism (Kerala, India) is designing a 'Spice Route Heritage Project', which was featured at the 6th International Meeting on Silk Road Tourism in China recently*
> Manaromaonline.com, 2013

> *The small emirate of Ajman had entered into an agreement with the UK's world famous Longstanton Spice Museum. The deal, said to be worth in excess of $500 [million], will see construction begin on Longstanton Spice Museum Arabia later this year, with opening expected sometime in 2013*
> The Pan-Arabia Enquirer, 2012

The quotes above reflect the growing awareness in various corners of the globe of both the significance of spice history and the potential for contributing to destination development by cultivating related attractions. These initiatives reflect the history of the spice trade at their respective locations while developing experiential products for contemporary tourism.

This concluding chapter draws out lessons from the content of the volume. This is followed by an analysis of the current state of spice-related tourism around the world. The chapter also proposes a spice-related tourism schema.

# Lessons for Spice-related Tourism

The chapter contributions have revealed a number of crosscutting themes in terms of the relationship of tourism to spices (see Table 12.1) that are discussed in the following sections.

## Sense of place and identity

At many of the destinations profiled (for example Grenada; Carriacou; Hungary and India's Goa Province) the production and use of spices is an inherent part of place-based culture and related traditions and the story of spices is integral to tourism experiences. In several cases (Grenada and Hungary) spices also are also symbolic of national identity (nutmeg and paprika respectively) and feature prominently in destination marketing strategies and even slogans, such as with Grenada's current tourism marketing slogan, 'Live the Rythmns of Spice' in reference to the tri-island state of Grenada, Carriacou and Petit Martinique. In this country, a significant global producer of nutmeg, whose member islands are also known as Spice Islands, the nutmeg is symbolic of the national identity. A dominant theme emerging here is of the incorporation of spices into national cuisines, for example in the cases of native spices of Australia reflecting a sense of place and the herbs used as spices that form part of the new Nordic cuisine in Iceland.

## Destination tourism branding and marketing

A convincing theme throughout the book is that of cultural identities through spices, revealed at the local, regional and national levels, as such spices are often closely related to tourism images and branding. Grenada provides an example of destination identity and branding using an agricultural product (in this case spices), which although it has been studied to some extent (Nelson, 2012) would be worthy of further study. Even nearby Carriacou, part of the nation of Grenada, while not being a major spice producer, benefits from the spice-related branding of the country.

**Table 12.1** Themes in the tourism and spice relationship

| Sense of place and identity (community and/or national) |
| --- |
| Destination tourism branding and marketing |
| Diversification from production towards tourism |
| Management and interpretation of spice attractions |
| Recognition of tangible and intangible aspects through cuisine |
| Synergistic forms of tourism (ecotourism, agri-tourism and sustainable rural tourism) |

## Management and interpretation of spice attractions

The primary spice-related attractions are popular spice gardens or farms, for the most part found at the tropical spice producing locations such as those discussed in the book of Zanzibar; Sri Lanka and Penang, Malaysia. The attraction studies demonstrate the possibilities and potentials for the diversification of spice gardens into visitor attractions, delving more into their development as touristic sites while augmenting incomes for spice farmers. A variety of management approaches are also demonstrated, from informally operated spice farms that depend on tour companies and guides to bring visitors who are often not charged admission but expected to purchase spices (Zanzibar and Sri Lanka) to the professionally operated award-winning visitor attraction, the Tropical Spice Garden (Malaysia). A significant finding is that in these situations the attractions provide an important component of the tourism supply, offering unique local experience to visitors, potentially extending lengths of stay in spice producing areas thus countering seasonality in visitor demand, at the same time contributing to the diversification of agriculture and its integration with tourism.

A human resource challenge to spice farms is both the availability and the training of guides who can interpret the spices to visitors. Lack of adequate training of guides in some cases may be inhibiting the development of the product as is evidenced by the cases of spice farm tours in both Zanzibar and Sri Lanka. In these locales spice farm attractions offer appealing but unsophisticated delivery of tours by local guides, rich in local lore, but lacking in the interpretive techniques that might be evident if the guides had professional training. The case of a more professional spice garden attraction in Penang, Malaysia could be a model for other spice gardens.

## Diversification from production towards tourism

Another significant trend is for the diversification of spice farms and gardens into spice-related destination attractions. This is evident on Grenada and also emergent in the Goa region of India, where the activities of spice farms have diversified to include tourism activities, but also using spices as an entry into the way of life of the region other cultural activities have been added to these attractions. Spice farms and plantations have the potential to contribute to diversifying the tourism offers at destinations, creating experiences that compliment agri-tourism and ecotourism within spice plantations and developing added value for the agricultural product through diversifying into food and handicraft items and medicinal products.

An important lesson in spice farm diversification was provided by the case of Zanzibar where organic spice growers and their industry association identified the opportunity for spice farmers to diversify their revenues by dedicating part of their farms as visitor attractions. This divergence from production to tourism, however, means that farmers need to plant an increased variety of spices for demonstration purposes, whereas production-orientated spice farmers concentrate on the few varieties that are most profitable.

### Recognition of tangible and intangible aspects through cuisine

There is potential for the intangible heritage of spices to be examined through the international designations related to cuisine. In particular the recognitions of cuisine through UNESCO designations contributes to enhancing the culinary images of destinations, potentially attracting more tourists to experience cuisines that may include both the tangible and intangible heritage of spices. Here there is the potential for destinations to be branded both for their spice production and forms of use. At these spice-related locations tourists can have new culinary experiences, but on the other hand the popularity of the recognitions may lead to the commoditization of the use of spices, threatening traditional knowledge by providing an altered form of the authentic in traditionally spicy foods.

### Synergistic forms of tourism

At a number of spice producing locales forms of ecotourism, agri-tourism and rural tourism are incorporating and featuring experiences related to spices. Agro-tourism in Grenada is clearly, at least on the main island of Grenada, a means of connecting the two dominant industries of spices and tourism. The fact that agricultural facilities related to spices have developed into visitor attractions is symbolic of this growing relationship. While spice production here has declined due to the impact of natural disasters (hurricanes), diversification into tourism provides an opportunity for the industry to recover some of its former strength in relationship to the local economy. The cases of both Goa and Sri Lanka articulate the concept of spice-related sustainable rural tourism.

## Analysis of Spice-related Tourism

This volume has provided insights into the existence of tourism related to spices. A number of distinct themes emerge from the chapters, as identified above. In a cultural context, spices and their production are initially place based. Where spices are produced and consumed spices can therefore provide a strong theme for destination identity and marketing, contributing to creating experiential tourism products reflecting spices. Where spices are traded there can likewise be an identity created by the spice routes, bazaars and markets as well as by the use of spices in cuisine. At spice-consuming destinations spices can still play a role in tourism through exhibitions and events related to them. The attractions hosting spice-related interpretation in various forms exhibit both the tangible and intangible aspects of spices. The tangible experience of seeing, tasting, smelling and feeling spices, both at their source and in interpretative situations away from the source can be powerful, reinforced by the intangible spice traditions that can be conveyed by hosts, tour guides and interpreters. The use of spices in cuisine is both tangible and intangible reflecting cultural characteristics and traditions regarding spicy foods.

There is thus a continuum of spice-related tourism, influenced by both people and place in terms of cultural traditions and the geography of both production and consumption. Spice-related tourism will be more evident at the places of production and trade than it is at destinations were spices are not produced, but are consumed. As Pearce (1995) indicates, tourism is essentially about people and places within an origin-linkage-destination system. Tourists travelling through this system will encounter spices as they travel, and since many of the tourism flows are to the tropical regions where the majority of spices are grown, it is evident that many travellers will encounter spices, either on a superficial basis through cuisine, casually through sight-seeing in spice growing regions or more intensely through visiting spice farms, gardens and related attractions. A few tourists may even have the opportunity to stay at spice-related accommodations. Since many spice-related destinations are tropical islands where accommodation is often clustered along the shorelines, the spice gardens inland provide activities for tourists in the form or agri-tourism and culinary tourism pursuits.

As reflected by the quotes at the beginning of this chapter, there seems to be a growing awareness, on the part of destinations in particular, of the value of recognizing their spice history and commemorating it through museums, routes and attractions. Returning to the components of spice-related tourism initially introduced in Chapter 1 it is evident that there are many variations of the relationship between the three factors of destinations, attractions and cuisine. Based on the chapter contributions and discussions a schema is proposed here (Figure 12.1).

Although it is clear that spice destinations are easily identified, spice-related attractions are not always featured as such, unless they are specifically related to either the production (as with spice farms, gardens and plantations), celebration (as with spice festivals) or history (as with spice

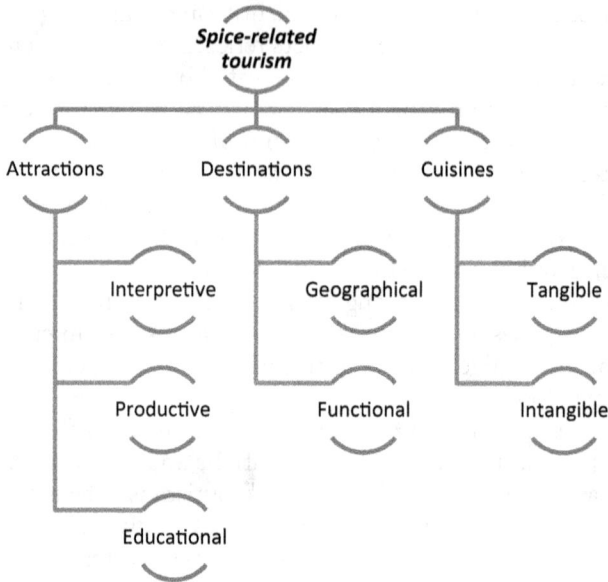

**Figure 12.1** Components of spice-related tourism

museums) of spices; however, a plethora of other types of attractions rely on spices, such as cooking schools, restaurants and culinary festivals. Destinations featuring spices can be examined from geographical and functional perspectives. Both the tangible (material) and intangible (immaterial) aspects of spices are worthy of more study, especially in light of the move by UNESCO towards identifying the intangible aspects of cuisine (and inherently spices) as global heritage.

# In Conclusion

This edited volume has explored the various ways in which spices and tourism are connected, and indeed how the two intersect in contemporary tourism product and experience. Spice-related tourism as discussed within this volume has a broad appeal, in both spice producing and consuming settings, owing to the potential for creating experiential and sensual experiences that enhance the tourism product and experience while also having the potential to contribute to sustainable forms of tourism at the local level. On a number of levels and at numerous locations, spices also contribute to national identities, through production, trade and use. The inherent branding of places with spices is an asset for tourism, as reflected by a number of locations known as spice-islands.

The contributions here in a scholarly gist on tourism related to spices (that in the broadest sense include herbs) provide only a glimpse of the potentials for employing spices in many aspects of tourism imagery, production and consumption, at spice gardens and markets, in culinary related settings, as souvenirs, and as a recall of the tourism experience in the home kitchen. Future research could study in more depth the development of spice-related attractions, destinations and cuisines, gaining insights from qualitative enquiries into the experience of tourists at dedicated spice themed destinations, attractions and food outlets. This research could contribute on a broader basis and in comparison to previous research on how other agricultural products (tea, coffee and sugar) are connected to tourism in terms of both the supply and demand for related niche tourism activities (Jolliffe, 2007, 2010, 2013).

It is hoped that this volume will advance the academic discussion related to both material culture and intangible heritage and foodways of spices in relation to tourism. The volume should in addition serve as a reference text for those both studying spice-related tourism and involved in the design and delivery of experiences related to this spicy form of tourism.

## References

Jolliffe, L. (2007) *Tea and Tourism: Tourists, Traditions and Transformations*. Clevedon: Channel View Publications.

Jolliffe, L. (2010) *Coffee Culture, Destinations and Attractions*. Bristol: Channel View Publications.

Jolliffe, L. (2013) *Sugar Heritage and Tourism in Transition*. Bristol: Channel View Publications.

Manaromaonline.com (2013) Kerala to add more spice to tourism, Wednesday 7 August 2013. Available: http://travel.manoramaonline.com (accessed 18 November 2013).

Nelson, V. (2012) Tourism, agriculture, and identity: Comparing Grenada and Dominica. *Journal of Tourism Insights* 3 (1), 1–22.

Pearce, D. (1995) *Tourism Today: A Geographical Analysis*. Essex, England: Longman Group Inc.

The Pan-Arabia Enquirer (2012) Longstanton Spice Museum to open in UAE 2013. Available: http://www.panarabiaenquirer.com/wordpress/ajman-signs-deal-with-longstanton-spice-museum/ (accessed 22 July 2013).

The Times of India (2013) Corporation eyes warehouses to set up spice museum. Available: http://articles.timesofindia.indiatimes.com/2013-04-19/kochi/38673948_1_kochi-corporation-french-team-lorient (accessed 19 April 2013).

# Index

For Product Safety Concerns and Information please contact our EU Authorised Representative:

Easy Access System Europe

Mustamäe tee 50

10621 Tallinn

Estonia

gpsr.requests@easproject.com

www.ingramcontent.com/pod-product-compliance
Lightning Source LLC
Chambersburg PA
CBHW050436280326
41932CB00013BA/2142